POLYNESIAN RESEARCHES
Polynesia

Fishing by Torch-light

Page 149

POMARE.

POLYNESIAN RESEARCHES
Polynesia

By WILLIAM ELLIS

A New Edition, Enlarged and Improved

CHARLES E. TUTTLE CO.: PUBLISHERS
Rutland, Vermont & Tokyo, Japan

Representatives
Continental Europe: BOXERBOOKS, INC., *Zurich*
British Isles: PRENTICE-HALL INTERNATIONAL, INC., *London*
Australasia: PAUL FLESCH & CO., PTY., *Melbourne*
Canada: M. G. HURTIG LTD., *Edmonton*

*Published by the Charles E. Tuttle Company, Inc.
of Rutland, Vermont & Tokyo, Japan
with editorial offices at Suido 1-chome, 2-6
Bunkyo-ku, Tokyo, Japan*

Copyright in Japan, 1969 by Charles E. Tuttle Co., Inc.

All rights reserved

Library of Congress Catalog Card No. 69-19601

Standard Book No. 8048 0475-3

First Tuttle edition published 1969

PRINTED IN JAPAN

TO

THE DIRECTORS AND SUPPORTERS

OF

THE LONDON MISSIONARY SOCIETY;

THESE VOLUMES,

DESCRIBING THE SCENES OF THEIR

EARLIEST EXERTIONS,

AND THE IMPORTANT RESULTS OF

THEIR OPERATIONS,

AMONG THOSE WHO WERE THE FIRST OBJECTS

OF THEIR BENEVOLENT SOLICITUDE,

ARE RESPECTFULLY INSCRIBED,

BY THEIR OBLIGED,

AND OBEDIENT SERVANT,

THE AUTHOR.

ADVERTISEMENT

TO THE SECOND EDITION.

In issuing the first Volume of his RESEARCHES in their present form, the Author begs to express his grateful sense of the favourable notice which the original publication received from several leading literary Journals, as well as its encouraging reception from the circle of his immediate friends, and the public at large. He is also happy in being thus able to comply with the suggestions of a number of highly respected individuals, who have expressed their wishes that the work might be published in a cheaper and more portable form. The reasonable price of the present Volumes, and their periodical publication, will, it is hoped, secure the object desired—their more extensive circulation. The less important parts have been slightly abridged, the whole has been arranged in a regular methodical order, and the history of the extension of Christianity in the South Seas continued to the date of the latest intelligence. As the Sandwich Islands form the northern boundary of Polynesia, in order to render the work more complete, the account of those islands originally entitled "Narrative of a Tour through Hawaii, or Owhyhee," is published in a corresponding manner, under the same title: this will constitute a fourth volume of POLYNESIAN RESEARCHES.—Thus improved, and imbodying much recent interesting information, the Author anticipates for the present Volumes a reception equal to that with which their predecessors were favoured.

London, Jan. 1, 1831,

TABLE OF CONTENTS

FOREWORD TO THE NEW EDITION .. xiii
PREFACE xvii

CHAP. I.
FROM PAGE 1 TO PAGE 29.

Historical notice of the discovery of the Pacific—Extent and limits of Polynesia—Voyages of Cook—Discovery of the Georgian and Society Islands — Origin of their designation—Number, names, and relative situation of the islands—Key to the pronunciation of native names—Extent and apparent structure of the islands—Beauty of the scenery—First approach to the shore of Matavai—Inland scenery — Description of Eimeo — Coral islands—Tetuaroa, the fashionable watering-place of Tahiti — Harbours — Islets on the reefs—Soil in the islands—Climate—Winds – Rains—and Tides.

CHAP. II.
FROM PAGE 30 TO PAGE 59.

Vegetable productions of the Islands—Forests—Various kinds of timber—The apape and faifai—The aito, or casuarina—Tiairi, candlenut tree—Callophylla Barringtonia— Thespesia populnea— Erythrina— Hibiscus —The anti, or cloth plant—Description, uses, and legends of the sacred aoa—Account of the bread-fruit tree and fruit—Various methods of preparing the fruit —Arum or taro, uhi or yam—U-ma-ra, or sweet potato—Culture, preparation, and method of dressing the arrow-root—Appearance and value of the cocoa-nut tree—Several stages of growth in which the fruit is used—Manufacture of cocoa-nut oil.

CHAP. III.
FROM PAGE 69 TO PAGE 77.

Varieties and appearance of the plantain and banana—Vi or Brazilian plum—A-hi-a or jambo—Singular growth of the inocarpus, or native chesnut—Different kinds of ti, or Dracanæ—To, or sugar-cane—Foreign fruits and vegetables that flourish in Polynesia—Value of a garden in the South Sea Islands—Unsuccessful attempts to introduce wheat—Introduction of coffee—Native and foreign flowers—Tradition of the origin of the bread-fruit—Quadrupeds—Absence of venomous animals and reptiles—Manner of rearing pigs—Birds of the South Sea Islands—Albatross— Pigeons — Domestic fowls—Number and variety of fish on the coasts, and in the lakes and rivers.

CHAP. IV.

FROM PAGE 78 TO PAGE 100.

Inhabitants of the islands of the Pacific—Oceanic negroes—Eastern Polynesians— General account of the South Sea Islanders—Physical character—Expression of countenance—Stature, colour, &c.—Mental capacity—Ancient division and computation of time—Tahitian numerals — Extended calculations — Aptness in receiving instruction—Moral character—Hospitality—Extensive and affecting moral degradation—Its enervating influence—Former longevity of the islanders.

CHAP. V.

FROM PAGE 101 TO PAGE 127.

Comparative numbers of the inhabitants—Indications and causes of depopulation—Beneficial tendency of Christianity—Origin of the inhabitants of the South Sea Islands—Traditions—Legends of Taaroa and Hina—Resemblance to Jewish history—Coincidences in language, mythology, &c. with the language, &c. of the Hindoos and Malays, Madagasse, and South Americans—Probable source of population—Difficulty of reaching the islands from the west—Account of the different native voyages—Geographical extent over which the Polynesian race and language prevail.

CHAP. VI.

FROM PAGE 128 TO PAGE 159.

Habits of the Islanders—Unsocial in domestic life—Humiliating circumstances of the females—Irregular mode of life—Time of taking food—Cleanliness—Frequent bathing—Manner of wearing the hair, and removing the beard—Artificial flowers—Native toilet—Occupations—Agriculture—Implements, &c.—Fishing—Enclosures—Salmon and other nets—Use of the spear—

Various kinds of hooks and lines—The vaa-tira—Fishing by torch light — Canoes used among the islands—Origin of the name — Skreened canoe and Maihi.

CHAP. VII.
FROM PAGE 160 TO PAGE 192.

Description of the vaa motu, or island-canoe—Methods of navigating native vessels—Danger from sharks—Affecting wreck—Accident in a single canoe—Tahitian architecture—Materials employed in building—Description of the various kinds of native houses—Dress of the Tahitians—Manufacture of native cloth—Variety of kinds—Durability and appearance—Methods of dyeing—Matting of Society and Paumotu islanders—Native pillow, seat, dishes, and other articles of household furniture.

CHAP. VIII.
FROM PAGE 193 TO PAGE 220.

Account of the music and amusements of the islanders—Description of the sacred drum—Heiva drum, &c. Occasions of their use—The bu or trumpet—Ihara—The vivo, or flute—General character of their songs—Elegiac singularly beautiful—Translation of a war song—Ballads, a kind of classical authority—Entertainments and amusements — Taupiti, or festival — Wrestling and boxing—Effects of victory and defeat—Foot-races — Martial games — Sham-fights — Naval reviews—Apai, bandy or cricket—Tuiraa, or foot-ball The haruraa puu, a female game—Native dances—Heiva, &c.—The te-a, or archery—Bows and arrows—Religious ceremonies connected with the game—Never used by the Society Islanders, except in their amusements—Discontinued since the introduction of Christianity.

CHAP. IX.
FROM PAGE 221 TO PAGE 247.

Cockfighting—Aquatic sports—Swimming in the surf—Danger from sharks—Juvenile amusements—Account of the Areois, the institution peculiar to the inhabitants of the Pacific—Antiquity of the Areoi society—Tradition of its origin—Account of its founders—Infanticide enjoined with its establishment—General character of the Areois—Their voyages—Public dances—Buildings for their accommodation—Marine exhibitions—Oppression and injury occasioned by their visits—Distinction of rank among them—Estimation in which they are held—Mode of admission—Ceremonies attending advancement to the higher orders—Demoralizing nature of their usages—Singular rites at their death and interment—Description of Rohutunoanoa, the Areois heaven—Reflections on the baneful tendency of the Areoi society, and its dissolution.

CHAP. X.

FROM PAGE 248 TO PAGE 274.

Customs of the islanders—Infanticide—Numbers destroyed—Universality of the crime—Mode of its perpetration—Reasons assigned for its continuance—Disproportion it occasioned between the sexes—Former treatment of children—Ceremonies performed at the temple on the birth of chiefs—Manner of carrying their children—Evils of neglecting parental discipline—Practice of tatauing—Tradition of its origin—Account of the dye instruments and process of tatauing—Variety of figures or patterns—The operation painful, and frequently fatal—Marriage contracts—Betrothment—Ancient usages—Ceremonies in the temple—Conduct of the relatives—Prevalence of polygamy.

CHAP. XI.

FROM PAGE 275 TO PAGE 294.

Frequency of war in the South Sea Islands—Polynesian war-god—Religious ceremonies and human sacrifices, prior to the commencement of hostilities—National councils—Mustering of forces—Emblems of the gods taken to the war—Strength of their fleets or armies—The battle of Hooroto—Women engaging in battle—Tahitian banners—Martial music—Modes of attack—Single combats, challenges, &c.—The rauti, or orators of battle—Sacrifice of the first prisoner—Manifestation of affection, and motives to revenge—Auguries of the war—Use of the sling—Singular custom of the chiefs marching to battle—Sanguinary and exterminating character of their engagements—Desolation of the country.

CHAP. XII.

FROM PAGE 295 TO PAGE 320.

Estimation in which fighting men were held—Weapons—Dress—Ornaments—Various kinds of helmet and armour—Ancient arms, &c. superseded by the introduction of fire-arms—Former ideas respecting the musket, &c.—Divination or augury—Savage and merciless conduct of the victors—Existence of wild men in the mountains—Account of one at Bunaauïa who had fled from the field of battle—Treatment of the captives and the slain—Division of the spoil, and appropriation of the country—Maritime warfare—Encampments—Fortifications—Instance of patriotism—Methods of concluding peace—Religious ceremonies and festivities that followed—Present sentiments of the people in reference to war—Triumph of the principles of peace—Incident at Rurutu.

CHAP. XIII.

FROM PAGE 321 TO PAGE 352.

General view of Polynesian mythology—Ideas relative to the origin of the world — Polytheism — Traditionary theogony—Taaroa supreme deity—Different orders of gods—Oro, Hiro, &c. gods of the wind—Power of spirits to raise tempests—Gods of the ocean, &c.—Supposed cause of an eclipse.—Gods of artificers and fishermen—Oramatuas, or demons—Emblems—Images—Uru, or feathers—Temples—Worship—Prayers—The awakening of the gods—Offerings—Sacrifices—Occasional and stated festivals and worship—Rau-mata-vehi-raa Maui-fata—Rites for recovery from sickness—Offering of first-fruits—The pae atua—The ripening of the year, a religious ceremony—Singular rites attending its close.

CHAP. XIV.

FROM PAGE 353 TO PAGE 381.

Description of Polynesian idols—Human sacrifices—Anthropophagism—Islands in which it prevails—Motives and circumstances under which it is practised—Tradition of its existence in Sir Charles Sanders' Island—Extensive prevalence of Sorcery and Divination—Views of the natives on the subject of satanic influence—Demons—Imprecations—Modes of incantation—Horrid and fatal effects supposed to result from sorcery—Impotency of enchantment on Europeans—Native remedies for sorcery—Native oracles—Buaatapena—Means of inspiration—Effects on the priest inspired—Manner of delivering the responses—Circumstances at Rurutu and Huahine—Intercourse between the priest and the god—Augury by the death of victims—Augury by the stars and clouds—Divination for the detection of theft.

CHAP. XV.
FROM PAGE 382 TO PAGE 414.

Tahitian prophets—Ancient predictions relative to the arrival of ships—Traditions of the Deluge corresponding with the accounts in sacred and profane writings—General ideas of the people relative to death and a future state—Death the consequence of Divine displeasure—State of spirits—Miru, or heaven—Religious ceremonies for ascertaining the causes of death—Embalming—The burying of the sins of the departed—Singular religious ceremony—Offerings to the dead—Occupation of the spirits of the deceased—Superstitions of the people—Otohaa, or lamentation—Wailing—Outrages committed under the paroxysms of grief—Use of sharks' teeth—Elegies—The heva—Absurdity and barbarism of the practice.

LIST OF PLATES

Vignette Title, Fishing by Torchlight
Head of Pomare .... Frontispiece
Map of Polynesia .... page 1

WOOD ENGRAVINGS.

Bread fruit Tree	page 37, 38	Tahitian Stool	page 189
Fishing Canoe	148	Wooden Dish	191
War Canoe	153	Tahitian Drums	194
Skreened Canoe	157	Trumpet Shell	196
Single or Island Canoe	162	National Temple	341
Adzes	177	Altar and Offerings	346
Cloth Mallet	180	Altar and Unus	351
Tahitian Pillow	189	Tahitian Idols	355, 356

FOREWORD TO THE NEW EDITION

THE peoples of Polynesia, who survived relatively unmolested for many hundreds of years in the broad Pacific Ocean, contributed some extremely interesting material for the study of independent cultural growth. Although many of the Polynesian cultures rapidly lost their identity following their discovery and conquest by Europeans, there were a few explorers and missionaries sufficiently interested in what they found in newly discovered Polynesia to record in their journals the social, cultural, and religious beliefs and practices of Polynesia.

Most of those who recorded their findings had a propensity to compare the Polynesian social and cultural system with European forms of government and ways of life. The Polynesian religious beliefs were compared in terms of classical mythology and an established Church based on the Judaic-Christian ethic. Through European eyes all Polynesians were savages. Little did the European realize that the Polynesian knew the world was round hundreds of years before the white man; that Polynesians had navigated by the stars and tides long before Europeans had discovered their importance; and that Polynesian religious beliefs were every bit as profound as, and practiced more sincerely than, most European religious beliefs. In the field of medicine the ancient Polynesian *kahunas* (medical practitioners) performed the delicate trephining operation and were well versed in the use of many dozens of plants with medicinal value.

At a time when European women were little more than chattels and slaves, women of Polynesia stood substantially on a social par with their men. Sometimes sisters were socially superior to their brothers, wives superior to their husbands. The first born child, either male or female, always had highest rank within the family and the ancestoral line was always traced through the ancestor of highest rank in each generation. It was a primogenitural arrangement found nowhere else in the world.

The Polynesian approach to life was orderly rather than emotional. The highest prestige was always accorded the most skilled technicians, be they boat builders, priests, navigators, warriors, or orators. Polynesians were realistic in their sexual concepts. Romantic love was for adolescents and sex was regarded as essential, natural, and enjoyable. It was a wholesome creation of their gods for man's well-being.

Into this unusual and little known world of Polynesia arrived an English missionary, the Rev. William Ellis, in the year 1816. His first important step was to learn the language of Tahiti and, in doing so, was readily adopted and respected as being a person worthy of the Polynesian's confidence. Once he had mastered the language he was on an equal footing with the Polynesians. It was by this means that he was brought to the awareness that Polynesia was possessed of a most unusual culture. Although he did not condone many of the practices then employed by the Polynesians, he quickly realized that he must first win their confidence if he was to be successful in introducing Christianity. His astucious approach in learning everything he could of Polynesian religious beliefs made it possible for him to draw realistic comparisions which the Polynesians could understand.

The Rev. Mr. Ellis kept voluminous notes on every phase of Polynesian life, culture, social organization, and beliefs. His records now constitute one of the finest historical records of their kind, free of foreign social intrusion and completely authentic. Unlike many other missionaries who came to Polynesia "to convert the savage and heathen" and who found the fun-loving, carefree Polynesians vile and beastly, Mr. Ellis treated them with respect and cultural justice, with the result that the Polynesians listened to him and freely discussed their ancient concepts and the differences between the Christian and the ancient Polynesian religious beliefs.

The Polynesian Researches of the Rev. Mr. Ellis cover all of the important areas of Polynesia, including Tahiti, Raiatea, Porapora (Borabora), Huahine, New Zealand, Hawaii, and dozens of small island groups within the Polynesian triangle of the Pacific Ocean. Despite Polynesia's isolation from the rest of the world, Ellis concludes that the Polynesian religious system was singularly complete and comprehensive. He was impressed with the fact that Polynesian "mental power" and ability to comprehend was not the least bit inferior to those of the generality of mankind. In *Polynesian Researches* will be found as fine a history of Polynesia as has ever been written. This book was originally published in the early nineteenth century by Peter Jackson, Late Fisher, Son, & Co., London.

Edouard R. L. Doty

PREFACE

Accurate information respecting the different parts of the world, is probably possessed in a greater degree, and diffused to a wider extent, at the present day, than it has been at any former period. The mariner has encountered the dangers of untraversed and hitherto impenetrable seas; and the traveller has explored remote and inhospitable countries, in order to increase general knowledge, and add new facilities to the prosecution of enlightened philosophical research.

Without depreciating the pursuits of science, or the advantages of a more enlarged acquaintance with the natural history of our globe, the Christian philanthropist directs his attention to objects still more important, and is led to contemplate, with growing intensity of interest, the moral and spiritual condition of mankind. The dominion and extent of delusive and sanguinary idolatries, with their moral debasement and attendant misery, have excited his liveliest concern; and to the melioration of human wretchedness thus induced, and the extension of true religion, as the only solid basis of virtue and happiness, his energies are directed, and his resources consecrated.— Animated by the predictions of inspiration which refer to the moral renovation of the world, and cheered by " the signs of the times," his anticipations of ultimate success are strengthened by the effects that already reward his exertions.

The results of efforts combined for the accomplishment of these objects, though various, have been such as materially to affect some of the most interesting portions of the human race. Their influence is at the present moment felt among the aborigines of Africa, the victims of colonial slavery, the millions of civilized China and India, the population of the inhospitable regions of Siberia and Greenland, and the inhabitants of the distant islands of the South Sea.

In this latter part of the world the author spent a number of years, endeavouring to promote the knowledge of Christianity among the natives; and while engaged in this pursuit, he regarded it as perfectly consistent with his office, and compatible with its duties, to collect, as opportunity offered, information on various subjects relative to the country and its inhabitants.

Although circumscribed in geographical extent, and comparatively insignificant in amount of population, the Society and Sandwich Islands have been regarded with unusual interest ever since their discovery; and the descriptions already given to the public, of the loveliness of their general appearance, and the peculiar character and engaging manners of their inhabitants, have excited a strong desire to obtain additional information relative to the varied natural phenomena of the Islands themselves; the early history; the moral, intellectual, and physical character of the people; and the nature of their ancient institutions.

All their usages of antiquity having been entirely superseded by the new order of things that has followed the subversion of their former system, the knowledge of but few of them is retained by the majority of the inhabitants, while the rising generation is growing up in total ignorance of all that distinguished their ancestors from themselves. The present, therefore, seems to be the only time in which a variety of facts, connected with the former state of the Inhabitants, can be secured; and to furnish, as far as possible, an authentic record of these, and thus preserve them from oblivion, is one design which the Author has always kept in view.

The following work will exhibit numerous facts, which may justly be regarded as illustrating the essential characteristics of idolatry, and its influence on a people, the simplicity of whose institutions affords facilities for observing its nature and tendencies, which could not be obtained in a more advanced state of society.

These volumes also contain a brief, but it is hoped satisfactory history of the origin, progress, and results of the Missionary enterprise, which, during the last thirty years, has, under the Divine blessing, transformed the barbarous, cruel, indolent, and idolatrous inhabitants of Tahiti, and the neighbouring Islands, into a comparatively civilized, humane, industrious, and Christian people. They also comprise a record of the measures pursued by the native governments, in changing the social economy of the people, and regulating their commercial intercourse with foreigners, in the promulgation of a new civil code, (a translation of which is given,) the establishment of courts of justice, and the introduction of trial by jury.

Besides information on these points, the present work furnishes an account of the intellectual culture, Christian experience, and general conduct, of the converts; the proceedings of the Missionaries in the several departments of their duty; the administration of the ordinances of Christianity; the establishment of the first churches, with their order and discipline; the advancement of education; the introduction of arts; the improvement in morals; and the progress of civilization.

During an absence of ten years from England, the author made copious notes of much that came under his notice, and, while residing in the South Seas, kept a daily journal. From these papers, from the printed and manuscript documents in the possession of the London Missionary Society, (to which the most ready access has been afforded,) from the very ample communications by the Missionaries in the islands, especially his respected colleagues, Messrs. Barff, Williams, and Orsmond, and from information derived by daily intercourse, for several years, with many of the natives, who have been identified with the most important events of the last thirty years in Tahiti, the present volumes have been written. He has studiously and constantly endeavoured to render the accounts accurate, and trusts they will prove, not only interesting, but useful.

From the defects that may appear in the execution of the work, he feels it necessary to apologize. It has been prepared amidst incessant public engagements, and some parts have passed through the press during his absence on a distant journey in behalf of the Missionary Society.

To the Rev. JOSEPH FLETCHER, A. M. of London, who, amidst his numerous and important engagements, has kindly inspected most of the sheets, and to Captain R. Elliot, R. N. who has favoured the Author with the use of his drawings for the embellishment of the work, he takes this opportunity of tendering his sincere and grateful acknowledgments.

POLYNESIAN RESEARCHES.

CHAP. I.

Historical notice of the discovery of the Pacific—Extent and limits of Polynesia—Voyages of Cook—Discovery of the Georgian and Society Islands — Origin of their designation—Number, names, and relative situation of the islands—Key to the pronunciation of native names—Extent and apparent structure of the islands—Beauty of the scenery—First approach to the shore of Matavai— Inland scenery — Description of Eimeo — Coral islands—Tetuaroa, the fashionable watering-place of Tahiti — Harbours — Islets on the reefs—Soil in the islands—Climate—Winds—Rains—and Tides.

PRELIMINARY REMARKS.

THE Pacific, the largest ocean in the world, extending over more than one-third of the surface of our globe, was discovered in the year 1513, by Vasco Nugnez de Balboa, a courageous and enterprising Spaniard, governor of the Spanish colony of Santa Maria, in the isthmus of Darien.

The desire of finding a more direct communication with the East Indies had prompted Columbus to the daring voyage which conducted him to the borders of the new world. In that immense and unexplored region, his followers pursued their career of enterprise, until Balboa, by discovering the great South Sea, accomplished what Columbus, notwithstanding his splendid achievements, had failed to perform. In his march across the isthmus which separates the Atlantic from the Pacific, (an enterprise designated by Robertson as the boldest on which the Spaniards had hitherto ventured in the New World,) Balboa, having been informed by his Indian guides, that he might view the sea from the next mountain, advanced alone to its summit; and beholding the vast ocean spread out before him in all its majesty, fell on his knees, and rendered thanks to God for having conducted him to so important a discovery. He hastened towards the object he had so laboriously sought, and, on reaching its margin, plunged up to his middle in its waves, with his sword and buckler, and took possession of it in the name of his sovereign, Ferdinand of Spain.

Seven years after this important event, Magellan, a Portuguese, despatched by the court of Spain to ascertain the exact situation of the Molucca Islands, sailed along the eastern coast of South America, discovered the straits that bear his name; and, passing through them, first launched the ships of Europe in the Southern Sea. It is, however, probable, that neither Balboa, while he gazed with transport on its mighty waters, nor Magellan, when he first whitened with his canvass the waves of that ocean whose smooth surface induced him to call it the PACIFIC, had any idea either of its vast extent, of the numerous islands that studded its bosom, the diversified and beautiful structure of those foundations, which myriads of tiny architects had reared from the depths of the ocean to the level of its highest wave, or of the varied tribes of man by whom they were inhabited. Boldly pursuing his way across the untraversed surface of this immense ocean, Magellan discovered the

NAME OF POLYNESIA.

Ladrone, and subsequently the Philippine islands. The object of the voyage was ultimately accomplished; the Victory, the vessel in which Magellan sailed, having performed the first voyage ever made round the world, returned to Europe: but the intrepid commander of the expedition terminated his life without reaching his original destination, having been killed in a quarrel with the natives of one of the Philippine Islands.

Several distinguished Spanish, Dutch, and British navigators followed the adventurous course of Magellan across the waters of the Pacific, and were rewarded by the discoveries they made in that part of the world, which, under the appellation of Polynesia,* from a Greek term signifying *many islands*, geographers have since denominated the sixth division of the globe. This designation was, in the sixteenth century, given by Portuguese authors to the Moluccas, the Philippines, and other islands to the eastward of Java; and was first appropriated to those clusters and islands, in reference to which it is employed in the present work, by President de Brosses, in his History of Navigation, published in Paris, 1756.

But, although many single islands and extensive groups, of diversified form and structure, some inhabited by isolated families of men, others peopled only by pelicans or aquatic birds, have been visited and explored, fresh discoveries continue to

---

* According to De Brosses, Malte Brun, Pinkerton, and others, Polynesia includes the various islands found in the Pacific, from the Ladrones to Easter Island. The principal groups are—the Ladrone Islands, the Carolinas, the Pelew Islands, the Sandwich Islands, the Friendly Islands, the Navigators' Islands, the Hervey Islands, the Society Islands, the Georgian Islands, and the Marquesas.

be made by almost every voyager; and it is by no means improbable, that there are yet many islands, and even groups of islands, which remain unknown to the inhabitants of the other parts of the globe.

Most of the early voyages of discovery in this ocean attracted unusual attention: those made in the sixteenth and seventeenth centuries, from the facilities they were expected to afford in the ultimate discovery of the long-sought southern continent; or the rich booty they furnished the daring adventurers, who often captured the Spanish vessels loaded with specie or precious metals. The narratives of voyages of a later period were equally attractive, by the fascinating descriptions they presented of countries and people before unknown. Among these, none appear to have excited a livelier interest, or produced a deeper impression, than those performed by Captain Cook, in the close of the eighteenth century. They were instrumental, in a great degree, in diverting public attention from the splendid and stupendous discoveries in the New World, and directing it to the clustering islands spread over the Pacific; exhibiting them in all the loveliness of their natural scenery, the interesting simplicity, and novel manners, of their inhabitants. The influence of Cook's discoveries appears to have been felt by voyagers and travellers of other countries, as well as by those of his own. Humboldt, speaking of his laborious researches in South America, remarks, that "the savages of America inspire less interest, since the celebrated navigators have made known to us the inhabitants of the South Sea, in whose character we find such a mixture of perversity and meekness: the state of half-civilization in which these islanders are found, gives a peculiar charm to the description of their manners. Here, a king, followed by a numerous suite, comes and presents the fruits of his orchard; there, the funeral festival embrowns the shade of the lofty forest. Such pictures, no doubt, have more attraction than those which portray the solemn gravity of the inhabitants of the Missouri or the Maranon."*

Since the death of Captain Cook, several intelligent and scientific men from England, France, and Russia, have undertaken voyages of discovery in the South Seas, and have favoured the world with the result of their enterprises. Their accounts are read with interest, not only by those engaged in nautical pursuits and the promotion of geographical science, but by the philosopher, who seeks to study human nature under all its diversified forms; and by the naturalist, who investigates the phenomena of our globe, and the varied productions of its surface. Voyages of discovery are also favourite volumes with the juvenile reader. They impart to the youthful mind many delightful and glowing impressions relative to the strange and interesting scenes they exhibit, which in after-life are seldom obliterated.—There are few who do not retain the vivid recollections of their first perusal of Prince Leeboo, or Captain Cook's Voyages. Often, when a school-boy, I have found the most gratifying recreation, for a winter's evening, in reading the account of the wreck of the Antelope, the discovery of Tahiti, and other narratives of a similar kind. Little, however, did I suppose, when in imagination I have followed the discoverer from island to island, and have gazed in fancy on their romantic hills and valleys, together with their strange but interesting inhabitants, that I should

* Humboldt Pers. Nar. preface.

ever visit scenes, the description of which afforded me so much satisfaction. This, however, in the providence of God, has since taken place; and I have been led, not indeed on a voyage of discovery, commercial adventure, or naval enterprise, but, as a Christian Missionary, on an errand of instruction; not only to visit, but to reside a number of years among the interesting natives of those isolated regions. The following pages record my observations in that part of the world. The account of the ancient customs, &c. of the people, and recent changes, have been derived principally from the people themselves, by my own inquiries, or the communications of my predecessors or companions in Missionary pursuits, with occasional illustrations from those who have visited the islands for purposes of commerce or science.

TAHITI, and the isles in its immediate vicinity, are situated between five and seven degrees of latitude within the southern tropic. The principal island is supposed by some to have been discovered by Quiros, towards the end of the sixteenth century: on this point, however, different opinions exist, and no authentic knowledge of Tahiti was obtained until Captain Wallis, in the Dolphin, crossed the Pacific, about 160 years ago. He anchored in Matavai bay on the 19th of June, 1767, gave to the harbour the name of Port Royal, and to the land, King George the Third's Island. The adjacent island of Eimeo was seen by Captain Wallis, and from him received the designation of Duke of York's Island. In 1769, Captain Cook, who, with a number of scientific gentlemen, had been despatched to the South Seas, for the purpose of observing the transit of Venus, anchored in Matavai bay. By him the native name was affixed to the island which, through a slight mistake that a foreigner might easily make, he called Otaheite. Bougainville, manifesting in this respect a nicer discrimination of sound, rejected the *O*, which is no part of the name, and called it Taiti; he however omitted the aspirate. By the natives their island is called Ta-hi-ti. The *i* having the sound of *e* in their language, it is pronounced as if written in English Ta-he-te. Captain Cook visited several parts of Tahiti, and the neighbouring islands; and, in honour of his majesty George III. by whom the expedition had been sent, he designated the cluster of which Tahiti is the principal, THE GEORGIAN ISLANDS: another cluster, which he discovered about 70 miles to the westward, he called THE SOCIETY ISLANDS, in honour of the Royal Society, at whose recommendation the expedition had been appointed. The Georgian Isles include Tahiti, Eimeo, Tabuaemanu or Sir Charles Sanders' Island, Tetuaroa, Matea, and Meetia. The Society Islands include Huahine, Raiatea, Tahaa, Borabora, Maurua, Tubai, Moupiha or Lord Howe's Island, and Fenuaura or Scilly Islands; with the small islets surrounding them.

The two clusters extend from 16 to 18 degrees S. lat. and from 149 to 155 degrees W. long. and are often included by geographical writers, among others by M. Malte Brun, under the general designation of the Society Islands.* As the islands are politically as well as geographically distinct, I have retained the designations given by Captain Cook, occasionally exchanging them for the terms Windward and Leeward Islands, which are frequently used by those residing and trading among them.

* System of Geography, vol. iii. p. 630.

The following table, principally from Wallis, Cook, and Wilson, will shew their relative situations:—

	SOUTH LAT.	WEST LONG.
Meatia,	17° 53′ 0″	148° 9′ 45″
Tahiti, north point,	17 29 17	149 33 15
Eimeo,	17 30 0	150 0 0
Maiaoiti, or Sir Charles Sander's Island,	17 28 0	150 40 0
Huahine,	16 43 0	151 6 45
Raiatea,	16 46 0	151 38 45
Tahaa, three miles northward of Raiatea.		
Borabora,	16 27 0	151 52 45
Maurua,	16 10 0	152 30 0
Lord Howe's Island,	16 46 0	154 12 45
Scilly Island,	16 28 0	155 24 45

In the preceding list I have adopted the orthography introduced by the first Missionaries, and by the press now established among the people. This has not been done from caprice or affectation, but because the letters approach the nearest to the signification of the sounds used by the natives themselves. In the words Otaheite, Otahaa, &c. sounds were exhibited which do not belong to the names they were intended to express, and on this account only they have been rejected.

As the native names of persons and places will unavoidably occur in the succeeding pages, a brief notice of the sounds of the letters, and the division of some of the principal words, will probably familiarize them to the eye of the reader, and facilitate their pronunciation.

The different Polynesian dialects abound in vowel sounds perhaps above any other language; they have also another striking peculiarity, that of rejecting all double consonants, possessing invariably vowel terminations, both of their syllables and words. Every final vowel is therefore distinctly sounded. Several consonants used in the English language, do not exist in that of the Georgian and Society Islanders. There is no sibilant, or hissing sound: s and c, and the corresponding letters, are therefore unnecessary. The consonants that are used retain the sound usually attached to them in English.

The natives sound the vowels with great distinctness: *a* has the sound of a in father, *e* the sound of a in fate, *i* that of i in marine or *e* in me, *o* that of o in no, and *u* that of oo in root. The diphthong *ai* is sounded as i in wine. The following are some of the names most frequently used in the present work.

The first column presents them in the proper syllabic divisions observed by the people. In the second column I have endeavoured to exhibit the native orthoëpy, by employing those letters which, according to their general use in the English language, would secure, as nearly as possible, the accurate pronunciation of the native words. The *h* is placed after the *a* only to secure to that vowel the uniform sound of *a* in father, or *a* in the interjection *ah*, or *aha*. *Y* is also placed after *a*, to secure for the Tahitian vowel *e*, invariably the sound of *a* in *day-light* or *may-pole*.

NAMES OF PLACES.

Ta-hí-ti	pronounced as	Tah-he-te
Ma-ta-vái	. . . . . .	Máh-tah-vye
Pá-re	. . . .	Pae-ray
Pá-pe-é-te	. . . . . .	Pah-pay-ay-tay
A'-te-hú-ru	. . . . . .	Ah-tay-hoo-roo
Tái-a-rá-bu	. . . . . .	Tye-ah-rah-boo
Eí-me-o	. . . . . .	Eye-may-o
Mo-o-ré-a	. . . . . .	Mo-o-ray-ah
A-fá-re-aí-tu.	. . . . . .	Ah-fah-ray-eye-too
O'-pu-nó-hu .	. . . . . .	O-poo-no-hoo
Hu-a-hí-ne	. . . . . .	Hoo-ah-he-nay

Fá-re	Fáh-ray
Raí-a-té-a	Rye-ah-tay-ah
O-pó-a	O-po-ah
U'-tu-maó-ro	Oo-too-mao-ro
Ta-há-a	Tah-ha-ah
Bó-ra-bó-ra	Bo-rah-bo-rah
Mau-rú-a	Mou-roo-ah
Rá-pa	Rah-pah
Aí-tu-tá-ke	Eye-too-tah-kay
Mi-ti-á-ro	Me-te-ah-ro
Ma-ú-te	Mah-oo-tay
A-ti-ú	Ah-tew
Ra-ro-tó-gna	Rah-ro-to-na
or	or
Ra-ro-tón-ga	Rah-ro-ton-ga
Tu-bu-aí	Too-boo-eye
Raí-va-vaí	Ry-vah-vye
Rí-ma-tá-ra	Re-mah-tah-rah

NAMES OF PERSONS.

Po-má-re	Po-mah-ray
I-dí-a	E-dee-ah
Ai-má-ta	Eye-mah-tah
Té-rii-tá-ri-a	Tay-ree-tah-re-ah
Tá-ro-á-ri-i	Tah-ro-ah-ree
Ma-hí-ne	Mah-he-nay
Té-rai-má-no	Tay-rye-mah-no
Taú-a	Tou-ah
Tá-ma-tó-a	Tah-mah-to-ah
Fe-nú-a-pé-ho	Fay-noo-ah-pay-ho
Mai	Mye
Au-ná	Ou-nah

A-tú-a	(God)		Ah-too-ah
Va-rú-a	(Spirit)		Vah-roo-ah
Tá-a-ta	(Man)		Tah-ah-tah
A-rí-i	(King)		Ah-re-e
Rá-a-tí-ra	(Chief)		Rah-ah-te-rah.

ORIGIN OF ISLANDS.

Tahiti, the principal of the Georgian Islands, is the most extensive and lofty of the group. It is formed by two peninsulas, united by a long broad isthmus. The largest is circular in form, and above twenty miles in diameter. The smaller is oval, and is sixteen miles long, and eight broad. The circumference of the whole island is 108 miles. The whole of the islands are mountainous in the interior, and have a border, from one to four miles wide, of rich level land, extending from the base of the high land to the sea, and though the outline of each has some peculiarity distinguishing it from the rest, in their general appearance they resemble each other. Tetuaroa, Tubai, Lord Howe's, and Scilly islands, however, form exceptions, as they are low coral islands, seldom rising many feet above the sea. Eimeo is supposed to be about twenty-five miles in circumference, Huahine probably more than thirty, and Raiatea somewhat larger. The others, though equally elevated, are of smaller extent.

A corresponding resemblance to each other prevails in the geological structure of the principal clusters and surrounding islands; the substances of which the majority are composed being the same, while each island has some distinguishing peculiarity.

There is no reason to suppose that either Tahiti, or any adjacent island, is altogether volcanic in its origin, as Hawaii, and the whole of the Sandwich Islands, are. The entire mass, composing the latter, has evidently been in a state of fusion, and in that condition has been ejected from the focus of an immense volcano, or volcanoes, originating, probably, at the bottom of the sea, and forming, by their action through successive ages, the whole group of islands; in which nothing like primitive or secondary rock has yet been found. In Tahiti, and other islands of the southern cluster, there are basalts, whinstone dykes, and homogeneous earthy lava, retaining all the convolutions which cooling lava is known to assume; there are also kinds of hornstone, limestone, silex, breccia, and other substances, which, under the action of fire, do not appear to have altered their original form. Some are found in detached fragments, others in large masses.

The variety of substances found in some of the smaller islands is greater than that which is met with in Tahiti, or the Georgian cluster. In Borabora there are masses of rock, apparently composed of feldspar and quartz; and in Maupiti, besides the common vesicular lava and the basalt common to all the islands, a species of granite is found in considerable abundance, which presents an anomaly as striking in the geology of these islands, as that furnished by the existence of carbonate of lime in the island of Rurutu, where garnets are also obtained. Hornblende and feldspar are found in Huahine, as well as in some of the other islands. Ancient lava, containing olivine, augite, and zeolite, are also met with, together with pumice and cellular lava, some kinds of which, found in Sir Charles Sanders' Island, are of a dark blue colour, and, though apparently containing a portion of iron, so light as to float on the water. Specimens of these I have by me; and a large one of the latter kind from Sir Charles Sanders' island, is more porous than any I ever met with among the volcanoes of the Sandwich Islands, and so completely honeycomb in its structure, that it is difficult to account for its formation.

Strata, or veins of basalt, are frequently met with in all the islands: they usually occur in mountains of amygdaloid rock, or cellular volcanic stone. The veins or strata are seldom, if ever, horizontal, but generally perpendicular, oblique, or curved. One of the most extensive and curious of these, is piled up in stupendous grandeur near the head of Matavai valley, and overhangs the mountain-stream that flows around its base. There are several in Huahine, which I have examined. One, on Huahiné-iti, intersects, in an oblique direction with an inclination towards the west, a large mass of pumice and ancient porous lava; another, situated on the south-east front of Vaiorea, in the midst of a pile of more compact and apparently recent lava, is nearly perpendicular; both resemble very much the whinstone dykes in the north of Ireland. The crystallized columns or prisms are very perfectly formed, and are laid at right angles with the position of the vein they compose. The greater part appear pentangular, but their shape and size is not uniform. On comparing a very small triangular crystal, which I brought from Vaiorea, with one which I procured from the dykes near the Giant's Causeway, the substance and structure of each appeared nearly the same.

Although so many unequivocal appearances of the action of fire occur in almost every island, especially in those in which I have had the best opportunity of pursuing inquiries, relative to the probable origin of the islands, viz., Huahine, and the small adjacent island of Vaiorea, where the cellular rocks often present a surface, exactly resembling that of the recently ejected and scarcely indurated lava in Hawaii; I never met with any cavern, aperture, or other formation resembling a crater; nor have I heard of the existence of any, with the exception of the large lake called by the natives Vaihiria, situated among the mountains of Tahiti. The wild and broken manner, however, in which the rocks and mountains now appear, warrants the inference, that since their formation, which was probably of equal antiquity with the bed of the ocean, they have been thrown up by some volcanic explosion, the disruptions of an earthquake, or other violent convulsions of the earth; and have, from this circumstance, assumed their bold, irregular, and romantic forms.

Every writer on the South Sea Islands has been lavish in praise of their scenery. Malte Brun observes, " A new Cythera emerges from the bosom of the enchanted wave. An amphitheatre of verdure rises to our view; tufted groves mingle their foliage with the brilliant enamel of the meadows; an eternal spring, combining with an eternal autumn, displays the opening blossom along with the ripened fruits."* When speaking of Tahiti, he remarks, that it " has merited the title of Queen of the Pacific Ocean." The descriptions in Cook's voyages are not exaggerated, and no scenery is adapted to produce a more powerful or delightful impression on the mind of those who traverse the wide ocean, in which they are situated, than the islands of the South Sea. The effect on my own mind, when approaching Tahiti for the first time, will not be easily obliterated.

The sea had been calm, the morning fair, the sky was without a cloud, and the lightness of the breeze had afforded us leisure for gazing upon the varied, picturesque, and beautiful scenery of this most enchanting island. We had beheld successively, as

* Syst. of Geog. vol. iii. p. 396. Ibid. p. 631.

we slowly sailed along its shore, all the diversity of hill and valley, broken or stupendous mountains, and rocky precipices, clothed with every variety of verdure, from the moss of the jutting promontories on the shore, to the deep and rich foliage of the bread-fruit tree, the Oriental luxuriance of the tropical pandanus, or the waving plumes of the lofty and graceful cocoa-nut grove. The scene was enlivened by the waterfall on the mountain's side, the cataract that chafed along its rocky bed in the recesses of the ravine, or the stream that slowly wound its way through the fertile and cultivated valleys, and the whole was surrounded by the white-crested waters of the Pacific, rolling their waves of foam in splendid majesty upon the coral reefs, or dashing in spray against its broken shore.

Cataracts and waterfalls, though occasionally seen, are not so numerous on any part of the Tahitian coast, as in the north-eastern shores of Hawaii. The mountains of Tahiti are less grand and stupendous than those of the northern group —but there is a greater richness of verdure and variety of landscape; the mountains are much broken in the interior, and deep and frequent ravines intersect their declivity from the centre to the shore. As we advanced towards the anchorage, I had time to observe, not only the diversified scenery, but the general structure and form, of the island. Tahiti, excepting the border of low alluvial land, by which it is nearly surrounded, is altogether mountainous, and highest in the centre. The mountains frequently diverge in short ranges from the interior towards the shore, though some rise like pyramids with pointed summits, and others present a conical, or sugar-loaf form, while the outline of several is regular, and almost circular. Orohena, the central and loftiest mountain in Tahiti, is six or seven thousand feet above the sea. Its summit is generally enveloped in clouds; but when the sky is clear, its appearance is broken and picturesque.

Matavai bay was the first place where we anchored, or had an opportunity of examining more closely the country. The level land at the mouth of the valley is broad, but along the eastern and southern sides, the mountains approach nearer to the sea. A dark-coloured sandy beach extends all round the bay, except at its southern extremity, near One-tree Hill, where the shore is rocky and bold. Groves of bread-fruit and cocoa-nut trees appear in every direction, and, amid the luxuriance of vegetation every where presented, the low and rustic habitations of the natives gave a pleasing variety to the delightful scene.

In the exterior or border landscapes of Tahiti and the other islands, there is a variety of objects, a happy combination of land and water, of precipices and plains, of trees often hanging their branches, clothed with thick foliage, over the sea, and distant mountains shewn in sublime outline and richest hues; and the whole, often blended in the harmony of nature, produces sensations of admiration and delight. The inland scenery is of a different character, but not less impressive. The landscapes are occasionally extensive, but more frequently circumscribed. There is, however, a startling boldness in the towering piles of basalt, often heaped in romantic confusion near the source or margin of some crystal stream, that flows in silence at their base, or dashes over the rocky fragments that arrest its progress: and

SOIL AND PRODUCTIONS.

there is the wildness of romance about the deep and lonely glens, around which the mountains rise like the steep sides of a natural amphitheatre, till the clouds seem supported by them—this arrests the attention of the beholder, and for a time suspends his faculties in mute astonishment. There is also so much that is new in the character and growth of trees and flowers, irregular, spontaneous, and luxuriant in the vegetation, which is sustained by a prolific soil, and matured by the genial heat of a tropic clime, that it is adapted to produce an indescribable effect. Often, when, either alone, or attended by one or two companions, I have journeyed through some of the inland parts of the islands, such has been the effect of the scenery through which I have passed, and the unbroken stillness which has pervaded the whole that imagination, unrestrained, might easily have induced the delusion, that we were walking on enchanted ground, or passing over fairy lands. It has at such seasons appeared as if we had been carried back to the primitive ages of the world, and beheld the face of the earth, as it was perhaps often exhibited, when the Creator's works were spread over it in all their endless variety, and all the vigour of exhaustless energy, and before population had extended, or the genius and enterprise of man had altered the aspect of its surface.

The valleys of Tahiti present some of the richest inland scenery that can be imagined. Those in the southern parts are remarkable for their beauty, but none more so than those of Hautaua, Matavai, and Apaiano. Those portions of them, in which the incipient effects of civilization appear, are the most interesting; presenting the neat white plastered cottages in beautiful contrast with the picturesque appearance of the mountains, and the rich verdure of the plains.

The outline of the mountains of Eimeo, and much of the low land, may, when the weather is clear, be distinctly seen from Tahiti.

Moorea is the name most frequently given by the natives to the island of Eimeo, which is situated about twelve or fourteen miles west from Tahiti. In the varied forms its mountains exhibit, the verdure with which they are clothed, and the general romantic and beautiful character of its scenery, this island surpasses every other in the Georgian or Society groups. The reef of coral which, like a ring, surrounds it, is in some places one or two miles distant from the shore, in others united to the beach. Several smal and verdant islands adorn the reef: one lies opposite the district of Afareaitu on the eastern side; and two others, a few miles south of Papetoai; the latter are covered with the elegantly growing casuarina, or aito-trees, and were a favourite retreat of Pomare the Second. Eimeo is not only distinguished by its varied and beautiful natural scenery, but also by the excellence of its harbours, which are better than those in any of the other islands.

On the north side is Taloo harbour, in lat. 17° 30 south, long. 150° west: one of the most secure and delightful anchoring places to be met with in the Pacific; Opunohu is the proper name of this harbour; near the mouth of which, on the right-hand side, there is a small rock, called by the natives *Tareu*, towards which, it is possible, Captain Cook was pointing, or looking, when he inquired of the natives the name of the harbour his ship was then entering. Tareu might be easily understood as if spelled Taloo, and the name of the rock thus mistaken for that of the harbour. Separated from Opunohu by a high mountain, is another capacious bay, called, after its discoverer, Cook's harbour; it is equally convenient for anchorage with the former, but rather more difficult of access.

On the north-eastern side of Eimeo, between the mountain and the sea, is an extensive and beautiful lake, called Tamai, on the border of which stands a sequestered village, bearing the same name. The lake is stocked with fish, and is a place of resort for flocks of wild ducks, which are sometimes taken in great numbers. The rivers of Eimeo, like those of the other islands, are but small, and are principally mountain streams, which originate in the high lands, roll down the rocky bottoms of the ravines, and wind their way through the valleys to the sea. The mountains are broken, and considerably elevated, but not so high as those of Tahiti, which are probably 7000 feet above the level of the sea.

The South Sea islands are not more distinguished by the elevation of their mountains, the picturesque outline of their landscapes, and the richness of their verdure, than by the extent, variety, and beauty, of those natural breakwaters of coral by which they are surrounded. The large islands, though not of coral formation, all share the advantages of that secure protection which the reefs afford. Among the smaller islands four, viz. Tetuaroa, Tobua, Moupiha, and Fenuaara, appear to rest on coral foundations. The former, which is about twenty miles north of Tahiti, includes five small islets, the names of which are Rimatu, Onehoa, Moturua, Hoatere, and Reiona. They are enclosed by one reef, in which there is an opening on the north-west, but only such as to admit with difficulty the narrow canoes of the natives. They are all low islands, the highest parts being seldom three or four feet above the water; the only soil they contain is composed of sand and fragments of coral, with which is mingled vegetable mould, produced on the spot, or carried from Tahiti. The chief article of food produced in these islands is the fruit of the cocoa-nut tree; with extensive and verdant groves of which they are adorned. They seem, at a distance, as if they were growing on the surface of the water, and the roots and stems of many are washed by the spray, or by the tide, when it rises a few inches higher than usual. Upon the kernel of the cocoa-nut, and the fish taken among the reefs, the inhabitants principally subsist.

Te-tua-roa, (the long, or distant, sea,) is part of the hereditary possessions of the reigning family of Tahiti; it is attached to the district of Pare, and is said formerly to have been the depository of the monarch's treasures. Most of the inhabitants of these little islets occupy, under the king, a part of his own land, from which they are supplied with bread-fruit and taro. They are much employed in fishing, and formerly brought over large quantities of fish, conveying in return bread-fruit, and other edible productions, from Tahiti. In the wars which disturbed the conclusion of the reign of Pomare the First, and the commencement of that of his successor, many of the inhabitants were cut off; and the decrease of population, thus occasioned, has diminished the intercourse between these islands and Tahiti.

In addition to the fishery carried on here, Tetuaroa has long been a kind of watering-place for the royal family, and a frequent resort for what might be called the fashionable and gay of Tahiti. Hither the areois, dancers, and singers, were accustomed to repair, together with those whose lives were professedly devoted to indolence and pleasure. It was also frequented by the females of the higher class, for the purposes of *haapori*, increasing the corpulency of their persons, and removing, by luxurious ease under the embowering shade of the cocoa-nut groves, the dark tinge which the vertical sun of Tahiti might have burnt upon their complexions. So great was the intercourse formerly, that a hundred canoes have sometimes been seen at one time on the beach.

The coral reefs, around the islands, not only protect the low land from the violence of the sea, but often exhibit one of the most sublime and beautiful marine spectacles that it is possible to behold. They are generally a mile, or a mile and a half, and occasionally two miles, from the shore. The surface of the water within the reef is placid and transparent; while that without, if there be the slightest breeze, is considerably agitated; and, being unsheltered from the wind, is generally raised in high and foaming waves.

The trade-wind, blowing constantly towards the shore, drives the waves with violence upon the reef, which is from five, to twenty or thirty yards wide. The long rolling billows of the Pacific, extending sometimes, in one unbroken line, a mile or a mile and a half along the reef, arrested by this natural barrier, often rise ten, twelve, or fourteen feet above its surface; and then, bending over it their white foaming tops, form a graceful liquid arch, glittering in the rays of a tropical sun, as if studded with brilliants. But, before the eyes of the spectator can follow the splendid aqueous gallery which they appear to have reared, with loud and hollow roar they fall in magnificent desolation, and spread the gigantic fabric in froth and spray upon the horizontal and gently broken surface of the coral.

In each of the islands, and opposite the large valleys, through which a stream of water falls into the ocean, there is usually a break, or opening, in the line of reef that surrounds the shore—a most wise and benevolent provision for the ingress and egress of vessels, as well as a singular phenomenon in the natural history of these marine ramparts. Whether the current of fresh water, constantly flowing from the rivers to the ocean, prevents the tiny architects from building their concentric walls in one continued line, or whether in the fresh water itself there is any quality inimical to the growth or increase of coral, is not easy to determine; but it is a remarkable fact, that few openings occur in the reefs which surround the South Sea Islands, excepting opposite those parts of the shore from which streams of fresh water flow into the sea. Reefs of varied, but generally circumscribed extent, are frequently observed within the large outer barrier, and near the shore, or mouth of the river; but they are formed in shallow places, and the coral is of a different and more slender kind, than that of which the larger reef, rising from the depths of the ocean, is usually composed. There is no coral in the lagoons of the large islands.

The openings in the reefs around Sir Charles Sanders' Island, Maurua, and other low islands, are small and intricate, and sometimes altogether wanting, probably because the land, composing these islands, collects but a scanty portion of water; and, if any, only small and frequently interrupted streams flow into the sea. The apertures in the coral beds around the larger islands, not only afford direct access to the indentations in the coast, and the mouths of the valleys, which form the best harbours, but secure to shipping a supply of fresh water, in equal, if not greater abundance, than it could be procured in any other part of the island. The circumstance, also, of the rivers near the harbours flowing into the sea, affords the greatest facility in procuring fresh water, which is so valuable to seamen.

These breaches in the reefs, in many places, especially at Papete, or Wilks' Harbour, in Tahiti and Afareaitu, in Moorea Fare, in Huahine, and along the eastern side of Raiatea and Tahaa, are not only serviceable to navigation, but highly ornamental, and contribute much to the beauty of the surrounding scenery. At the *Ava Moa*, or Sacred Entrance leading to Opoa, there is a small island, on which a few cocoa-nut trees are growing. At Tipaemau there are two, one on each side of the opening, rising from the extremity of the line of reef. The little islets, elevated three or four feet above the water, are clothed with shrubs and verdure, and adorned with a number of lofty cocoa-nut trees. At Te-Avapiti, several miles to the northward of Tipaemau, and opposite the Missionary settlement—where, as its name indicates, are two openings—there are also two beautiful, green, and woody islands, on which the lowly hut of the fisherman, or of the voyager waiting for a favourable wind, may be often seen. Two large and very charming islands adorn the entrance at Tomahahotu, leading to the island of Tahaa. The largest of these is not more than half a mile in circumference, but both are covered with fresh and evergreen shrubs and trees.

Detached from the large islands, and viewed in connexion with the ocean rolling through the channel on the one side, or the foaming billows dashing, and roaring, and breaking over the reef on the other, they appear like emerald gems of the ocean, contrasting their solitude and verdant beauty with the agitated element sporting in grandeur around. They are useful, as well as ornamental. The tall cocoa-nuts that grow on their surface, can be seen many miles distant; and the native mariner is thereby enabled to steer directly towards the spot where he knows he shall find a passage to the shore. The constant current passing the opening, probably deposited on the ends of the reef fragments of coral, sea-weeds, and drift-wood, which in time rose above the surface of the water. Seeds borne thither by the waves, or wafted by the winds, found a soil on which they could germinate—decaying vegetation increased the mould—and by this process it is most likely these beautiful little fairy-looking islands were formed on the ends of the reefs at the entrance to the different harbours.

The *Soil* of the islands presents considerable variety. The sides of the mountains are frequently covered with a thin layer of light earth, but the summits of many of the inferior hills present a thick strata, or covering, of stiff red ochre, or yellow marl. The ochre greatly resembles burnt clay, and in the island of Rurutu, and some others of the group, its colour is so strong as to enable the natives to form a bright red pigment for staining or painting their doors, window-shutters, canoes, and, when mixed with lime, the walls of

FERTILITY AND CAPABILITIES.

their houses. This kind of ochre is seldom found in the lofty mountains composed of basalt, or cellular volcanic stone, but generally covers the lower hills that rise between the interior mountains and the shore. It is not peculiar to any single island, and in some places it appears several feet in thickness. Besides the soil on the sides of the mountains and the bottom of the valleys, around each of the islands there are level borders of varied breadth, sometimes three or four miles wide. This, to the inhabitants, is the most valuable portion of land; here their gardens are enclosed, and hence their chief subsistence and greatest luxuries are derived. The soil here is a rich alluvial deposit, with a considerable admixture of vegetable mould. It is remarkably prolific; the only manure ever used is decayed leaves, and these are employed more to loosen than enrich the soil. Near the base of the mountains, though stony, it is fertile; but nearer to the sea, where a considerable portion of sand is incorporated, it is less fruitful. In many places the sea has thrown up an embankment along the shore, considerably higher than the intervening space between the shore and the mountains; extensive swamps are thus formed. Though the effluvia arising from these marshy places must be highly prejudicial to health, they are generally prized by the natives, and, though not drained, enclosed for the culture of the different kinds of arum which constitute so great a portion of the food of the people, when the bread-fruit is out of season. The soil of the South Sea Islands is not only rich, but extensive, and capable, if cultivated, of supporting a population nearly ten times as large as that which it now sustains.

The *Climate* of the South Sea Islands is in general regular, and, though considerably hotter than in Europe, is more temperate than that of the East or West Indies, or those parts of the continent of America that are situated in the same latitude. This is probably occasioned by the vast expanse of ocean around; for though only 17 degrees from the equator, the thermometer, in the shade, seldom rises higher than 90, while the general average in some of the islands is not more than 74. During the time the Duff remained in Tahiti, from March to August, 1797, the thermometer was never lower than 65, and seldom higher than 73; and between the months of April and August, 1819, it ranged in the morning from 68 to 78, at noon from 75 to 84, and in the evening from 70 to 78. Sometimes it rises for a short time much higher than 90, but I never saw it so low as 60. The heat is constant, and, to an European, debilitating, though much less so than that of an Indian climate. To the natives it is genial, and, excepting in the immediate neighbourhood of their stagnant waters or marshy ground, is salubrious. They experience no inconvenience from the heat, and often, when the mornings have been gratefully cool to a European, they wrap themselves in their warmest clothing.

The climate is remarkably serene and equable; its changes are neither violent, frequent, nor sudden. This circumstance, were it not for the constant heat, would render it remarkably salubrious. The atmosphere is moist, and the agreeable alternations of land and sea breezes are experienced during the greater part of the year. The refreshing land breeze sweeps down the valleys soon after sunset, but, though grateful to the inhabitants on the shore, it extends only a short distance over the ocean. The sea breeze sets in in the forenoon. These breezes are, however, from the circumscribed surface of land, which in comparison with the surrounding waters is exceedingly limited, more feeble and transient than those which prevail on the shores of the continents in the same latitude.

Strong currents of air, resembling whirlwinds, occasionally sweep across the islands, and produce considerable devastations among the plantations and habitations of the people: tempests are sometimes heavy and destructive, but the islands are never visited with those fearful hurricanes or tornadoes, that occur in the West Indies, or in the Indian and Chinese seas. In general, the winds are moderate, and peculiarly refreshing.

The east, with its variations from north-east to south-east, being the regular trade-wind, is most prevalent, but is seldom unpleasantly violent. Winds from the north are often tempestuous, more so than from the south, yet, although during the season of variable winds, viz. from December to March, they are strong, and continue several days, they are not dangerous. The wind seldom prevails from the west, among the Society Islands, excepting in the months of December, January, and February. At this season, though the westerly winds are usually of short duration, they are often heavy and boisterous. The sky is dark and lowering, rain frequently falls in torrents, and the weather is remarkably unsettled.

Rain is much more frequent in the Society than in the Sandwich Islands, during the whole of the year; but, except in the rainy season, it is seldom heavy or lasting: gentle showers fall, during many of the months, almost every alternate day, though sometimes there are some weeks of dry weather. The rainy season, the only variation of the tropical year, occurs when the sun is vertical, and generally continues from December to March, At this season the rains are heavy, and often incessant for several weeks — the streams are swollen and muddy—the low lands overflowed— fences washed away—and, unless great care is taken, many plantations destroyed. The winds are also variable and tempestuous, the climate is more insalubrious, and sickness among the people greater, than at any other period. Thunder and lightning are frequent on the islands, especially during the rainy season. The lightnings are vivid and awful, though not frequently injurious to the dwellings, or fatal to the inhabitants. The thunder is sometimes loud and terrific, often more appalling than any I ever heard in any other parts of the world. The awful effects of the loud and quick-succeeding thunders is probably much increased by the hilly nature of the country, which greatly augments the reverberations of the deafening reports.

Among the natural phenomena of the South Sea Islands, the tide is one of the most singular, and presents as great an exception to the theory of Sir Isaac Newton as is to be met with in any part of the world. The rising and falling of the waters of the ocean appear, if influenced at all, to be so in a very small degree only, by the moon. The height to which the water rises, varies but a few inches during the whole year, and at no time is it elevated more than a foot, or a foot and a half. The sea, however, often rises to an unusual height, but this appears to be the effect of a strong wind blowing for

PHENOMENA OF TIDES.

some time from one quarter, or the heavy swells of the sea, which flow from different directions, and prevail equally during the time of high and low water. But the most remarkable circumstance is, the uniformity of the time of high and low water. During the year, whatever be the age or situation of the moon, the water is lowest at six in the morning, and the same hour in the evening, and highest at noon and midnight. This is so well established, that the time of night is marked by the ebbing and flowing of the tide; and, in all the islands, the term for high water and for midnight is the same.

CHAP. II.

Vegetable productions of the Islands—Forests—Various kinds of timber—The Apape and faifai—The aito, or casuarina—Tiairi, candlenut tree—Callophylla Barringtonia—Thespesia populnea—Erythrina—Hibiscus—The auti, or cloth plant—Description, uses, and legends of the sacred aoa—Account of the bread-fruit tree and fruit—Various methods of preparing the fruit—Arum or taro, uhi or yam—U-ma-ra, or sweet potato—Culture, preparation, and method of dressing the arrow-root—Appearance and value of the cocoanut tree—Several stages of growth in which the fruit is used—Manufacture of cocoa-nut oil.

THE warmth of a tropical climate, and a humid atmosphere, operating on a prolific soil, combine to render vegetation in the South Sea Islands rapid and luxuriant. The botany, however, of the islands was rather abundant than diversified, when compared with that of New Holland, or other intertropical countries. But though the flora of Polynesia is less varied and brilliant than that of New South Wales, and among its valuable trees there be neither the oak of Europe, the teak of India, the cedar of America, the eucalypti of New Holland, nor the pine of New Zealand, it is not deficient in valuable timber.

Many of the inferior hills, and the sides of the loftiest mountains, are clothed with forests of stately trees. Among these, the most valuable is the apape, a tree resembling, in its habits of growth, the gum of New Holland, and the pine of New Zealand, rearing its straight and branchless trunk, two or three feet in diameter, forty or fifty feet, and spreading above a light crown of pale green leaves, not much unlike the leaves of the English ash. The wood, which is harder than the pine, and of a beautiful pink or salmon colour, is easily worked and durable. It is frequently used by the natives in building their canoes. The faifai is another tree resembling this, but rather smaller in size, of a bright yellow colour, and hard texture. Numbers of small kinds of timber are found in the mountains, but these two are the most valuable.

Next to these there is a numerous class that grow on the sides of the hills, and connect the forests of the mountains with the woods of the valley or the plain. The principal of these is the aito, or toa, *casuarina equasitifolia;* the shape of this tree is remarkably light and elegant, and its appearance is superior to that of the most graceful of the firs. The wood when first cut has a deep red, but on exposure to the air it assumes a dark chesnut or black colour. It is exceedingly hard, and more durable than any other in the islands: by foreigners it is often called iron wood; and was formerly employed by the inhabitants in the manufacture of their implements of war. The reva, *galaxa sparta*, is another large and useful tree, growing on the sides of the mountains, where is also found the tiairi, or candle-nut tree, *al rites triloba.* The form of this tree is stately; the foliage, beautifully white, gives a pleasing relief to the verdure of the mountain sides.

The most valuable and beautiful trees are those that grow in the valleys or plains: the chief of these is the splendid tamanu, or ati, *callophyllum inophyllum*; this, like most of the trees in the islands, is an evergreen; the leaves resemble those of the laurel in shape, but are more dark and shining; the trunk seldom rises above twelve or twenty feet without branching, yet it is one of the most magnificent trees in the country: the stem is often four feet in diameter; the grain of the wood resembles mahogany; the colour is rather lighter, but the texture equally close, and the wood more durable. It is one of the most valuable kinds of timber, and is not only used by the natives in the manufacture of their household furniture, but as keels for their largest canoes, as it is a kind of wood which the insects never perforate. Next to this, the hutu, *Barringtonia speciosa*, is the most splendid tree. Its growth and foliage greatly resemble the magnolia; and when in full bloom, its gigantic figure, adorned with large white flowers, whose petals are edged with bright pink, render it a most imposing object. The trunk is frequently three or four feet in diameter, but though occasionally used, it is less prized than the tamanu or tou, which is a species of *cordia*, and is a valuable tree. Next to the ati, the miro, *thespesia populnea*, though of smaller growth, is most highly prized by the people; the wood is durable, the grain is close, and the colour a variegated chesnut. The atai, though deciduous, is a beautiful tree; it is the *erythrina coralodendron*, and when in blossom, its light green acacia foliage, adorned with a bright red papilionaceous flowers, render it a most pleasing object. The branches are occasionally employed in fencing, but the wood of the trunk, being remarkably spongy, is seldom used. The sea shore is generally ornamented with several kinds of mimosa, but none of any great beauty or value. One of the most serviceable trees is the purau, or fau, *hibiscus tiliaceus.* In all the islands it is more abundant than any other, and though generally crooked and branching, the wood is light, tough, and durable. On account of its lightness, elasticity, and strength, it is selected for paddles and bows; it furnishes the best boards for the native vessels, and its long slender branches make excellent rafters for the ordinary dwellings. The mara and the pua, the *beslaria laurifolia* of Parkinson, is also a useful as well as an elegant tree, while its blossoms are among the most fragrant of native flowers.

To the above catalogue many others might be added, which, though inferior in size and number, are highly serviceable to the natives. With the exception of the purau, most of them are of slow growth. In consequence of the recent alteration in their habits of life, timber is much more in demand than formerly, and has of late years become less abundant. As the natives are generally averse to planting bread-fruit trees, and for general purposes always expect a supply of timber from the spontaneous growth of the forests, there is great fear that, without more regard to the future than they have hitherto been induced to manifest, timber will in a few years become very scarce among them. It is, however, to be hoped that the great quantity they are now using, will cause them to feel the necessity of providing for a continued supply. We have often urged it upon their attention, but they seem to think it unnecessary, and perhaps the spontaneous growth may be more rapid and abundant than we have anticipated.

Next to the trees that furnish them with timber, those plants from which they formerly procured their clothing, require to be noticed. The most valuable of these is the auti, *morus papyrifera*, or the Chinese paper-mulberry. The greater part of the cloth worn in the islands is made with the bark of this plant, which is cultivated as osiers or willow-twigs are cultivated in England, excepting that, instead of a low and wet, a rich and dry soil is selected. The bark of the bread-fruit is also used for this purpose; but the most singular tree is the aoa.

Among the beautiful and diversified vegetable productions that adorn the banks of the lake of Maeva, is one of these trees. It stands near the large temple of Tane, at Tama-pua, and is one of the most ancient and extensive that I have met with in the islands. In its growth, the aoa resembles the banian tree of the East, and is probably a variety of the species. The bark has a light tinge and shining appearance, the leaf lance-shaped and small, of a beautiful pea-green colour. It is an evergreen, and is propagated by slips or branches, which readily take root. When the stem of the young tree is about two or three inches in diameter, the bark immediately below the branches, which generally spread from the trunk about six feet above the ground, begins to open near the lower part of the limbs. A number of fine yellow-pointed roots protrude, and increase in size and length every year. The branches grow horizontally, and rather bending than otherwise: from different parts of these, fibres shoot forth through the bursting bark, and hang like fine dark-brown threads. The habits of growth in these pendulous roots are singular: sometimes they appear like a single line, or rope, reaching from the highest branches nearly to the ground, where they terminate in a bunch of spreading fibres, not unlike a tassel. At other times, while there is one principal fibre, a number of others branch off from this at unequal distances, from its insertion in the bough above, and terminate in a cluster of small fibres. The different threads are sometimes separate from each other for a considerable distance, and, near the bottom, unite in one single root.

As soon as these depending fibres reach the ground, they take root, and, in the course of a number of years, become solid stems, covered with a bark resembling that of the original tree, and forming so many natural pillars to the progressively extending branches above.

By this singular process, the aoa, at Tamapua, appears more like a clump or grove than a single tree. The original stem was joined by one or two, of such dimensions, that it was not easy to distinguish the parent from the offspring; and the fibres that had united with the ground, and thus became so many trunks or stems of the tree, covered a space many yards in circumference. The lateral branches continue to extend, and tendrils of every length and size are seen in all directions depending from them, appearing as if in time it would cover the face of the country with a forest, which yet should be but a single tree.

The most remarkable appearance, however, which the aoa presents, is when it grows near some of the high mountain precipices that often occur in the islands. A short distance from Buaoa, where the rocks are exceedingly steep, and almost perpendicular for a hundred feet or more, an aoa appears to have been planted near the foot of the rocky pile, and the tender fibres protruded from the branches, being nearer the rocks at the side than the ground below, have been attracted towards the precipice. From this, fresh nourishment has been derived; the tree has continued to ascend, and throw out new fibres still higher, till it has reached the top. Here a branching tree has flourished, exhibiting all the peculiarities of the aoa; while the root, and that part growing along the face of the rock, resemble a strong interwoven hedge, extending from the base to the summit of the precipice.

The account of the origin of this tree is one of the most fabulous of native legends: it states that the moon is diversified with hill and valley like our earth, that it is adorned with trees, and among these the aoa, the shadow of whose spreading branches, the Polynesians suppose, occasions the dark parts in her surface. They state that, in ancient times, a bird flew to the moon, and plucked the berries of the aoa; these are smaller than grapes; the bird readily carried them, and, flying over the islands, dropped some of the seeds, which, germinating in the soil, produced the aoa tree.

Nearly allied to the aoa, is the mate, *ficus prolixa*, an useful tree, its berries furnishing a beautiful scarlet dye, and its bark supplying the cord for the manufacture of the large and durable nets employed in taking salmon. The romaha, *urtica argentea*, is also a valuable plant, with the bark of which, the natives twist their strong and elastic fishing-lines, and the cord for their smaller nets.

The vegetable productions, from which the inhabitants derive a great part of their subsist-

Bread Fruit Tree.

ence, are numerous, varied, and valuable: among these, the first that demands notice is the breadfruit tree, *artocarpus*, being in greater abundance, and in more general use, than any other. The tree is large and umbrageous; the bark is light-coloured and rough; the trunk is sometimes two or three feet in diameter, and rises from twelve to twenty feet without a branch. The outline of the tree is remarkably beautiful, the leaves are broad, and indented somewhat like those of the fig-tree, frequently twelve or eighteen inches long, and rather thick, of a dark green colour, with a surface glossy as that of the richest evergreen.

The fruit is generally circular or oval, and is, on an average, six inches in diameter; it is covered with a roughish rind, which is marked with small square or lozenge-shaped divisions, having each a small elevation in the centre, and is at first of a light pea-green colour; subsequently it changes to brown, and when fully ripe assumes a rich yellow tinge. It is attached to the small branches of the tree by a short thick stalk, and hangs either singly, or in clusters of two or three together. The pulp is soft; in the centre there is a hard kind of core extending from the stalk to the crown, around which a few imperfect seeds are formed.

There is nothing very pleasing in the blossom; but a stately tree, clothed with dark shining leaves, and loaded with many hundreds of large light green or yellowish coloured fruit, is one of the most splendid and beautiful objects to be met with among the rich and diversified scenery of a Tahitian landscape. Two or three of these trees are often seen growing around a rustic cottage, and embowering it with their interwoven and prolific branches. The tree is propagated by shoots from the root, it bears in about five years, and will probably continue bearing fifty or sixty.

The bread-fruit is never eaten raw, except by pigs; the natives, however, have several methods of dressing it. When travelling on a journey, they often roast it in the flame or embers of a wood-fire; and, peeling off the rind, eat the fruit: this mode of dressing is called *tunu pa*, crust or shell roasting. Sometimes, when thus dressed, it is immersed in a stream of water, and, when completely saturated, forms a soft, sweet, spongy pulp, or sort of paste; of which the natives are exceedingly fond.

The general and best way of dressing the breadfruit, is by baking it in an oven of heated stones. The rind is scraped off, each fruit is cut into three or four pieces, and the core carefully taken out; heated stones are then spread over the bottom of the cavity forming the oven, and covered with leaves, upon which the pieces of bread-fruit are placed; a layer of green leaves is strewn over the fruit, and other heated stones are laid on the top; the whole is then covered with earth and leaves, several inches in depth. In this state, the oven remains half an hour or longer, when the earth and leaves are removed, and the pieces of breadfruit taken out; the outsides are in general nicely browned, and the inner part presents a white or yellowish, cellular, pulpy substance, in appearance slightly resembling the crumb of a small wheaten loaf. Its colour, size, and structure are, however, the only resemblance it has to bread. It has but little taste, and that is frequently rather sweet; it is somewhat farinaceous, but not so much so as several other vegetables, and probably less so than the English potato, to which in flavour it is also inferior. It is slightly astringent, and, as a vegetable, it is good, but is a very indifferent substitute for English bread.

To the natives of the South Sea Islands it is the principal article of diet, and may indeed be called their staff of life. They are exceedingly fond of it, and it is evidently adapted to their constitutions, and highly nutritive, as a very perceptible improvement is often manifest in the appearance of many of the people, a few weeks after the bread-fruit season has commenced. For the chiefs, it is usually dressed two or three times a day; but the peasantry, &c. seldom prepare more than one oven during the same period; and frequently *tihana*, or bake it again, on the second day.

During the bread-fruit season, the inhabitants of a district sometimes join, to prepare a quantity of *opio*. This is generally baked in a prodigious oven. A pit, twenty or thirty feet in circumference, is dug out; the bottom is filled with stones, logs of firewood are piled upon them, and the whole is covered with large stones. The wood is then kindled, and the heat is often so intense, as to reduce the stones to a state of liquefaction. When thoroughly heated, the stones are removed to the sides; many hundred ripe bread-fruit are then thrown in, just as they have been gathered from the trees, and are piled up in the centre of the pit; a few leaves are spread upon them, the remaining hot stones built up like an arch over the heap, and the whole is covered, a foot or eighteen inches thick, with leaves and earth. In this state it remains a day or two; a hole is then dug on one side, and the parties to whom it belongs take out what they want, till the whole is consumed. Bread-fruit baked in this manner, will keep good several weeks after the oven is opened.

Although the general or district ovens of opio were in their tendency less injurious than the public stills, often erected in the different districts they were usually attended with debauchery and excess, highly injurious to the health and debasing to the morals of the people, who frequently relinquished their ordinary employment, and devoted their nights and days to mere animal existence, of the lowest kind—rioting, feasting, and sleeping, until the opio was consumed. Within the last ten years, very few ovens of opio have been prepared, those have been comparatively small, and they are now almost entirely discontinued.

Another mode of preserving the bread-fruit is by submitting it to a slight degree of fermentation, and reducing it to a soft substance, which they call *mahi*. When the fruit is ripe, a large quantity is gathered, the rind scraped off, the core taken out, and the whole thrown in a heap. In this state it remains until it has undergone the process of fermentation, when it is beaten into a kind of paste. A hole is now dug in the ground, the bottom and sides of which are lined with green *ti* leaves; the mahi is put into the pit, covered over with *ti* leaves, and then with earth or stones. In this state it may be preserved several months; and, although rather sour and indigestible, it is generally esteemed by the natives as a good article of food during the scarce season. Previous to its being eaten, it is rolled up in small portions, enclosed in bread-fruit leaves, and baked in the native ovens.

The tree on which the bread-fruit grows, besides producing two, and in some cases three crops in a year, of so excellent an article of food, furnishes a valuable gum, or resin, which exudes from the bark, when punctured, in a thick mucilaginous fluid, which is hardened by exposure to the sun, and is serviceable in rendering water-tight the seams of their canoes. The bark of the young branches is used in making several varieties of native cloth. The trunk of the tree also furnishes one of the most valuable kinds of timber which the natives possess, it being used in building their canoes and houses, and in the manufacture of several articles of furniture. It is of a rich yellow colour, and assumes, from the effects of the air, the appearance of mahogany; it is not tough, but durable when not exposed to the weather.

It is very probable, that in no group of the Pacific Islands is there a greater variety in the kinds of this valuable fruit, than in the South Sea Islands. The several varieties ripen at different seasons, and the same kinds also come to perfection at an earlier period in one part of Tahiti than in another; so that there are but few months in the year in which ripe fruit is not to be found in the several parts of this island. The Missionaries are acquainted with nearly fifty varieties, for which the natives have distinct names—these, as collected by one of the first Missionaries, I have by me, but it is unnecessary to insert them—the principal are, the *paea*, artocarpus incisa, and the *uru maohe*, artocarpus integrifolia.

Next to the bread-fruit, the *taro*, or *arum*, is the most serviceable article of food the natives possess, and its culture receives a considerable share of their attention. It has a large, solid, tuberous root, of an oblong shape, sometimes nine or twelve inches in length, and five or six in diameter. The plant has no stalk; the broad heart-shaped leaves rise from the upper end of the root, and the flower is contained in a sheath or spathe. There are several varieties; for thirty-three of which the natives have distinct names; and, as the plant is found to thrive best in moist situations, it is cultivated in low marshy parts. A large kind, called ape, *arum costatum*, which is frequently planted in the dry grounds, is also used in some seasons, but is considered inferior to the taro.

All the varieties are so exceedingly acrid and pungent in their raw state, as to cause the greatest pain, if not excoriation, should they be applied to the tongue or palate. They are always baked in the same manner as bread-fruit is dressed; the rind, or skin, being first scraped off with a shell. The roots are solid, and generally of a mottled green or gray colour; and when baked, are palatable, farinaceous, and nutritive, resembling the Irish potato as much as any other root in the islands.

The different varieties of arum are propagated either by transplanting the small tubers, which they call *pohiri*, that grow round the principal root, or setting the top or crown of those roots used for food. When destitute of foreign supplies, we have attempted to make flour with both the bread-fruit and the taro, by employing the natives to scrape the root and fruit into a kind of pulpy paste, then drying it in the sun, and grinding it in a hand-mill. The taro in this state was sometimes rather improved, but the bread-fruit seldom is so good as when dressed immediately after it has been gathered.

The *uhi*, or yam, *dioscoria alata*, a most valuable root, appears to be indigenous in most of the South Sea Islands, and grows remarkably well. Several kinds flourish in the mountains; the shape of the root is generally long and round, and the substance rather fibrous, but remarkably farinaceous and sweet. The kind most in use is generally of a dark brown colour, with a roughish skin; it is called by the natives *obura*.

The yam is cultivated with much care, though to no very great extent, on account of the labour and attention required. The sides of the inferior hills, and the sunny banks occasionally met with in the bottoms of the valleys, are selected for its growth. Here, a number of small terraces are formed one above another, covered with a mixture of rich earth and decayed leaves. The roots intended for planting are kept in baskets till they begin to sprout; a yam is then taken, and each eye, or sprout, cut off, with a part of the outside of the root, an inch long and a quarter of an inch thick, attached to it; these pieces, sometimes containing two eyes each, are spread upon a board, and left in some part of the house to dry; the remainder of the root is baked and eaten. This mode of preparing the parts for planting does not appear to result from motives of economy, as is the case in some parts where the Irish potato is prepared for planting in a similar manner; but because the natives imagine it is better thus to plant the eyes when they first begin to open, or germinate, with only a small part of the root, than to plant the whole yam, which they say is likely to rot. Whether the same plan might be adopted in planting the sweet potato, and other roots, I am not prepared to say, as it is only in raising the yam that it is practised in the horticulture of the natives. When the pieces are sufficiently dry, they are carefully put in the ground with the sprouts uppermost, a small portion of dried leaves is laid upon each, and the whole lightly covered with mould. When the roots begin to swell, the cultivators watch their enlargement, and keep them covered with light rich earth, which is generally spread over them about an inch in thickness.

The yam is one of the best flavoured and most nutritive roots which the islands produce. The natives usually bake them; they are, however, equally good when boiled; and, as they may be preserved longer out of the ground than any other, they are the most valuable sea-stock to be procured; and it is to be regretted that they are not more generally cultivated. Few are reared in the Georgian Islands; more perhaps in the Society cluster; but Sir Charles Sanders' Island is more celebrated for its yams than any other of the group.

The *umara*, or sweet potato, *convolvulus batatus*, or *chrysorizus*, is grown by the natives as an article of food. The richest black mould is chosen for its culture; and the earth is raised in mounds nine or ten feet in diameter, and about three feet high. They do not plant the roots; but in the top of these mounds insert a small bunch of the vines, which germinating, produce the tuberous roots eaten by the natives. In the Sandwich Islands, the sweet potato is one of the principal means of subsistence; here it is only partially cultivated, and is greatly inferior to those grown in the northern islands, probably from the difference of soil and climate. The roots are large, and covered with a thin smooth skin. In size, shape, and structure, they resemble several kinds of the Irish potato. The umara is very sweet, seldom mealy, and sometimes quite soft, but altogether less palatable than the taro or the yam. It is dressed by the natives in their stone ovens, and is only used when the bread-fruit is scarce.

Patara, is a root growing wild in the valleys, in shape and taste resembling a potato more than any other root found in Tahiti. It is highly farinaceous, though less nutritive than the yam; the stem resembles the woodbine or convolvulus. The natives say the flower is small and white; I never saw one, for it is not cultivated, and but seldom sought, as the tuberous root is small, and more than two are seldom found attached to the same vine or stalk.

The natives are acquainted with rice; but, although both the soil and climate would probably favour its growth, it has not yet been added to the edibles of Tahiti. We have not been very anxious to introduce it, as the quantity of water required for its culture, would, we have supposed, induce in such a climate a state of atmosphere by no means conducive to health. But though they have not rice, they have a plant which they call *hoi*, the shape and growth of which resemble the patara; but in taste and appearance it is so much like rice, that the natives call the latter by the native designation of the former. It is very insipid, and only sought in seasons of scarcity.

The *pia*, or arrow-root, *chailea tacca*, is indigenous and abundant. It is sometimes cultivated; but in most of the islands it grows spontaneously on the high sandy banks near the sea, or on the sides of the lower mountains, and appears to thrive in a light soil and dry situation. Though evidently of a superior quality, and capable of being procured in any quantity, it requires some labour to render it fit for food, and on this account it was not extensively used by the natives, but formed rather a variety in their dishes at public feastings, than an article of general consumption.

The growth of the arrow-root resembles that of the potato. Although indigenous, and growing spontaneously, it is occasionally cultivated in the native gardens, by which means finer roots are procured. When it is raised in this manner, a single root uncut is planted; a number of tuberous roots, about the size of large new potatoes, are formed at the extremities of fibres, proceeding from the root which had been planted. The leaves are of a light green colour, and deeply indented; they are not attached to one common stem, but the stalk of each distinct leaf proceeds from the root. The stalk, bearing the flower, rises in a single shaft, resembling a reed, or arrow, three or four feet high, crowned with a tuft of light pea-green petalled flowers. These are succeeded by a bunch of green berries, resembling the berries of the potato. To the shape and size of the reed or shaft bearing the flower, the *arrow*-root is probably indebted for its name.

When the leaves from the stalk dry or decay, the roots are dug up and washed; after which the rind is scraped off with a cowrie shell. The root is then grated on a piece of coral, and the pulp pressed through a sieve made with the wiry fibrous matting of the cocoa-nut husk. This is designed to remove the fibres and other woody matter which the root may contain. The pulp, or powder, is received in a large trough of water, placed beneath the rustic sieve. Here, after having been repeatedly stirred, it is allowed to subside to the bottom, and the water is poured off. Fresh water is applied and removed, until it flows from the pulp, tasteless and colourless; the arrow-root is then taken out, dried in the sun, and is fit for use.

Simple as this process is, it requires considerable care to dry it properly. When partially dry, the natives were formerly accustomed to knead or roll it up in circular masses, containing six or seven pounds each, and in this state expose it to the sun till sufficiently dry to be preserved for use. By this process they prepared much that has been exported from the islands, which may account for its inferior colour, as the whole mass was seldom sufficiently dry to prevent its turning mouldy, and assuming a brown or unfavourable colour.

They had no means of boiling it, but were accustomed to put a quantity of the arrow-root powder with the expressed milk from the kernel of the cocoa-nut into a large wooden tray, or dish; and, having mixed them well together, to throw in a number of red-hot stones, which being moved about by thin white sticks, heated the whole mass nearly to boiling, and occasioned it to assume a thick, broken, jellied appearance. In this state it is served up in baskets of cocoa-nut leaves, and is a very rich sweet kind of food, usually forming a part of every public entertainment.

Arrow-root has recently been prepared in large quantities, as an article of exportation to England; but although it is equal to that brought from the West Indies, it has not been so well cleaned, dried, or packed, and has consequently appeared very inferior when it has been brought into the market. There is reason, however, to believe, that when the natives shall have acquired better methods of preparing their arrow-root, it may become a valuable article of commerce.

There is a very large and beautiful species of fern, called by the natives *nahe;* the leaves of which are fragrant, and, in seasons of scarcity, the large tuberous kind of root is baked and eaten. It is insipid, affords but little nutriment, and is only resorted to when other supplies fail. It is altogether a different plant from the fern, the root of which is eaten by the natives of New Zealand. The berries, or apples, of the nono, *morindo citrifolia,* and the stalks of the pohue, *convolvulus Brasiliensis,* are also eaten in times of famine.

The fruits of the islands are not so numerous as in some continental countries of similar temperature, but they are valuable; and, next to the bread-fruit, the *haari,* or cocoa-nut, *coccos nucifera,* is the most serviceable. The tree on which it grows is also one of the most useful and ornamental in the islands, imparting to the landscape, in which it forms a conspicuous object, all the richness and elegance of intertropical verdure.

The stem is perfectly cylindrical, three or four feet in diameter at the root, very gradually tapering to the top, where it is probably not more than eighteen inches round. It is one single stem from the root to the crown, composed apparently of a vast number of small hollow reeds, united by a kind of resinous pith, and enclosed in a rough, brittle, and exceedingly hard bark. The stem is without branch or leaf, excepting at the top, where a beautiful crown or tuft of long green leaves appears like a graceful plume waving in the fitful breeze, or nodding over the spreading wood, or the humble shrubbery. The nut begins to grow in a few months after it is planted; in about five or six years, the stem is seven or eight feet high, and the tree begins to bear. It continues to grow and bear fifty or sixty years, or perhaps longer, as there are many groves of trees, apparently in their highest perfection, which were planted by Pomare nearly forty years ago. While the plants are young, they require fencing, in order to protect them from the pigs; but after the crown has reached a few feet above the ground, the plants require no further care.

The bread-fruit, the plantain, and almost every other tree furnishing any valuable fruit, arrives at perfection only in the most fertile soil; but the cocoa-nut, although it will grow in the rich bottoms of the valleys, and by the side of the streams that flow through them, yet flourishes equally on the barren sea-beach, amid fragments of coral and sand, where its roots are washed by every rising tide; and on the sun-burnt sides of the mountains, where the soil is shallow, and remote from the streams so favourable to vegetation.

The trunk of the tree is used for a variety of purposes: their best spears were made with cocoa-nut wood; wall plates, rafters, and pillars for their larger houses, were often of the same material; their instruments for splitting bread-fruit, their rollers for their canoes, and also their most durable fences, were made with its trunk. It is also a valuable kind of fuel, and makes excellent charcoal.

The timber is not the only valuable article the cocoa-nut tree furnishes. The leaves, called *niau*, are composed of strong stalks twelve or fifteen feet long. A number of long narrow pointed leaflets are ranged alternately on opposite sides. The leaflets are often plaited, when the whole leaf is called *paua*, and forms an excellent skreen for the sides of their houses, or covering for their floors. Several kinds of baskets are also made with the leaves, one of which, called *arairi*, is neat, convenient, and durable. They were also plaited for bonnets or shades for the foreheads and eyes, and were worn by both sexes. In many of their religious ceremonies they were used, and the *niau*, or leaf, was also an emblem of authority, and was sent by the chief to his dependents, when any requisition was made: through the cocoa-nut leaf tied to the sacrifice the god was supposed to enter; and by the same road the evil spirits, who, it was imagined, tormented those affected with diseases were driven out. Bunches or strings of the leaflets were also suspended in the temple on certain occasions, and answered the same purpose as beads in Roman Catholic worship, reminding the priest or the worshipper of the order of his prayers. On the tough and stiff stalks of the leaflets, the candle-nuts, employed for lighting their houses, were strung when used.

Round that part of the stem of the leaf which is attached to the trunk of the tree, there is a singular provision of nature, for the security of the long leaves against the violence of the winds. A remarkably fine, strong, fibrous matting, attached to the bark under the bottom of the stalk, extending half way round the trunk, and reaching perhaps two or three feet up the leaf, acting like a bracing of network to each side of the stalk, keeps it steadily fixed to the trunk. While the leaves are young, this substance is remarkably white, transparent, and as fine in texture as silver paper. In this state it is occasionally cut into long narrow slips, tied up in bunches, and used by the natives to ornament their hair. Its remarkable flexibility, beautiful whiteness, and glossy surface, render it a singularly novel, light, and elegant plume; the effect of which is heightened by its contrast with the black and shining ringlets of the native hair it surmounts. As the leaf increases in size, and the matting is exposed to the air, it becomes coarser and stronger, assuming a yellowish colour, and is called *aa*.

There is a kind of seam along the centre, exactly under the stem of the leaf, from both sides of which long and tough fibres, about the size of a bristle, regularly diverge in an oblique direction. Sometimes there appear to be two layers of fibres, which cross each other, and the whole is cemented with a still finer, fibrous, and adhesive substance. The length and evenness of the threads or fibres, the regular manner in which they cross each other at oblique angles; the extent of surface, and the thickness of the piece, corresponding with that of coarse cotton cloth; the singular manner in which the fibres are attached to each other— cause this curious substance, woven in the loom of nature, to present to the eye a remarkable resemblance to cloth spun and woven by human ingenuity.

This singular fibrous matting is sometimes taken off by the natives in pieces two or three feet wide, and used as wrapping for their arrow-root, or made into bags. It is also occasionally employed in preparing articles of clothing. Jackets, coats, and even shirts, are made with the *aa*, though the coarsest linen cloth would be much more soft and flexible. To these shirts the natives generally fix a cotton collar and wristbands, and seem susceptible of but little irritation from its wiry texture and surface. It is a favourite dress with the fishermen, and others occupied on the sea.

The fruit, however, is the most valuable part of this serviceable, hardy, and beautiful plant. The flowers are small and white, insignificant when compared with the size of the tree or the fruit. They are ranged along the sides of a tough, succulent, branching stalk, surrounded by a sheath, which the natives call *aroe*, and are fixed to the trunk of the tree, immediately above the bottom of the leaf. Fruit in every stage, from the first formation after the falling of the blossom, to the hard, dry, ripe, and full-grown nut, that has almost begun to germinate, may be seen at one time on the same tree, and frequently fruit in several distinct stages on the same bunch, attached to the trunk of the same stalk.

The tree is slow in growth, and the fruit does not, probably, come to perfection in much less than twelve months after the blossoms have fallen. A bunch will sometimes contain twenty or thirty nuts, and there are, perhaps, six or seven bunches on the tree at a time. Each nut is surrounded by a tough fibrous husk, in some parts two inches thick; and when it has reached its full size, it contains, enclosed in a soft white shell, a pint or a pint and a half of the juice usually called cocoa-nut milk.

There is at this time no pulp whatever in the inside. In this stage of its growth the nut is called *oua*, and the liquid is preferred to that found in the nut in any other state. It is perfectly clear, and in taste combines a degree of acidity and sweetness, which renders it equal to the best lemonade. No accurate idea of the consistence and taste of

FRUIT, AND GERMINATING PROCESS.

the juice of the cocoa-nut can be formed from that found in the nuts brought to England. These are old and dry, and the fluid comparatively rancid; in this state they are never used by the natives, except for the purpose of planting or extracting oil. The shell of the *oua*, or young cocoanut, is used medicinally.

In a few weeks after the nut has reached its full size, a soft white pulp, remarkably delicate and sweet, resembling, in consistence and appearance, the white of a slightly boiled egg, is formed around the inside of the shell. In this state it is called *niaa*, and is eaten by the chiefs as an article of luxury, and used in preparing many of what may be called the made-dishes of Tahitian banquets. After remaining a month or six weeks longer, the pulp on the inside becomes much firmer, and rather more than half an inch in thickness. The juice assumes a whitish colour, and a sharper taste. It is now called *omoto*, and is not so much used. If allowed to hang two or three months longer on the tree, the outside skin becomes yellow and brown, the shell hardens, the kernel increases to an inch or an inch and a quarter in thickness, and the liquid is reduced to less than half a pint. It is now called *opaa*, and, after hanging some months on the tree, falls to the ground. The hard nut is sometimes broken in two, and broiled, or eaten as taken from the tree, but is generally used in making oil

If the cocoa-nut be kept long after it is fully ripe, a white, sweet, spongy substance is formed in the inside, originating at the inner end of the germ which is enclosed in the kernel, immediately opposite one of the three apertures or eyes, in the sharpest end of the shell, which is opposite to that where the stalk is united to the husk. This fibrous sponge ultimately absorbs the water, and fills the concavity, dissolving the hard kernel, and combining it with its own substance, so that the shell, instead of containing a kernel and milk, encloses only a soft cellular substance. While this truly wonderful process is going on within the nut, a single bud or shoot, of a white colour but hard texture, forces its way through one of the holes in the shell, perforates the tough fibrous husk, and, after rising some inches, begins to unfold its pale green leaves to the light and the air; at this time, also, two thick white fibres, originating in the same point, push away the stoppers or coverings from the other two holes in the shell, pierce the husk in an opposite direction, and finally penetrate the ground. If allowed to remain, the shell, which no knife would cut, and which a saw would scarcely penetrate, is burst by an expansive power, generated within itself; the husk and the shell gradually decay, and, forming a light manure, facilitate the growth of the young plant, which gradually strikes its roots deeper, elevates its stalk, and expands its leaves, until it becomes a lofty, fruitful, and graceful tree.

There are many varieties of the cocoa-nut tree, in some of which the fruit is rather small and sweet. For each variety the natives have a distinct name, as well as for the same nut in its different stages of perfection. I have the names of six sorts, but it is unnecessary to insert them.

The juice of the nuts growing on the sea-shore does not appear to partake, in any degree, of the saline property of the water that must constantly moisten the roots of the tree. The milk of the nuts from the sandy beach or the rocky mountain, is often as sweet and as rich as that grown in the most fertile parts of the valley.

On first arriving in the islands, we used the cocoa-nut milk freely, but subsequently preferred plain water as a beverage; not that the milk became less agreeable, but because we supposed, perhaps erroneously, the free use of it predisposed to certain dropsical complaints prevalent among the people.

The cocoa-nut trees are remarkably high, sometimes sixty or seventy feet, with only a tuft of leaves, and a number of bunches of fruit, on the top; yet the natives gather the fruit with comparative ease. A little boy strips off a piece of bark from a *purau*, branch, and fastens it round his feet, leaving a space of four or five inches between them, and then, clasping the tree, he vaults up its trunk with greater agility and ease than a European could ascend a ladder to an equal elevation. When they gather a bunch at a time, they lower them down by a rope; but when they pluck the fruit singly, they cast them on the ground. In throwing down the nuts, they give them a whirling motion, that they may fall on the point, and not on the side, whereby they would be likely to burst.

Cocoa-nuts were formerly a considerable article of food among the common people, and were used with profusion on every feast of the chiefs; but for some years past they have been preserved, and allowed to ripen on the tree, for the purpose of preparing oil, which has recently become an article of exportation, although the value is so small as to afford but little encouragement to its extended manufacture.

The cocoa-nut oil is procured from the pulp, and is prepared by grating the kernel of the old nut, and depositing it in a long wooden trough, usually the hollow trunk of a tree. This is placed in the sun every morning, and exposed during the day; after a few days the grated nut is piled up in heaps in the trough, leaving a small space between each heap. As the oil exudes, it drains into the hollows, whence it is scooped in bamboo canes, and preserved for sale or use. After the oil ceases to collect in the trough, the kernel is put into a bag, of the matted fibres, and submitted to the action of a rude lever press; but the additional quantity of oil, thus obtained, is inferior in quality to that produced by the heat of the sun. This process requires considerable labour for the grating of the kernel by the hand; but it is probable, should its manufacture be continued, that mills will be erected for bruising the pulp.

In addition to these advantages, the shells of the large old cocoa-nuts are used as water-bottles, the largest of which will hold a quart; they are of a black colour, often highly polished, and, with care, last a number of years. All the cups and drinking vessels of the natives are made with cocoa-nut shells, usually of the omoto, which is of a yellow colour. It is scraped very thin, and is often slightly transparent. Their ava cups were generally black, highly polished, and sometimes ingeniously carved with a variety of devices, but the Tahitians did not excel in carving. The fibres of the husk are separated from the pulp by soaking them in water, and are used in making various kinds of cinet and cordage, especially a valuable coiar rope; and, as the pious Herbert sung two hundred years ago,

> "The Indian's nut alone
> Is clothing, meat and trencher, drink and can,
> Boat, cable, sail and needle, all in one."

It is impossible to contemplate either the bread-fruit or cocoa-nut tree, in their gigantic and spontaneous growth, their majestic appearance, the value and abundance of their fruit, and the varied purposes to which they are subservient, without admiring the wisdom and benevolence of the Creator, and his distinguishing kindness towards the inhabitants of these interesting islands.

CHAP. III.

Varieties and appearance of the plantain and banana—Vi or Brazilian plum—A-hi-a or jambo—Singular growth of the inocarpus, or native chesnut—Different kinds of ti, or Dracanæ—To, or sugar-cane—Foreign fruits and vegetables that flourish in Polynesia—Value of a garden in the South Sea Islands—Unsuccessful attempts to introduce wheat—Introduction of coffee—Native and foreign flowers—Tradition of the origin of the bread-fruit—Quadrupeds—Absence of venomous animals and reptiles—Manner of rearing pigs—Birds of the South Sea Islands—Albatross—Pigeons—Domestic fowls—Number and variety of fish on the coasts, and in the lakes and rivers.

MORE rich and sweet to the taste, though far less serviceable as an article of food, is the *maia*, plantain and banana, *musa paradisaica* and *musa sapientum*. These are also indigenous, although generally cultivated in the native gardens. They are a rich nutritive fruit, common within the tropics, and so generally known as to need no particular description here. There are not, perhaps, fewer than thirty varieties cultivated by the natives, besides nearly twenty kinds, very large and serviceable, that grow wild in the mountains. The *orea*, or maiden plantain, with the other varieties, comes to the highest perfection in the South Sea Islands, and is a delicious fruit. The stalk, or tree, on which these fruits grow, is seldom above eight or twelve feet high; the leaves are fine broad specimens of the luxuriance of tropical vegetation, being frequently twelve or sixteen feet long, eighteen inches or two feet wide, of a beautiful pea-green colour when fresh, and a rich bright yellow when dry. The fruit is about nine inches long, and in shape somewhat like a cucumber, excepting that the angles are frequently well defined, which gives to the fruit, when ripe, the appearance of a triangular or quadrangular prism of a bright delicate yellow colour. Sixty or seventy single fruit are occasionally attached to one stalk. Each plantain stem, or tree, produces only one bunch of fruit; and when the fruit is ripe, it is cut down, and its place supplied by the suckers that rise around the root whence it originally sprung. If the suckers, or offsets, be four or five feet high when the parent stem is cut down, they will bear in about twelve months.

The fruit is not often allowed to ripen on the trees, but it is generally cut down as soon as it has reached its full size, and while yet green; the bunch is then hung up in the native houses to ripen, and is eaten as the fruit turns yellow. When they wish to accelerate their ripeness for a public entertainment, they cut them down green, wrap them in leaves, and bury them thirty-six or forty-eight hours in the earth, and on taking them out they are quite soft, and apparently ripe, but much more insipid than those which had gradually ripened on the tree, or even in the house. The kinds growing in the mountains are large, and, though rich and agreeable when baked, are most unpalatable when raw; they have a red skin, and a bright yellow pulp. Their native name is *fei*: their habits of growth are singular; for, while the fruit of all the other varieties is pendent from the stem, this rises erect from a short thick stalk in the centre of the crown or tuft of leaves at the top. In several of these islands, the *fei* is the principal support of the inhabitants. The plantain is a fruit that is always acceptable, and resembles in flavour a soft, sweet, but not juicy pear; it is very good in milk, also in puddings and pies, and, when fermented, makes excellent vinegar.

The *vi*, or Brazilian plum, a variety of *spondias*, (*spondias dulcis* of Parkinson,) is an abundant and excellent fruit, of an oval or oblong shape, and bright yellow colour. In form and taste it somewhat resembles a magnum-bonum plum, but it is larger, and, instead of a stone, has a hard and spiked core, containing a number of seeds. The tree on which it grows is deciduous, and one of the largest found in the islands, the trunk being frequently four or five feet in diameter. The bark is gray and smooth, the leaf pinnate, of a light green colour; the fruit hangs in bunches, and is often so plentiful, that the ground underneath the trees is covered with ripe fruit, while the satisfied, and almost surfeited pigs, lie sleeping round its roots.

The *ahia*, or jambo, *eugenia Mallaccensis*, is perhaps the most juicy of the indigenous fruits of the Society Islands. It resembles, in shape, a small oblong apple, is of a bright beautiful red colour, and has a white, juicy, but rather insipid pulp. Though grateful in a warm climate like Tahiti, its flavour is by no means so good as that of the ahia growing on the Sandwich Islands. Like the vi, it bears but one crop in the year, and does not continue in season longer than two or three months. Both these trees are propagated by seed.

In certain seasons of the year, if the bread-fruit be scarce, the natives supply the deficiency thus occasioned with the fruit of the ma-pe or rata, a native chesnut, *tuscarpus edulis*. Like other chesnut-trees, the ma-pe is of stately growth and splendid foliage. It is occasionally seen in the high grounds, but flourishes only in the rich bottoms of the valleys, and seldom appears in greater perfection than on the margin of a stream. From the top of a mountain I have often been able to mark the course of a river by the winding and almost unbroken line of chesnuts, that have towered in majesty above the trees of humbler growth. The ma-pe is branching, but the trunk, which is the most singular part of it, usually rises ten or twelve feet without a branch, after which the arms are large and spreading.

During the first seven or eight years of its growth, the stem is tolerably round, but after that period, as it enlarges, instead of continuing cylindrical, it assumes a different shape. In four or five places round the trunk, small projections appear, extending in nearly straight lines from the root to the branches. The centre of the tree seems to remain stationary; while these projections increasing, at length seem like so many planks covered with bark, forming a number of natural buttresses round the tree. The centre of the tree often continues many years with perhaps not more than two or three inches of wood round the medula, or pith; while the buttresses, though only about two inches thick, extend two, three, and four feet, being widest at the bottom. I have observed buttresses, not more than two inches in thickness, projecting four feet from the tree, and forming between each, natural recesses, in which I have often taken shelter during a shower. When the tree becomes old, its form is still more picturesque, as a number of knots and contortions are formed on the buttresses and branches, which render the outlines more broken and fantastic.

The wood of the rata has a fine straight grain, but being remarkably perishable, is seldom used, excepting for fire-wood. Occasionally, however, they cut off one of the buttresses, and thus obtain a good natural plank, with which they make the long paddles for their canoes, or axe-handles. The leaf is large and beautiful, six or eight inches in length, oblong in shape, of a dark green colour, and, though an evergreen, exceedingly light and delicate in its structure. The tree bears a small white racimated panicle flower, esteemed by the natives on account of its fragrance. The fruit, which hangs singly or in small clusters from the slender twigs, is flat, and somewhat kidney-shaped. The same term is used by the natives for this fruit, and the kidney of an animal. The nut is a single kernel, in a hard, tough, fibrous shell, covered with a thin, compact, fibrous husk. It is not eaten in a raw state; but, though rather hard when fully ripe, it is, when roasted in a green state, soft, and pleasant to the taste.

In addition to these, the *ti*-root, *dracanæ terminalis*, resembling exactly that found in the Sandwich Islands, is baked and eaten; and the *to*, or sugar-cane, *saccharum officinarum*, which grows spontaneously, and perhaps in greater perfection than in any other part of the world, was formerly cultivated, and eaten raw. On a journey, the natives often carry a piece of sugar-cane, which furnishes a sweet and nourishing juice, appeasing at once, to a certain degree, both thirst and hunger. Within a few years they have been taught to extract the juice, and, by boiling it, to prepare a very good sugar.

Most of the native fruits are delicious; and their number has been greatly increased by the addition of many of the most valuable tropical fruits. Vines, oranges, shaddocks, limes, and other plants, were introduced by Captains Cook, Bligh, and Vancouver. It is stated, that as soon as the young grapes were formed, the natives plucked and ate them, but were so displeased at their acidity, that they tore up the plant. Vines were also taken by the Missionaries, but nearly destroyed by the natives in their wars. In 1824 I brought a number of plants from the Sandwich Islands; which were thriving when I last heard. Citrons, tamarinds, pine-apples, guavas, Cape mulberries and figs, custard apples and coffee plants, have at different times been introduced, and successfully cultivated, by the Missionaries. Many foreign vegetables have been tried, yet few of them thrive. The growth of corn has been more than once attempted without success. Pumpkins, melons, water-melons, cucumbers, cabbages, and French-beans, flourish better than any other foreign vegetables.

To a European, a garden is a valuable acquisition in this part of the world; and, next to our dwellings, we regarded it as an important part of our domestic establishment. As soon as the sites of our houses were fixed, we employed natives to enclose a piece of ground adjoining them. I received, in December, 1816, from governor Macquarie in New South Wales, a hundred ears of Egyptian wheat, which being a kind frequently grown in a warm climate, it was supposed might flourish in the islands. The grain was planted with care, and grew remarkably well; the leaf was green, the stalks high and strong, and the ears large; but as they began to turn yellow, few of them contained a single grain, and those that were found were shrivelled and dry. Potatoes were also tried, and have been repeatedly planted since, in different situations and seasons; but although, after the first growth, they usually appear like young potatoes,—if planted again, they are invariably soft and sweet, very small, and less palatable than the indigenous sweet potato.

At Afareaitu I had sown a number of seeds from England, Rio Janeiro, and New South Wales. Coffee and cashew-nuts, *anacardium occidentale*, I had before planted in boxes; they grew well, but the coffee and the cashew-nuts were totally destroyed by the goats, which, leaping the fence one day, in a few minutes ate up the plants on which I had bestowed much care. The custard-apple, *anona triloba* or *squamosa*, that I had brought from Rio, were preserved, and plants from it are now bearing fruit in several of the islands. In addition to these, I was enabled to cultivate the papaw apple, *carica papaya*, French-beans, carrots, turnips, cabbages, and Indian corn; while our little flower-garden, in Huahine, was adorned with the convolvulus major and minor, capsicum, helianthus, and amaranthus, with several brilliant native flowers, among which the *gardenia* and *hibiscus rosea chinensis* were always conspicuous. The front of our house was shaded by orange trees, and our garden enclosed with a citron hedge.

The comfort connected with a garden, and the means of support derived therefrom, were not our only inducements to its culture; we were desirous to increase the vegetable productions of the island,

and anxious also that our establishments should become models for the natives in the formation of their own, and in this we were not disappointed. A neat little garden was afterwards considered by numbers as a necessary appendage to their habitation. The natives display a taste for the beautiful, in their fondness of flowers. The gardenia, hibiscus, and amaranthus, were often woven in graceful wreaths or garlands, and worn on their brows. They were delighted when the helianthus was added to their flowers. Pomare and his queen passed by my garden when the first ever grown in the islands was in flower, and came in, to admire its size and brilliancy. Soon after their return, I received a note from the king, asking for a flower for the queen, and also one for her sister; I sent them each a small one; and the next time they appeared in public, the large sunflowers were fixed as ornaments in their hair.

To the list of the edible vegetables, fruits, and roots of the Society Islands, already given, others might probably be added, but these are sufficient to show the abundance, diversity, nutritiveness, delicacy, and richness of the provision spontaneously furnished to gratify the palate, and supply the necessities, of their inhabitants. Here man seemed to live only for enjoyment, and appeared to have been placed in circumstances, where every desire was satisfied, and where it might be imagined that even the apprehension of want was a thing unknown. Amid the unrestrained enjoyment of a bounty so diversified and profuse, it is hardly possible to suppose that the divine Author of all should neither be recognized nor acknowledged; or, that his very mercies should foster insensibility, and alienate the hearts of the participants in his bounty. Such, however, was the melancholy fact. Although

> ——————————————— " the soil untill'd
> Pour'd forth spontaneous and abundant harvests,
> The forests cast their fruits, in husks or rind,
> Yielding sweet kernels or delicious pulp,
> Smooth oil, cool milk, and unfermented wine,
> In rich and exquisite variety;
> On these the indolent inhabitants
> Fed without care or forethought."

We have often endeavoured to learn from the natives whether the vegetable productions used as food when the islands were discovered by Captain Wallis, were found there by those who first peopled them; whether these colonists, from whatsoever country they may have come, had brought any seeds or roots with them; or whether they had been, at a more recent period, conveyed thither from any other islands: but their answers, with regard to the origin of most of them, have been so absurd and fabulous, that no correct inference can be drawn from them. Most of them are, in their traditions, stated to have been formed by their gods, at the same time that the fishes of the sea, the fowls of the air, and the inhabitants of the earth, were produced.

In reference to the origin of the bread-fruit, one of their traditionary legends states, that in the reign of a certain king, when the people ate *araea*, red earth, a husband and wife had an only son, whom they tenderly loved. The youth was weak and delicate; and one day the husband said to the wife, " I compassionate our son, he is unable to eat the red earth. I will die, and become food for our son." The wife said, " How will you become food?" He answered, " I will pray to my god; he has power, and he will enable me to do it." Accordingly, he repaired to the family marae, and presented his petition to the deity. A favourable answer was given to his prayer, and in the evening he called his wife to him, and said, " I am about to die; when I am dead, take my body, separate it, plant my head in one place, my heart and stomach in another, &c. and then come into the house and wait. When you shall hear first a sound like that of a leaf, then of a flower, afterwards of an unripe fruit, and subsequently of a ripe round fruit falling on the ground, know that it is I, who am become food for our son." He died soon after. His wife obeyed his injunctions, planting the stomach near the house, as directed. After a while, she heard a leaf fall, then the large scales of the flower, then a small unripe fruit, afterwards one full grown and ripe. By this time it was daylight; she awoke her son, took him out, and they beheld a large and handsome tree, clothed with broad shining leaves, and loaded with bread-fruit. She directed him to gather a number, take the first to the family god and to the king; to eat no more red earth, but to roast and eat the fruit of the tree growing before them.—This is only a brief outline of the tradition which the natives give of the origin of the bread-fruit. The account is much longer, and I wrote it out in detail once or twice from the mouth of the natives; but though not unpleasant as a specimen of the natives' faculty of invention, it is ill adapted to afford information. It was probably invented by some priest, to uphold the influence of the gods, and the tribute of first-fruits paid to the king. The origin of the cocoa-nut, chesnut, and yam, are derived from similar sources; the cocoa-nut having grown from the head of a man, the chesnut from his kidneys, the yams from his legs,—and other vegetable productions from different parts of his body. The importance of the bread-fruit and cocoa-nut, in the estimation of the natives, may also be gathered from the fact of their fabulous traditions assigning their origin to the head and the heart of him whose affection for his son was stronger than his love of life.

There are no serpents in the islands, and the only venomous reptiles are a species of centipede, and a small kind of scorpion. The natives are seldom stung by them; and though the bite of the latter is painful, it is not attended with danger or serious inconvenience. There are no beasts of prey, nor wild animals, with the exception of a few boars or hogs, and dogs, in the mountains, and these are not often troublesome.

With the exception of the fish on the coasts, the variety and abundance in the animal is much inferior to that in the vegetable productions of the South Sea Islands. Hogs, dogs, rats, and lizards were the only quadrupeds originally found among them. Hogs, called by the natives *puaa*, or *buaa*, and which they say were brought by the first inhabitants, were found in the island by Wallis and Cook. These, however, differed considerably from the present breed, which is a mixture of English and Spanish. They are described as having been smaller than the generality of hogs now are, with long legs, long noses, curly or almost woolly hair, and short erect ears. An animal of this kind is now and then seen, and the people say such were the only hogs formerly in Tahiti. It was also said, that they, unlike all other swine, were wholly averse to the mire; and a phenomenon so novel among the habits of their species, produced a poetical effusion, which appeared in a monthly periodical about five or six and twenty years ago. If such were the cleanly habits of the swine in Tahiti at that time, they have degenerated very much since, for I have often seen them stretched out at ease in a miry slough, apparently as much at home as the greatest hog would be in such a situation, in any other part of the world.

The swine now reared are large, and often well fed; they are never confined in sties, but range about in search of food. Those that feed in the heads of the valleys live chiefly upon fruit and roots, while those kept about the houses of the natives are fed occasionally with bread-fruit or cocoa-nuts. Unless well fed, they are very destructive to the fences and the native gardens, and bite through a stick, one or two inches in diameter, with very little effort: sometimes the natives break their teeth, or put a kind of yoke upon them; which, in some of the islands of the Pacific, is rather a singular one. A circular piece, as large as a shilling or a half-crown, is cut out of each ear, and when the wound has healed, a single stick, eighteen inches or two feet long, is passed through the apertures. This wooden bar lies horizontally across the upper part of the pig's head, and, coming in contact with the upright sticks of a fence, arrests his progress, even when he has succeeded in forcing his head through. The flesh of the pig, though in general soft, rich, and sweet, is not so fine as English-fed pork, neither has it the peculiarly agreeable taste by which the latter is distinguished. This is probably caused by the Tahitian swine feeding so much upon cocoa-nuts, and other sweet fruit. For the kind, however, native pork is very good; but, having little meat besides, we soon became tired of it. Although capable, when all the bones are taken out, of being preserved by salt, the natives never, till lately, thought of sitting down to less than a hog baked whole. Several of the chiefs, however, now only dress so much as is necessary for the immediate use of their families, and salt the remainder.

Next to the flesh of swine, that of the dog was formerly prized by the Tahitians, as an article of food. Nevertheless, dogs do not appear to have been reared for food so generally as among the Sandwich Islanders; here they were fed rather as an article of luxury, and principally eaten by the chiefs. They were usually of a small or middling size, and appear a kind of terrier breed, but were by no means ferocious; and, excepting their shape and habits, they have few of the characteristics of the English dog: this probably arises from their different food. The hog and the dog were the only quadrupeds whose flesh was eaten by the Tahitians. Rats were occasionally eaten uncooked by the Friendly Islanders; but, although numerous, they do not appear to have been used for that purpose here. Cats are now domesticated in most of the houses, and appear great favourites with the people.

To these, horses, asses, horned cattle, goats, and sheep, have been added, and, excepting the latter, appear to thrive exceedingly well. Rabits have been several times taken to the islands, and either turned loose, or fed in pens; but the climate, or food, does not seem to have been suitable, and they seldom lived long.

The feathered tribes of the South Sea Islands, like those of the northern Pacific, are not distinguished by brilliancy of plumage, or melody of song. There are, however, several varieties, and some of them in amazing numbers. The most numerous class are the aquatic birds. These skim the surface of the ocean, derive their subsistence from the sea or the inland lakes and streams, build their nests in the hollows of the craggy rocks, or haunt the lagoons and streams, rearing their young, and reposing by the side of the inland waters, or among the tall grass and rushes that border the extensive lakes or marshy hollows. Among the former may be reckoned the stately albatross, *diomedia exulans*, called by the natives obutu; the tropic bird, *phaeton aetherius*, called otaha; several kinds of petrels, called otatare, and others: these abound in all the islands, but appear to resort in greater multitudes to the unnumbered clefts in the rocky sides of the mountains of Borabora and Maurua, than to the more eastern islands. Among the lakes are several kinds of heron, that stand like sentinels on the broken rocks, watching for their prey, or march with solemn gravity along the margin of the stream: wild ducks resort to the lagoons and marshes.

There are several kinds of birds of prey, and a number of the woodpecker tribe, with some small paroquets, of rich and splendid plumage. In the inland parts of some of the islands, the turtle-dove, which is called uupa, and among the mountains pigeons, which, for the sound of their notes, the natives call uuairao, are found in considerable numbers. Among the singing birds, which are not numerous, the omaomao is the most conspicuous. It is about the size of the English thrush, is of a yellow and brown speckled colour, and in its note resembles the thrush more than any other bird.

The most useful bird, however, is the common domestic fowl, called moa by the natives. These were found among the islands by their discoverers, and appear to have been there as long as the people. They are of the same kind as those reared in England; the bodies are smaller, and the legs longer, but this may perhaps have arisen from their not being confined, and seldom fed by the people. Those that are tame usually live upon what they find in the garden, or the fragments of bread-fruit, &c. left after the native meal. During the day they seldom wander far from their owner's dwelling, and at night, either take shelter under the same roof, or roost on the boughs of the trees by which it is overshadowed. Eggs are often plentiful, and the flesh of the fowls, though inferior to that of those fed in England, is generally good. Besides the tame fowls, there are numbers wild in different parts of the island, which range the woods, feeding on fruits or insects; these are occasionally taken by the natives, but are inferior to those that are domesticated. Fowls are not much used by the inhabitants, but are now reared chiefly to supply the vessels that touch at the islands for refreshment.

Fish are numerous in the seas that surround the islands; they abound on their coasts among the reefs, and in their extensive lagoons. The enormous whale, called by the people *tohora*, is often seen by the natives in their canoes, pursuing his gigantic pastime, raising his unwieldy bulk above the water, or spouting it in the air. The black-fish pass along their straits, and the porpoises often appear in shoals, or exhibit their gambols to the great amusement of the people, frequently throwing their whole bodies several feet out of the water, curving their tails, and falling headlong into the sea. The natives call them *oua*, a word which also signifies to spring or jump. Here, also, are seen a great number of the ray species, from the large unsightly diabolus, to the smallest kind, and a great variety of the medusa, or cuttle-fish. The fleet, beautiful, and sportive dolphin, and the anomalous creature called the flying-fish, that pursues its way alternately through the water and the air, and seems the uniting link between the feathered and the finny tribes. The natives call it marara. The totara, or hedge-hog fish, is also found among their reefs. The operu, *scomber scomber* of Linneus, resort to their coasts in large shoals, at stated seasons of the year, and are taken in great numbers by the people.

The islanders are usually expert fishermen, and fish is a principal means of support for those who reside near the shore. The albicore, bonito, ray, swordfish and shark, the porpoise and the dolphin, are among the larger sea-fish that are eaten by them; in addition to which, they have an almost endless variety of rock-fish, which are remarkably sweet and good.

In the rivers they find prawns and eels, and in their lakes, where there is an opening to the sea, multitudes of excellent fish are always found; among others is a salmon, which, at certain seasons of the year, is taken in great abundance. It exactly resembles the northern salmon in size, shape, and structure, but the flesh is much whiter than that of the salmon of Europe, or of those taken on the northern coasts of America; the taste is also the same, excepting that the Tahitian salmon is rather drier than the other. In the sand they find muscles and cockles, and on the coral reefs a great variety of shell-fish; among which, the principal are crabs, lobsters, welks, a large species of cham, and several varieties of echinis, or sea-egg. Numbers of turtle are also found among the reefs and low coralline or sandy islands. The turtle was formerly considered sacred; a part of every one taken was offered to the gods, and the rest dressed with sacred fire, was eaten only by the king and chiefs; and then, I think, either within the precincts of the temple, or in its immediate vicinity; now they are eaten by whomsoever they are caught. Most of their fish is very good, and furnishes a dish of which we never tired.

The rivers furnish few fresh-water fish; eels are the principal, and they are very fine. Eels being great favourites, are sometimes tamed, and fed till they attain an enormous size. Taaroarii had several in different parts of the island. These pets were kept in large holes, two or three feet deep, partially filled with water. On the sides of these pits, the eels formed or found an aperture in a horizontal direction, in which they generally remained, excepting when called by the person who fed them. I have been several times with the young chief, when he has sat down by the side of the hole, and, by giving a shrill sort of whistle, has brought out an enormous eel, which has moved about the surface of the water, and eaten with confidence out of its master's hand. Connected with the fresh-water fish, a phenomenon is often observed, for which the natives are puzzled to account. In the hollows of the rocks, and in other places, to which they suppose the sea and the river never gain access, and where the water collected is entirely what falls from the clouds, small but regularly formed fish are sometimes found. The people have frequently expressed their surprise at finding them, and appeared to wonder how they ever came there. They call them *topataua*, literally, rain-drop, supposing they must have fallen from the clouds with the rain.

The accounts the natives give of the introduction of the animals found on the islands by the first European visitors, are most of them as fabulous as those relating to their own origin. Some, indeed, say that pigs and dogs were brought from the west by the first inhabitants; but others refer their origin to man. One of their traditions states, that after Taaroa had made the world and mankind, he created the quadrupeds of the earth, the fowls of the air, and the fishes of the sea; but one of their most indelicate accounts states, that in ancient times a man died, and after death his body was destroyed by worms, which ultimately grew into swine—and were the first known in the islands. We never observed among them any traces of the Asiatic doctrine of the transmigration of souls; although they believed that hogs had souls, and that there was a distinct place, called Ofetuna, whither they supposed the souls of the pigs repaired after their death. This idea some carried so far as to suppose, that, not only animals had souls, but to imagine that even flowers and plants were organized beings, also possessing souls. Another singular practice in reference to their pigs was, that of giving them some distinct, though often arbitrary name; so that each pig had his own proper name, by which he, as well as the several members of the family, was distinguished. This difference, however, prevailed—a man frequently changed his name, but the name of the pig, once received, was usually retained.

CHAP. IV.

Inhabitants of the islands of the Pacific—Oceanic negroes—Eastern Polynesians—General account of the South Sea Islanders—Physical character—Expression of countenance—Stature, colour, &c.—Mental capacity—Ancient division and computation of time—Tahitian numerals—Extended calculations—Aptness in receiving instruction—Moral character—Hospitality—Extensive and affecting moral degradation—Its enervating influence—Former longevity of the islanders.

THE islands of the Pacific are inhabited by two tribes of men totally distinct, and in some respects entirely different from each other. The most ancient tribe is composed of what are designated Oceanic negroes, who are distinguished by the darkness of the skin, smallness of stature, and particularly by their black woolly or crisped hair. The other tribe exhibits many of the distinguishing features which belong to the physical character of the Malayan and aboriginal American tribes. The former race more properly belong to Australasia, as by them New Holland, New Guinea, New Britain, New Caledonia, and the New Hebrides, are peopled, while on one of the islands, still farther to the westward, both tribes take up their abode, and yet remain distinct; the Oceanic negroes dwelling in the interior, and among the mountain fastnesses, while those of a fairer complexion form their settlements along the shore. In the vicinity of the Friendly Islands they appear to be blended. The greater part of Polynesia appears to be inhabited by those who present in their physical character many points of resemblance to the Malays and South Americans, but yet differ materially from either, and seem to form an intermediate race.

Although, with very few exceptions, all the inhabitants of these islands, to which the designation of Polynesia is given, exhibit the leading marks of the tribe to which they belong, the people of each cluster are distinguished by some minor peculiarities. The following description refers to the inhabitants of the Georgian, Society, and adjacent islands, which, for the sake of brevity, are designated Tahitians, or Society Islanders.

The Tahitians are generally above the middle stature; but their limbs are less muscular and firm than those of the Sandwich Islanders, whom in many respects they resemble. They are, at the same time, more robust than the Marquesans, who are the most light and agile of the inhabitants of Eastern Polynesia. In size and physical power they are inferior to the New Zealanders, and probably resemble in person the Friendly Islanders, as much as any others in the Pacific; exhibiting, however, neither the gravity of the latter, nor the vivacity of the Marquesans. Their limbs are well formed, and although, where corpulency prevails, there is a degree of sluggishness, they are generally active in their movements, graceful and stately in their gait, and perfectly unembarrassed in their address. Those who reside in the interior, or frequently visit the mountainous parts of the islands, form an exception to this remark. The constant use of the naked feet in climbing the steep sides of the rocks, or the narrow defiles of the ravines, probably induces them to turn their toes inwards, which renders their gait exceedingly awkward.

Among the many models of perfection in the human figure that appear in the islands, (presenting to the eye of the stranger all that is beautiful in symmetry and graceful in action,) instances of deformity are now frequently seen, arising from a loathsome disease, of foreign origin, affecting the features of the face, and muscular parts of the body. There is another disease, which forms such a curvature of the upper part of the spine, as to produce what is termed a humped or broken back. The disease which produces this distortion of shape, and deformity of appearance, is declared, by the natives, to have been unknown to their ancestors; and, according to the accounts some of them give of it, was the result of a disease left by the crew of Vancouver's ship. It does not prevail in any of the other groups; and although such numbers are now affected with it, there is no reason to believe, that, formerly, except the many disfigurements produced by the elephantiasis, which appears to have prevailed from their earliest antiquity, a deformed person was seldom seen.

The countenance of the Society Islander is open and prepossessing, though the features are bold, and sometimes prominent. The facial angle is frequently as perpendicular as in the European structure, excepting where the frontal and the occipital bones of the skull were pressed together in infancy. This was frequently done by the mothers, with the male children, when they were designed for warriors. The forehead is sometimes low, but frequently high, and finely formed; the eye-brows are dark and well defined, occasionally arched, but more generally straight; the eyes seldom large, but bright and full, and of a jet-black colour; the cheek-bones not high; the nose either rectilinear or aquiline, often accompanied with a fulness about the nostrils; it is seldom flat, notwithstanding it was formerly the practice of the mothers and nurses to press the nostrils of the female children, a flat and broad nose being by many regarded as more handsome than otherwise. The mouth in general is well formed, though the lips are sometimes large, yet never so much so as to resemble those of the African. The teeth are always entire, excepting in extreme old age, and, though rather large in some, are remarkably white, and seldom either discoloured or decayed. The ears are large, and the chin retreating or projecting, most generally inclining to the latter. The form of the face is either round or oval, and but very seldom exhibits any resemblance to the angular form of the Tartar visage, while their profile frequently bears a most striking resemblance to that of the European. Their hair is a shining black or dark brown colour; straight, but not lank and wiry like that of the American Indian, nor, excepting in a few solitary instances, woolly like the New Guinea or New Holland negroes. Frequently it is soft and curly, though seldom so fine as that of the civilized nations inhabiting the temperate zones.

There is a considerable difference between the stature of the male and female sex here, as well as in other parts of the world, yet not so great as that which often prevails in Europe. The females, though generally more delicate in form and smaller in size than the men, are, taken altogether, stronger and larger than the females of England, and sometimes remarkably tall and stout. A roundness and fulness of figure, without extending to corpulency, distinguishes the people in general, particularly the females.

It is a singular fact in the physiology of the inhabitants of this part of the world, that the chiefs, and persons of hereditary rank and influence in the islands, are, almost without exception, as much superior to the peasantry or common people, in stateliness, dignified deportment, and physical strength, as they are in rank and circumstances; although they are not elected to their station on account of their personal endowments, but derive their rank and elevation from their ancestry. This is the case with most of the groups of the Pacific, but peculiarly so in Tahiti and the adjacent isles. The father of the late king was six feet four inches high; Pomare was six feet two. The present king of Raiatea is equally tall. Mahine, the king of Huahine, but for the effects of age, would appear little inferior. Their limbs are generally well formed, and the whole figure is proportioned to their height; which renders the difference between the rulers and their subjects so striking, that Bougainville and some others have supposed they were a distinct race, the descendants of a superior people, who at a remote period had conquered the aborigines, and perpetuated their supremacy. It does not, however, appear necessary, in accounting for the fact, to resort to such a supposition; different treatment in infancy, superior and more regular diet, bathing, distinct habits of life, and the relation that often prevails between the physical character of parents and their children, are sufficient. Some individuals among the lower classes exhibit a stature equal to that of the chiefs; but this is of rare occurrence, and that circumstance alone does not facilitate the admission of its possessor to the higher ranks in society, though in the matrimonial alliances of their chiefs, they undoubtedly had respect to the physical superiority of their rulers. Hence, in one of their songs, the following sentiments are inculcated:—" If black be the complexion of the mother, the son will sound the conch-shell; if vigorous and strong the mother, the son will be a governor."

The prevailing colour of the natives is an olive, a bronze, or a reddish brown—equally removed from the jet-black of the African and the Asiatic, the yellow of the Malay, and the red or copper-colour of the aboriginal American, frequently presenting a kind of medium between the two latter colours. Considerable variety, nevertheless, prevails in the complexion of the population of the same island, and as great a diversity among the inhabitants of different islands. The natives of the Paliser or Pearl Islands, a short distance to the eastward of Tahiti, are darker than the inhabitants of the Georgian group. It is not, however, a blacker hue that their skin presents, but a darker red or brown. The natives of Maniaa, or Mangeea, one of the Harvey cluster, and some of the inhabitants of Rurutu, and the neighbourhood to the south of Tahiti, designated by Malte Brun, " the Austral Islands," and the majority of the reigning family in Raiatea, are not darker than the inhabitants of some parts of southern Europe.

At the time of their birth, the complexion of Tahitian infants is but little if any darker than that of European children, and the skin only assumes the bronze or brown hue as they grow up under repeated or constant exposure to the sun. Those parts of the body that are most covered, even with their loose draperies of native cloth, are, through every period of life, much lighter coloured than those that are exposed; and, notwithstanding the dark tint with which the climate appears to dye their skin, the ruddy bloom of health and vigour or the sudden blush, is often seen mantling the youthful countenance under the light brown tinge, which, like a thin veil, but partially conceals its glowing hue. The females who are much employed in beating cloth, making mats, or other occupations followed under shelter, are usually fairer than the rest; while the fishermen, who are most exposed to the sun, are invariably the darkest portion of the population.

Darkness of colour was generally considered an indication of strength; and fairness of complexion, the contrary. Hence, the men were not solicitous either to cover their persons, or avoid the sun's rays, from any apprehension of the effect it would produce on the skin. When they searched the field of battle for the bones of the slain, to use them in the manufacture of chisels, gimlets, or fish-hooks, they always selected those whose skins were dark, as they supposed their bones were strongest. When I have seen the natives looking at a very dark man, I have sometimes heard them say, *Taata ra e, te ereere! ivi maitai tona:* "The man, how dark! good bones are his." A fair complexion was not an object of admiration or desire. They never considered the fairest European countenance seen among them, handsomer than their own; and sometimes, when a fine, tall, well-formed, and personable man has landed from a ship, they have remarked as he passed along, " A fine man that, if he were but a native." They formerly supposed the white colour of the European's skin to the effect of illness, and hence beheld it with pity. This opinion probably originated from the effects of a disease with which they are occasionally afflicted—a kind of leprosy, which turns the skin of the parts affected, white.

This impression, however, is now altogether removed by the lengthened intercourse they have had with foreigners, and the residence of European families among them.

The mental capacity of the Society Islanders has been hitherto much more partially developed than their physical character. They are remarkably curious and inquisitive, and, compared with other Polynesian nations, may be said to possess considerable ingenuity, mechanical invention, and imitation. Totally unacquainted with the use of letters, their minds could not be improved by any regular continued culture; yet the distinguishing features of their civil polity—the imposing nature, numerous observances, and diversified ramifications of their mythology—the legends of their gods—the historical songs of their bards—the beautiful, figurative, and impassioned eloquence sometimes displayed in their national assemblies—and, above all, the copiousness, variety, precision, and purity of their language, with their extensive use of numbers—warrant the conclusion, that they possess no contemptible mental capabilities. This conclusion is supported by a variety of circumstances connected with their former state.

Though unacquainted with the compass, they have names for the cardinal points. The north they call Apatoa; the south, Apatoerau; the east, Te hitia o te ra, the rising of the sun; and the west, the Tooa o te ra, the falling or sinking of the sun.

Their genealogies and chronological traditions do not appear to have been so correctly preserved as those of the Hawaiians, one or two of which I have, that appear, at least for nearly thirty generations, tolerably correct, though they go back one hundred generations. They were, however, as correct in their methods of computing time as their northern neighbours, if not more so. One mode of reckoning time was by *ui's*, or generations; but the most general calculation was by the year, which they call matahiti, and which consisted of twelve or thirteen lunar months, by the tau or matarii, season or half-year, by the month of thirty days, and by the day or night. They had distinct names for each month; and though they all agreed about the length of the year, they were not unanimous as to the beginning of it, or the names of the months, each island having a computation peculiar to itself.

The following is a statement of their divisions of time, copied from a small book on arithmetic, &c. prepared by Mr. Davies, which I printed at Huahine in 1819. It is the method of computation adopted by the late Pomare and the reigning family.

1. Avarehu	. . .	The new moon that appears about the summer solstice of Tahiti, and generally answers to the last ten days of December or the beginning of January.
2. Faaahu	. . .	January, and part of February—The season of plenty.
3. Pipiri	. . . .	February, and part of March.
4. Taaoa	. . . .	March, and part of April—The season of scarcity.
5. Aununu	. . .	April, and part of May.
6. Apaapa	. . .	May, and a part of June.
7. Paroro mua	. .	June, and a part of July.
8. Paroro muri	. .	July, and a part of August.
9. Muriaha	. . .	August, and a part of September.
10. Hiaia	. . . .	September, and part of October.
11. Tema	. . . .	October, and part of November—The season of scarcity.
12. Te-eri	. . .	The whole, or a part of, November—The uru, or young bread-fruit, begins to flower.

DIVISION OF TIME. 87

13. Te-tai . . . . The whole, or a part of, December—The uru, or bread-fruit, nearly ripe.

Their calculations, however, were not very exact. Thirteen moons exceed the duration of the solar year. But, in order to adapt the same moons to the same seasons, as they successively occur, the moon generally answering to March, or the one occurring about July, is omitted; and, in some years, only twelve moons are enumerated.

Another computation commenced the year at the month *Apaapa*, about the middle of May, and gave different names to several of the months. They divided the year into two seasons, of the *Matarii*, or Pleiades. The first they called *Matarii i nia*, Pleiades above. It commenced when, in the evening, these stars appeared on or near the horizon; and the half year, during which, immediately after sunset, they were seen above the horizon, was called *Matarii i nia*. The other season commenced when, at sunset, the stars were invisible, and continued until at that hour they appeared again above the horizon. This season was called *Matarii i raro*, Pleiades below.

The islanders had three seasons besides these. The first they called *Tetau*, autumn, or season of plenty, the harvest of bread-fruit. It commenced with the month *Tetai*, December, and continued till Faahu. This is not only the harvest, but the summer of the South Sea Islands. It is also the season of most frequent rain. The next is *Te tau miti rahi*, the season of high sea. This commences with *Tieri*, November, and continues until January. The third is the longest, and is called the *Te tau Poai*, the winter, or season of drought and scarcity. It generally commences in *Paroromua*, July, and continues till *Tema*, October.

The natives have distinct names for each day

and each night of the month or moon. They do not, however, reckon time by days, but by nights. Hence, instead of saying, How many days since? they would inquire, *Rui hia aenei?* "How many nights?" The following are the different nights of each moon.

THE NIGHTS OF THE MOON.

1. Ohirohiti.
2. Hoata.
3. Hami-ami-mua.
4. Hami-ami-roto.
5. Hami-ami-muré.
6. Ore-ore-mua.
7. Ore-ore-muri.
8. Tamatea.
9. Ohuna.
10. Oari.
11. Omaharu.
12. Ohua.
13. Omaitu.
14. Ohotu.
15. Omarae. — Te-marama-ati, or the moon with a round and full face.
16. Oturu-tea.
17. Raau-mua.
18. Raau-roto.
19. Raau-muri.
20. Ore-ore-mua.
21. Ore-ore-roto.
22. Ore-ore-muri.
23. Taaroa-mua.
24. Taaroa-roto.
25. Taaroa-muri.
26. O-Tane.
27. O-Roomie.
28. O-Roomaori.
29. O-mutu.
20. O-Terieo.—This is the night or day the moon dies, or is changed.

The seventeenth, eighteenth, and nineteenth nights, or nights immediately succeeding the full moon, were considered as seasons when spirits wander more than at any other time; they were also favourable to the depredations of thieves. They do not appear to have divided their months into weeks, or to have had any division between months and days. Totally ignorant of clocks or watches, they could not divide the day into hours. They, however, marked the progress of the day with sufficient exactness, by noticing the position of the sun in the firmament, the appearance of the atmosphere, and the ebbing and flowing of the tide.

DIVISION OF TIME.

Midnight they called the Tui ra po.

One or two in the morning—Maru ao.

Cock-crowing, or about three o'clock in the morning—Aaoa te moa; aaoa being an imitation of the crowing of a cock.

The dawn of day—Tatahiata.

Morning twilight—Marao rao.

When the flies begin to stir—Ferao-rao.

When a man's face can be known—Itea te mata taata.

The first appearance of the upper part of the sun—Te hatea ra o te ra.

Sunrise, or morning—Poi poi.

The sun above the horizon—Ofao tuna te ra.

The sun a little higher, sending his rays on the land—Matiti titi te ra.

About seven o'clock—Tohe pu te ra.

Eight o'clock—Pere tia te ra.

About nine—Ua paare te ra.

Ten or eleven—Ua medua te ra.

Noon-day, or the sun on the meridian—Avatea.

One or two in the afternoon—Taupe te ra.

About three in the afternoon—Tape-tape te ra.

Nearly four—Tahataha te ra.

About five—Hia-hia te ra.

Between five and six—Ua maru maru te ra.

Sun-setting, Ahiahi—Evening—Mairi te ra, Falling of the sun.

The beginning of darkness—Arehurehu.

Night, or the light quite gone—Po.

When the sea begins to flow towards the land—Pananu te tai.

About eleven at night—Tia rua te rui.

In order to facilitate their commercial transactions, and their intercourse with civilized nations, the names for the months, and the days of the week, used in England, have been introduced. They have also been instructed in our methods of calculating the leap-years, &c.

The English method of mensuration has been introduced, and, with regard to short distances, they begin to understand it. The word *hebedoma* has been introduced, to signify a week. It is not, however, so frequently employed by the people, as the word Sabbath. If a native wished to say he had been absent on a voyage or journey six weeks, he would generally say six Sabbaths, or one moon and two Sabbaths.

Considering their uncivilized state, and want of letters, their method of computing time is matter of astonishment, and shews that they must have existed as a nation for many generations, to have rendered it so perfect. It is also an additional proof that they are not deficient in mental capacity.

Their acquaintance with, and extensive use of numbers, under these circumstances, is still more surprising. They did not reckon by forties, after the manner of the Mexicans and the Sandwich Islanders, but had a decimal method of calculation. These numerals were,

Atahi, one.	Aono, six.
Arua, two.	Ahitu, seven.
Atoru, three.	Avaru, eight.
Amaha, four.	Aiva, nine.
Arima, five.	Ahuru, ten.

Eleven would be Ahuru matahi, ten and one; and so on to twenty, which was simply Erua ahuru, two tens; twenty-one, two tens and one; and proceeding in this way till ten tens, or one hundred, which they called a *Rau*. The same method was repeated for every successive rau, or hundred, till ten had been enumerated, and these they called one *Mano*, or thousand. They continued in the same way to enumerate the units, ahurus or tens, raus or hundreds, and manos or thousands, until they had counted ten manos, or thousands; this they called a *Manotini*, or ten thousand. Continuing the same process, they counted ten manotinis, which they called a *Rehu*, or one hundred thousand. Advancing still farther, they counted ten rehus, which they called an *Iu*, which was ten hundred thousand, or one million.

They had no higher number than the *iu*, or million: they could, however, by means of the above terms or combinations, enumerate, with facility, tens, hundreds, thousands, tens of thousands, or hundreds of thousands of millions.

The precision, regularity, and extent of their numbers has often astonished me; and how a people, having, comparatively speaking, but little necessity to use calculation, and being destitute of knowledge of figures, should have originated and matured such a system, is still wonderful, and appears, more than any other fact, to favour the opinion that these islands were peopled from a country whose inhabitants were highly civilized.

Many of their numerals are precisely the same as those used by the people of several of the Asiatic islands, and also in the remote and populous island of Madagascar. Occasionally the islanders double the number, by simply counting two instead of one. This is frequently practised in counting fish, bread-fruit, or cocoa-nuts, and is called double counting, by which all the above terms signify twice as large a number as is now affixed to them.

In counting, they usually employ a piece of the stalk of the cocoa-nut leaf, putting one aside for every ten, and gathering them up, and putting a longer one aside for every rau, or hundred. The natives of most of the islands, adults and children, appear remarkably fond of figures and calculations, and receive the elements of arithmetic with great facility, and seeming delight.

They estimate the distance of places by the length of time it takes to travel or sail from one to the other. Thus, if we wished to give them an idea of the distance from the islands to England, we should say it was five months; and they would say the distance from Tahiti to Huahine was a night and a day, and from Huahine to Raiatea, from sunrise to nearly noon, &c.

That their mental powers are not inferior to those of the generality of mankind, has been more fully shown since the establishment of schools, and the introduction of letters. Not only have the children and young persons learned to read, write, cipher, and commit their lessons to memory with a facility and quickness not exceeded by individuals of the same age in any country; but the education of adults, and even persons advanced in years—which in England, with every advantage, is so difficult an undertaking, that nothing but the use of the best means and untiring application ever accomplished it—has been effected here with comparative ease. Multitudes, who were upwards of thirty or forty years of age when they commenced with the alphabet, have, in the course of twelve months, learned to read distinctly in the New Testament, large portions, and even whole books of which, some of them have in a short period committed to memory.

They acquired the first rules of arithmetic with equal facility, and have readily received the different kinds of instruction hitherto furnished, as fast as their teachers could prepare lessons in the native language. It is probable that not less than ten thousand persons have learned to read the Scriptures, and that nearly an equal number are either capable of writing, or are under

APTITUDE FOR INSTRUCTION. 93

instruction. In the several stations and branch stations, many thousands are still receiving daily instruction in the first principles of human knowledge and divine truth.

The following extract from the journal of a Tahitian, now a native Missionary in the Sandwich group, is not only most interesting from the intelligence it conveys, but creditable to the writer's talents. It was published in the American Missionary Herald, and refers to the young princess of the Sandwich Islands, the only sister of the late and present king.

"Nahienaena, in knowledge and words, is a woman of matured understanding. All the fathers and mothers of this land are ignorant and left-handed; they become children in the presence of Nahienaena, and she is their mother and teacher. Her own men, women, and children, those composing her household, (or domestic establishment,) listen to the good word of God from her lips. She also instructs Hoapiri and wife in good things. She teaches them night and day. She is constantly speaking to her steward, and to all her household. Very numerous are the words which she speaks, to encourage, and to strengthen them in the good way.

"The young princess has always been pleasant in conversation. Her words are good words. She takes pleasure in conversation, like a woman of mature years. She orders her speech with great wisdom and discretion, always making a just distinction between good and evil. She manifests much discernment in speaking to others the word of God, and the word of love. It was by the maliciousness of the people, old and young, that she was formerly led astray. She was then ignorant of the devices of the wicked. They have given her no rest; but have presented every argument before her that this world could present, to win her over to them.

"Nahienaena desires now to make herself very low. She does not wish to be exalted by men. She desires to cast off entirely the rehearsing of names; for her rejoicing is not now in names and titles. This is what she desires, and longs to have rehearsed—'Jesus alone; let him be lifted up; let him be exalted; let all rejoice in him; let our hearts sing praise to him.' This is the language of her inmost soul."

On a public occasion, in the island of Raiatea, during the year 1825, a number of the inhabitants were conversing on the wisdom of God; which, it was observed, though so long unperceived by them, was strikingly exhibited in every object they beheld. In confirmation of this, a venerable and gray-headed man, who had formerly been a sorcerer, or priest of the evil spirit, stretched forth his hand, and, looking at the limbs of his body, said, " Here the wisdom of God is displayed. I have *hinges* from my toes to my finger ends. This finger has its hinges, and bends at my desire—this arm, on its hinge, is extended at my will—by means of these hinges, my legs bear me where I wish; and my mouth, by its hinge, masticates my food. Does not all this display the wisdom of God?"

The above will show, that the inhabitants of these distant isles, though shut out for ages from intercourse with every other part of the world, and deprived of every channel of knowledge, are, notwithstanding, by no means inferior in intellect or capacity to the more favoured inhabitants of other parts of the globe. These statements also warrant the anticipation, that they will attain an elevation equal to that of the most cultivated and enlarged intellect, whenever they shall secure the requisite advantages.

They certainly appear to possess an aptness for learning, and a quickness in pursuit of it, which is highly encouraging, although in some degree counteracted by the volatile disposition and fugitive habits of their early life, under the influence of which their mental character was formed; and a love of indolence, fostered by the warmth of the climate, and the fertility of the soil.

The moral character of the South Sea Islanders, though more fully developed than their intellectual capacity, often presents the most striking contradictions. Their hospitality has, ever since their discovery, been proverbial, and cannot be exceeded. It is practised alike by all ranks, and is regulated only by the means of the individual by whom it is exercised. A poor man feels himself called upon, when a friend from a distance visits his dwelling, to provide an entertainment for him, though he should thereby expend every article of food he possessed; and he would generally divide his fish or his bread-fruit with any one, even a stranger, who should be in need, or who should ask him for it.

I am willing to afford them every degree of credit for the exercise of this amiable disposition; yet, when it is considered that a guest is not entertained day after day at his friend's table, but that after one large collection of food has been presented, the visitor must provide for himself, while the host frequently takes but little further concern about him—we are induced to think, that the force of custom is as powerful in its influence on his mind, as that of hospitality. In connexion with this, it should be recollected, that for every such entertainment, the individual expects to be reimbursed in kind, whenever he may visit the abode of his guest. Their ancient laws of government, also, imperiously required the poor industrious landholder, or farmer, to bring forth the produce of his garden or his field for the use of the chiefs, or the wandering and licentious Areois, whenever they might halt at his residence; and more individuals have been banished, or selected as sacrifices, for withholding what these daring ramblers required than perhaps for all other crimes. To withhold food from the king or chiefs, when they might enter a district, was considered a crime next to resisting the royal authority, or declaring war against the king; and this has in a great degree rendered the people so ready to provide an entertainment for those by whom they may be visited.

Next to their hospitality, their cheerfulness and good nature strike a stranger. They are seldom melancholy or reserved, always willing to enter into conversation, and ready to be pleased, and to attempt to please their associates. They are, generally speaking, careful not to give offence to each other: but though, since the introduction of Christianity, families dwell together, and find an increasing interest in social intercourse, yet they do not realize that high satisfaction experienced by members of families more advanced in civilization. There are, however, few domestic broils; and were fifty natives taken promiscuously from any town or village, to be placed in a neighbourhood or house—where *they* would disagree once, fifty Englishmen, selected in the same way, and placed under similar circumstances, would quarrel perhaps twenty times. They do not appear to delight in provoking one another, but are far more accustomed to jesting, mirth, and humour, than irritating or reproachful language.

Their jests and raillery were not always confined to individuals, but extended to neighbourhoods, or the population of whole islands. The inhabitants of one of the Leeward Islands, (Tahaa, I believe,) even to the present time furnish matter for mirthful jest to the natives of the other islands of the group, from the circumstance of one of their people, the first time she saw a foreigner who wore boots, exclaiming, with astonishment, that the individual had *iron legs.* It is also said, that among the first scissors possessed by the Huahineans, one pair became exceedingly dull, and the simple-hearted people, not knowing how to remedy this defect, tried several experiments, and at length *baked the scissors* in a native oven, for the purpose of sharpening them. Hence the people of Huahine are often spoken of in jest by the Tahitians, as the *feia eu paoti,* or people that baked the scissors. The Tahitians themselves were in their turn subjects of raillery, from some of their number, who resided at a distance from the sea, attempting, on one occasion, to kill a turtle by pinching its throat, or strangling it, when the neck was drawn into the shell, on which they were surprised to find they could make no impression with their fingers. The Huahineans, therefore, in their turn, spoke of the Tahitians as the *feia uumi honu,* the people that strangled the turtle.

Their humour and their jests were, however, but rarely what might be termed innocent sallies of wit; they were in general low and immoral to a disgusting degree. Their common conversation, when engaged in their ordinary avocations, was often such as the ear could not listen to without pollution, presenting images, and conveying sentiments, whose most fleeting passage through the mind left contamination. Awfully dark, indeed, was their moral character, and notwithstanding the apparent mildness of their disposition, and the cheerful vivacity of their conversation, no portion of the human race was ever perhaps sunk lower in brutal licentiousness and moral degradation, than this isolated people,

> "The Paphian Venus driven from the west,
> In Polynesian groves long undisturbed,
> Her shameful rites and orgies foul maintained.
> The wandering voyager at Tahiti found
> Another Daphne."

The veil of oblivion must be spread over this part of their character, of which the appalling picture, drawn by the pen of inspiration in the hand of the apostle, in the first chapter of his epistle to the Romans, revolting and humiliating as it is, affords but too faithful a portraiture.

The depraved moral habits of the South Sea Islanders undoubtedly weaken their mental energies, and enervate their physical powers; and although remarkably strong men are now and then met with among them, they seem to be more distinguished by activity, and capability of endurance, than by muscular strength. They engage in various kinds of work with great spirit for a time, but they soon tire. Regular, steady habits of labour are only acquired by long practice. When a boat manned with English seamen, and a canoe with natives, have started together from the shore—at their first setting out, the natives would soon leave the boat behind, but, as they became weary, they would relax their vigour; while the seamen, pulling on steadily, would not only overtake them, but, if the voyage occupied three or four hours, would invariably reach their destination first.

The natives take a much larger quantity of refreshment than European labourers, but their food is less solid and nutritive. They have, however, the power of enduring fatigue and hunger in a greater degree than those by whom they are visited. A native will sometimes travel, in the course of a day, thirty or forty miles, frequently over mountain and ravine, without taking any refreshment, except the juice from a piece of sugar-cane, and apparently experience but little inconvenience from his excursion. The facility with which they perform their journeys is undoubtedly the result of habit, as many are accustomed to traverse the mo'ntains, and climb the rocky precipices, even from their childhood.

The longevity of the islanders does not appear to have been, in former times, inferior to that of the inhabitants of more temperate climates. It is, however, exceedingly difficult to ascertain the age of individuals in a community destitute of all records; and although many persons are to be met with, whose wrinkled skin, decrepit form, silver hair, impaired sight, toothless jaws, and tremulous voice, afford every indication of extreme age; these alone would be fallacious data, as climate, food, and habits of life might have prematurely induced them. Our inferences are therefore drawn from facts connected with comparatively recent events in their history, the dates of which are well known. When the Missionaries arrived in the Duff, there were natives on the island who could recollect the visit of Captain Wallis: he was there in 1767. There are, in both the Sandwich and Society Islands, individuals who can recollect Captain Cook's visit, which is fifty years ago; there are also two now in the islands, that were taken away in the Bounty, forty years since; and these individuals do not look more aged, nor even so far advanced in years, as others that may be seen. The opinion of those Missionaries who have been longest in the islands is, that many reach the age of seventy years, or upwards. There is, therefore, every reason to believe, that the period of human life, in the South

Sea Islands, is not shorter than in other parts of the world, unless when it is rendered so by the inordinate use of ardent spirits, and the influence of diseases prevailing among the lower classes, from which they were originally exempt, and the ravages of which they are unable to palliate or remove.

The mode of living, especially among the farmers, their simple diet, and the absence of all stimulants, their early hours of retiring to rest, and rising in the morning with or before the break of day, their freedom from irritating or distressing cares, and sedentary habits, which so often, in artificial or civilized society, destroy health, appear favourable to the longevity of this portion of the inhabitants, and present a striking contrast to the dissipated and licentious habits of the Areois dancers, and votaries of dissipation and pleasure.

CHAP. V.

Comparative numbers of the inhabitants—Indications and causes of depopulation—Beneficial tendency of Christianity—Origin of the inhabitants of the South Sea Islands—Traditions—Legends of Taaroa and Hina—Resemblance to Jewish history—Coincidences in language, mythology, &c. with the language, &c. of the Hindoos and Malays, Madagasse, and South Americans—Probable source of population—Difficulty of reaching the islands from the west—Account of the different native voyages—Geographical extent over which the Polynesian race and language prevail.

It is impossible for any one who has visited these islands, or traversed any one of the districts, to entertain the slightest doubt that the number of inhabitants in the South Sea Islands was formerly much greater than at present. What their number, in any remote period of their history, may have been, it is not easy to ascertain: Captain Cook estimated those residing in Tahiti at 200,000. The grounds, however, on which he formed his conclusions were certainly fallacious. The population was at all times so fugitive and uncertain, as to the proportion it bore to any section of geographical surface, that no correct inference, as to the amount of the whole, could be drawn from the numbers seen in one part. Captain Wilson's calculation, in 1797, made the population of Tahiti only about 16,000; and, not many years afterwards, the Missionaries declared it as their opinion, that this island did not contain more than 8000 souls; and I cannot think that, within the last thirty years, it has ever contained fewer inhabitants.

The present number of natives is about 10,000; that of Eimeo and Tetuaroa probably 2,000. The Leeward Islands perhaps contain nearly an equal number. The Austral Islands have about 5,000 inhabitants; 4,000 of whom reside in the islands of Rapa and Raivavai.* Rarotogna, or Rarotoa, has a population of nearly 7,000; and the whole of the Harvey Islands contain not less than ten or eleven thousand. Connected with these may be considered the Paumotu, or Pearl Islands, of whose population it is difficult to form any correct estimate, as there are no means of ascertaining their numbers, excepting from the reports of the natives, and the observations of masters of vessels, who generally make a very short stay among them. Anaa, or Prince of Wales's Island, is said to be inhabited by several thousands, and as the islands are numerous, though small, it is to be presumed that their population does not amount to less than ten thousand. From these statements it will appear, that the population of the Georgian and Society Islands, together with the adjacent clusters, with which the natives maintain constant intercourse, and to which Christianity has been conveyed by native or European teachers, comprises between forty-eight and fifty thousand persons. In this number, the Marquesas, to which native teachers have gone, and which one of the Missionaries has recently visited, are not included. Their population is probably about thirty or forty thousand.

With respect to the Society and neighbouring

* Since this estimate was first published, a severe epidemic has swept through these two latter islands, and considerably diminished the population.

islands, although no ancient monuments are found indicating that they were ever inhabited by a race much further advanced in civilization than those found on their shores by Wallis, Cook, and Bougainville; yet that race has evidently, at no very remote period, been much more numerous than it was when discovered by Europeans. In the bottom of every valley, even to the recesses in the mountains, on the sides of the inferior hills, and on the brows of almost every promontory, in each of the islands, monuments of former generations are still met with in great abundance. Stone pavements of their dwellings and court-yards, foundations of houses, and ruins of family temples, are numerous. Occasionally they are found in exposed situations, but generally amidst thickets of brushwood or groves of trees, some of which are of the largest growth. All these relics are of the same kind as those observed among the natives at the time of their discovery, evidently proving that they belong to the same race, though to a more populous æra of their history. The stone tools occasionally found near these vestiges of antiquity demonstrate the same lamentable fact.

The present generations, deeply sensible of the depopulation that has taken place even within the recollection of those most advanced in years, have felt acutely in prospect of the annihilation that appeared inevitable. Their priests formerly denounced the destruction of the nation, as the greatest punishment the gods could inflict, and the following was one of the predictions: *E tupu te fau, e toro te farero, e mou te taata:* "The fau (*hibiscus*) shall grow, the *farero* (coral) shall spread or stretch out its branches, but man shall cease."— The fau is one of the most spreading trees, and is of quickest growth; it soon over-runs uncultivated lands; while the branching coral, *farero*, is perhaps more rapid in its formation than any of the corallines that close up the openings in the reefs, and, wherever it is shallow, rises to the water's surface, so as to prevent the passage of the canoe, and destroy the resort of the fish. This was denounced as the punishment that would follow disobedience to the injunctions or requisitions of the priest, delivered in the name, and under the authority, of the gods. Tati, however, remarked to Mr. Davies, that it was the observing, not the neglecting of the directions of the priest, that had nearly produced its actual accomplishment.

At the time when the nation renounced idolatry, the population was so much reduced, that many of the more observant natives thought the denunciation of the prophet was about to be literally fulfilled. Tati, the chief of Papara, talking with Mr. Davies on this subject, in 1815, said, with great emphasis, that "if God had not sent his word at the time he did, wars, infant-murder, human sacrifices, &c. would have made an end of the small remnant of the nation." A similar declaration was pathetically made by Pomare soon after, when some visitors from England, I think the Deputation from the Missionary Society, waited upon him at his residence. He addressed them to the following effect: "You have come to see us under circumstances very different from those under which your countrymen formerly visited our ancestors. They came in the æra of men, when the islands were inhabited, but you are come to behold just the remnant of the people." I have often heard the chiefs speak of themselves and of the natives as only a small *toea*, remainder, left after the extermination of Satani, or the evil spirit; comparing themselves to a firebrand unconsumed among the mouldering embers of a recent conflagration. These figures, and others equally affecting and impressive, were but too appropriate, as emblems of the actual state to which they were reduced. Under the depopulating influence of vicious habits—the dreadful devastation of diseases that followed, and the early destruction of health—the prevalence of infanticide—the frequency of war—the barbarous principles upon which it was prosecuted, and the increase of human sacrifices, it does not appear possible that they could have existed, as a nation, for many generations longer.

An inquiry naturally presents itself in connexion with this subject, viz.—To what cause is this recent change in the circumstances of the people to be attributed? It is self-evident, that if these habits had always prevailed among the Tahitians, they must long since have been annihilated. Society must, at some time, have been more favourable, not only to the preservation, but to the increase of population, or the inhabitants could never have been so numerous as they undoubtedly were a century or a century and a half ago. There is no question that depopulation had taken place to a considerable extent prior to their discovery by Captain Wallis, and it is not easy to discover the causes which first led to it. Infanticide and human sacrifices, together with their wars, appear to have occasioned the diminution of the inhabitants before the period alluded to. Whether wars were more frequent immediately preceding their discovery, than it had been in earlier ages, we have not the means of knowing, nor have we been able to ascertain, with any great accuracy, how long the Areoi society had existed, or child-murder was practised. There is reason to believe that infanticide is not of recent origin, and the antiquity of the Areoi fraternity, according to tradition, is equal to that of the first inhabitants.

Human sacrifices, we are informed by the natives, are comparatively of modern institution: they were not admitted until a few generations antecedent to the discovery of the islands. They were first offered at Raiatea, in the national marae at Opoa, having been demanded by the priest in the name of the god, who had communicated the requisition to his servant in a dream. Human sacrifices were presented at Raiatea and the Leeward Islands for some time before they were introduced among the offerings to the deities of Tahiti; but soon after they began to be employed, they were offered with great frequency, and in appalling numbers: but of this, an account will hereafter be given.

The depopulation that has taken place during the last two or three generations, viz. since their discovery, may be easily accounted for. In addition to a disease, which, as a desolating scourge, spread, unpalliated and unrestrained, its unsightly and fatal influence among the people, two others are reported to have been carried thither—one by the crew of Vancouver in 1790; and the other by means of the Britannia, an English whaler, in 1807. Both these disorders spread through the islands; the former almost as fatal as the plague, the latter affecting nearly every individual throughout all the islands. The maladies originally prevailing among them, appear, compared with those by which they are now afflicted, to have been few in number and mild in character.

Next to these diseases, the introduction of fire-arms, although their use in war has not perhaps rendered their engagements more cruel and murderous than when they fought hand to hand with club and spear—has most undoubtedly cherished, in those who possessed them, a desire for war, as a means of enlarging their territory, and augmenting their power. Pomare's dominion would never have been so extensive and so absolute, but for the aid he derived, in the early part of his reign, from the mutineers of the Bounty, who attended him to battle with arms which they had previously learned to use with an effect, which his opponents could not resist. Subsequently, the hostile chieftains, having procured fire-arms, and succeeding in attaching to their interest European deserters from their ships, considered themselves, if not invincible, at least equal to their enemies, and sought every opportunity for engaging in the horrid work of accelerating the depopulation of their country. Destruction was the avowed design with which they commenced every war, and the principle of extermination rendered all their hostilities fatal to the vanquished party.

Another cause most influential in the diminution of the Tahitian race, has been the introduction of the art of distillation, and the extensive use of ardent spirits. They had, before they were visited by our ships, a kind of intoxicating beverage called *ava*, but the deleterious effects resulting from its use were confined to a comparatively small portion of the inhabitants. The growth of the plant from which it was procured was slow; its culture required care; it was usually tabued for the chiefs; and the common people were as strictly prohibited from appropriating it to their own use, as the peasantry are in reference to game in England.

Its effects also were rather sedative, than narcotic or inebriating.

But after the Tahitians had been taught by foreign seamen, and natives of the Sandwich Islands, to distil spirits from indigenous roots, and rum had been carried to the islands in abundance as an article of barter, intoxication became almost universal; and all the demoralization, crimes, and misery, that follow in its train, were added to the multiplied sorrows and wasting scourges of the people. It nurtured indolence, and spread discord through their families, increased the abominations of the Areoi society, and the unnatural crime of infanticide. Before going to the temple to offer a human sacrifice to their gods, the priests have been known to intoxicate themselves, in order that they might be insensible to any unpleasant feelings this horrid work might excite.

These causes operating upon a people, whose simple habits of diet rendered their constitutions remarkably susceptible of violent impressions, are, to a reflecting mind, quite sufficient to account for the rapid depopulation of the islands within the last fifty or sixty years.

The philanthropist, however, will rejoice to know, that although sixteen years ago the nation appeared on the verge of extinction, it is now, under the renovating and genial principles of true religion, and the morality with which this is inseparably connected, rapidly increasing. When the people in general embraced Christianity, we recommended that a correct account of the births and deaths occurring in each of the islands should be kept. From the operation of the causes above enumerated, for some years even after the crimes in which they originated had ceased, the number of deaths exceeded that of births. About the years 1819 and 1820 they were nearly equal, and since that period population has been rapidly increasing,

It was not till the account of deaths and births was presented, that we had an adequate idea of the affecting depopulation that had been going on; and if, for several years after infanticide, inebriation, human sacrifices, and war, were discontinued, the number of deaths exceeded that of the births; how appalling must that excess have been, when all these destructive causes were in full operation! There is now, however, every ground to indulge the expectation that the population will become greater than it has been in any former period of their history; and it is satisfactory, in connexion with this anticipation, to know—that an extent of soil capable of cultivation, and other resources, are adequate to the maintenance of a population tenfold increased above its present numbers.

The origin of the inhabitants of the South Sea Islands, in common with other parts of Polynesia, is a subject perhaps of more interest and curiosity, than of importance and practical utility. The vast extent of geographical surface covered by the race of which they form an integral portion, the analogy in character, the identity in language, &c., the remote distance at which the different tribes are placed from each other, and the isolated spots which they occupy in the vast expanse of surrounding water, render the source whence they were derived, one of the mysteries connected with the history of our species.

To a Missionary, the business of whose life is with the people among whom he is stationed, every thing relating to their history is, at least, interesting; and the origin of the islanders has often engaged our attention, and formed the subject of our inquiries. The early history of a people destitute of all records, and remote from nations in whose annals contemporaneous events would be preserved, is necessarily involved in obscurity. The greater part of the traditions of this people are adapted to perplex rather than facilitate the investigation.

A very generally received Tahitian tradition is, that the first human pair were made by Taaroa, the principal deity formerly acknowledged by the nation. On more than one occasion, I have listened to the details of the people respecting his work of creation. They say, that after Taaroa had formed the world, he created man out of *araea*, red earth, which was also the food of man until bread-fruit was produced. In connexion with this, some relate that Taaroa one day called for the man by name. When he came, he caused him to fall asleep, and that, while he slept, he took out one of his *ivi*, or bones, and with it made a woman, whom he gave to the man as his wife, and that they became the progenitors of mankind. This always appeared to me a mere recital of the Mosaic account of creation, which they had heard from some European, and I never placed any reliance on it, although they have repeatedly told me it was a tradition among them before any foreigner arrived. Some have also stated that the woman's name was Ivi, which would be by them pronounced as if written *Eve*. Ivi is an aboriginal word, and not only signifies a bone, but also a widow, and a victim slain in war. Notwithstanding the assertion of the natives, I am disposed to think that *Ivi*, or Eve, is the only aboriginal part of the story, as far as it respects the mother of the human race. Should more careful and minute inquiry confirm the truth of their declaration, and prove that this account was in existence among them prior to their intercourse with Europeans, it will be the most remarkable and valuable oral tradition of the origin of the human race yet known.

Another extensive and popular tradition referred the origin of the people to Opoa, in the island of Raiatea, where the *tiis*, or spirits, formerly resided, who assumed of themselves, or received from the gods, human bodies, and became the progenitors of mankind. The name of one was Tii Maaraauta; *Tii*, branching or extending towards the land, or the interior: and of the other, Tii Maaraatai; *Tii*, branching or spreading towards the sea. These, however, are supposed to be but other names for Taaroa. It is supposed that prior to the period of Tii Maaraauta's existence, the islands were only resorted to by the gods or spiritual beings, but that these two, endowed with powers of procreation, produced the human species. They first resided at Opoa, whence they peopled the island of Raiatea, and subsequently spread themselves over the whole cluster. Others state, that Tii was not a spirit, but a human being, the first man made by the gods; that his wife was sometimes called Tii, and sometimes Hina; that when they died, their spirits were supposed to survive the dissolution of the body, and were still called by the same name, and hence the term *tii* was first applied to the spirits of the departed, a signification which it retained till idolatry was abolished.

In the Ladrone Islands, departed chiefs, or the spirits of such, are called *aritis*, and to them prayers were addressed. The *tiis* of Tahiti were also considered a kind of inferior deities, to whom, on several occasions, prayers were offered. The resemblance of this term to the demons or *dii* of the ancients, is singular, and might favour the conjecture that both were derived from the same source.

The origin of the islands, as well as their inhabitants, was generally attributed to Taaroa, or the joint agency of Taaroa and Hina; and although one of their traditions states that all the islands were formerly united in one *fenua nui*, or large continent, which the gods in anger destroyed, scattering in the ocean the fragments, of which Tahiti is one of the largest; yet others ascribe their formation to Taaroa, who is said to have laboured so hard in the work of creation, that the profuse perspiration induced thereby, filled up the hollows, and formed the sea; accounting, by this circumstance, for its transparency and saltness. Others attribute the origin of the world, the elements, the heavenly bodies, and the human species, to the procreative powers of their deities; and, according to their account, one of the descendants of Taaroa, and the son of the sun and moon, and, in reference to his descent, the Manco Capac of their mythology, embracing the sand on the sea shore,—begat a son, who was called Tii, and a daughter, who was called Opiira. These two, according to their tradition, were the father and mother of mankind.

But the most circumstantial tradition, relative to the origin of mankind, is one for which, as well as for much valuable information on the mythology and worship of the idols of the South Sea Islanders, I am indebted to the researches of my esteemed friend and coadjutor, Mr. Barff. According to this legend, man was the fifth order of intelligent beings created by Taaroa and Hina, (of whom an account will hereafter be given,) and was called the *Rahu tuata i te ao ia Tii*, " The class, or order of the world, of, or by, Tii." Hina is reported to have said to Taaroa, " What shall be done, how shall man be obtained ? Behold, classed or fixed are gods of the *po*, or state of night, and there are no men." Taaroa is said to have answered, " Go on the shore to the interior, to your brother." Hina answered, " I have been inland, and he is not." Taaroa then said, " Go to the sea, perhaps he is on the sea ; or if on the land, he will be on the land." Hina said, " Who is at sea ?" The god answered, " Tiimaaraatai." Who is Tiimaaraatai ? is he a man ?" " He is a man, and your brother," answered the god ; " Go to the sea, and seek him." When the goddess had departed, Taaroa ruminated within himself as to the means by which man should be formed, and went to the land, where he assumed the appearance and substance which should constitute man. Hina returning from her unsuccessful search for Tiimaaraatai at sea, met him, but not knowing him, said, " Who are you ?" " I am Tiimaaraatai," he replied. " Where have you been?" said the goddess : " I have sought you here, and you were not ; I went to the sea, to look for Tiimaaraatai, and he was not." " I have been here in my house, or abode," answered Tiimaaraatai," and behold you have arrived, my sister, come to me." Hina said, " So it is, you are my brother ; let us live together." They became man and wife ; and the son that Hina afterwards bore, they called Tii. He was the first-born of mankind. Afterwards Hina had a daughter, who was called Hinaereeremonoi ; she became the wife of Tii, and bore to him a son, who was called Taata, the general name (with slight modification) for *man* throughout the Pacific. Hina, the daughter and wife of Taaroa, the grandmother of Taata, being transformed into a beautiful young woman, became the wife of *Taata* or Man, bore him a son and a daughter, called Ouru and Fana, who were the progenitors of the human race.

One account states that the visible creation has two foundations or origins, that Taaroa made the earth, the sun, moon, and stars, heaven and hell: and that Tii made man of the earth. According to this tradition, they believed that of the earth at Ati-auru, a place in Opoa, Tii made a woman, dwelt with her in a house called Fare-pouri, in Opoa, that she bore him a daughter who was called Hina-tumararo; she became the wife of Tiimaaraatai, and from these the world was peopled: Tii and Taaroa, the people imagined to be one and the same being, but that Taaroa dwelt in the region of *chaos*, and Tii in the world of *light*.

Another tradition stated, that the first inhabitants of the South Sea Islands originally came from a country in the direction of the setting sun, to which they say several names were given, though none of them are remembered by the present inhabitants.

Their traditions are numerous, often contradictory, and though it is difficult to obtain a correct recital of them from any of the present inhabitants; yet more might have been inserted, but they can scarcely be said to impart any valuable information as to the country whence the inhabitants originally came. Some additional evidence, small indeed in quantity, but rather more conclusive, may be gathered from the traditions of the mythology, customs, and language preserved among the Tahitians, and inhabitants of other isles of the Pacific, when they are compared with those prevailing in different parts of the world. One of their accounts of creation, that in which Taaroa is stated to have made the first man with earth or sand, and the very circumstantial tradition they have of the deluge, if they do not, as some have supposed, (when taken in connexion with many customs, and analogies in language,) warrant the inference that the Polynesians have an Hebrew origin; they show that the nation, whence they emigrated, was acquainted with some of the leading facts recorded in the Mosaic history of the primitive ages of mankind. Others appear to have a striking resemblance to several conspicuous features of the more modern Hindoo, or Braminical mythology. The account of the creation given in Sir W. Jones's translation of the Institutes of Menu, accords in no small degree with the Tahitian legends of the production of the world, including waters, &c., by the procreative power of their god. The Braminical account is, that "He (i. e. the divine Being) having willed to produce various beings from his own Divine substance, first, with a thought, created the waters, and placed in them a productive seed. That seed became an egg, bright as gold, blazing like the luminary with a thousand beams, and in that egg he was born himself, in the form of Brama, the great forefather of all spirits. The waters were called *nara*, because they were the production of *narau*, the Spirit of God; and since they were his first *ayana*, or place of motion, he is thence named *Narayana*, or moving in the waters. In the egg the great power sat inactive a whole year (of the creator;) at the close of which, by his thought alone, he caused the egg to divide itself. From its two divisions he formed the heavens (above) and the earth (beneath)" &c. It is impossible to avoid noticing the identity of this account, contained in one of the ancient writings of the Bramins, with the ruder version of the same legend in the tradition prevailing in the Sandwich Islands, that the islands were produced by a bird, a frequent emblem of deity, a medium through which the gods often communicated with men; which laid an egg upon the waters, which afterwards burst of itself, and produced the islands; especially, if with this we connect the appendages Tahitian tradition furnishes, that at first the heavens joined the earth, and were only separated by the *teva*, an insignificant plant, *draconitum polyphillum*, till their god, Ruu, lifted up the heavens from the earth. The same event is recorded in one of their songs, in the following line:

> Na Ruu i to te rai:
> Ruu did elevate or raise the heavens.

Meru, or Mount Meru, the abode of the gods, the heaven of the Hindoos, is also the paradise of some classes of the South Sea Islanders, the dwelling-place of departed kings, and others who have been deified.

The institutes of Menu[*] also forbade a Bramin to eat with his wife, or to be present when she ate; and in this injunction may have originated the former universal practice among these islands, of the man and his wife eating their meat separately.

---

[*] Menu was the Noah of the Hindoos; and Miru, pronounced Meru, was the first king of the Sandwich Islands.

Varuna and *Vahni* are among the gods of the Hindoos; the latter, among the eight guardian deities of the world, appears to have been the Neptune of the Bramins, as we learn from the following lines in Sir W. Jones's beautiful translation of the hymn to Indra; " Green Varuna, whom foaming waves obey:" and also, " Vahni flaming like the lamp of day." Both the terms in the South Sea language for spirit, or spiritual being, bear a strong resemblance to these names; the one being *varua*, in which the *n* only is omitted; and in many words, as they are used among the other islanders, some of their consonants are omitted by the Tahitians. *Vaiti* is also another apparently more ancient term for spirit used by them, which somewhat resembles the *Vahni* of the Hindoos. Bishop Heber, the most recent writer on the usages and appearance of the Hindoos, informs us, in his admirable Journal, that many things which he saw among the inhabitants of India, especially of Ceylon, reminded him of the plates in Cook's voyages.

The points of resemblance between the Polynesians and the Malayan inhabitants of Java, Sumatra, and Borneo, and the Ladrone, Caroline, and Philippine Islands, are still greater. In some parts the word for god or spirit is *dewa*. Among the Battas of Sumatra, men and women eat separately, cannibalism prevails, and they are much addicted to gaming. War is determined, and its results predicted, by observing the entrails, and the appearance, of the animals offered in sacrifice; these all prevail in the isles of the Pacific.

The principal portion of the marriage ceremony, in some of these islands, consists in the bridegroom throwing a piece of cloth over the bride, or the friends throwing it over both. This is also practised among the Tahitians. The bodies of the dead are kept by the inhabitants of the Caroline Islands, in a manner resembling the tupapaus of Tahiti; and, in the Ladrones, they feast round the tomb, and offer food, &c. to the departed. This practice also prevailed extensively in the South Sea Islands. The fables of the inhabitants of the Ladrone Islands, which led them to regard a rock as the father of their race, accords with some of the Tahitian traditions.

In the former also, according to the accounts of the Jesuit Missionaries, a licentious society existed, called by the people *Uritoy*, strikingly analogous, in all its distinguishing features, to that institution in the South Seas called the Areoi society. Their implements of war are alike. Dr. Buchanan states, that in Pulo Panang he saw a chief of the Malay tribe, who had a staff, the head of which was ornamented with a bushy lock of human hair, which the chief had cut from the head of his enemy when he lay dead at his feet. This exactly accords with the conduct of the Marquesans; many of whose clubs, and even walking-sticks, I have seen decorated with locks of human hair taken from those slain in battle.

Between the canoes and the language, of these islands and the southern groups, there is a more close resemblance. Their language has a remarkable affinity with that of the eastern Polynesia. There are also many points of resemblance in language, manners, and customs, between the South Sea Islanders and the inhabitants of Madagascar in the west; the inhabitants of the Aleutian and Kurile islands in the north, which stretch along the mouth of Behring's straits, and form the chain which connects the old and the new worlds; and also between the Polynesians and the inhabitants of Mexico, and some parts of South America. The general cast of feature, and frequent shade of complexion—the practice of tatauing, which prevails among the Aleutians, and some of the tribes of America—the process of embalming the dead bodies of their chiefs, and preserving them uninterred—the form and structure of their massy pyramidal stone temples and places of sepulture—the game of chess among the Araucanians—the word for God being *tew* or *tev*—the exposure of their children—their games—their mode of dressing the hair, ornamenting it with feathers—the numerous words in their language resembling those of Tahiti, &c.; their dress, especially the *poncho*, and even the legend of the origin of the Incas, bear no small resemblance to that of Tii, who was also descended from the sun.

The points of resemblance are not so many as in the Asiatic continent and islands; but that probably arises from the circumstance of the great facilities furnished by the Hindoo records, and the absence of all original writings relating to the history, mythology, manners, language, &c. of the aborigines of South America. Were we better acquainted with the history and institutions of the first inhabitants of the new world, more numerous points of resemblance would be discovered.

Other coincidences, of a more dubious character, occur in the eastern, western, and intermediate or oceanic tribes; among which might be mentioned the account given by Sir John Mandeville. He is stated to have commenced his travels early in the fourteenth century. In a country near the river Indus, he met with the fountain of youth, the water of which being odoriferous, tasted of all manner of spices; and of this, whoever drank for a few days upon a fasting stomach, was quickly cured of every internal disorder with which he might be afflicted. To this description he added, it was certain those who lived near, and drank frequently of it, had a wonderful appearance of youth through their whole lives, and that he himself drank of it three or four times, and imagined his health was better afterwards. The expedition which led to the discovery of Florida was undertaken not so much from a desire to explore unknown countries, as to find an equally celebrated fountain, described in a tradition prevailing among the inhabitants of Puerto Rico, as existing in Binini, one of the Lucayo Islands. It was said to possess such restorative powers as to renew the youth and vigour of every person who bathed in its waters. It was in search of this fountain, which was the chief object of their expedition, that Ponce de Leon ranged through the Lucayo Islands, and ultimately reached the shores of Florida.* Although it may throw no light on the origin of the South Sea Islanders, nor furnish any evidence of their former connexion with the inhabitants either of India or America, the coincidence is striking between these fabulous traditions, and those so circumstantially detailed by the natives of some of the islands of the Pacific, especially in the Hawaiian account of the voyage of Kamapiikai, to

---

* In reference to this enterprise, Robertson remarks: "That a tale so fabulous should gain credit among the uninstructed Indians, is not surprising; that it should make any impression on an enlightened people, appears, in the present age, altogether incredible. The fact, however, is certain.

the land where the inhabitants enjoyed perpetual health and youthful beauty, where the *wai ora* (life-giving fountain) removed every internal malady, and external deformity or decrepitude, from all those who were plunged beneath its salutary waters. A tabular view of a number of words in the Malayan, Asiatic, or the Madagasse, the American, and the Polynesian languages, would probably show, that at some remote period, either the inhabitants of these distant parts of the world maintained frequent intercourse with each other, or that colonies from some one of them, originally peopled, in part or altogether, the others. The striking analogy between the numerals and other parts of the language, and several of the customs, of the aborigines of Madagascar, and those of the Malays who inhabit the Asiatic islands, many thousands of miles distant in one direction, and of the Polynesians more remote in another, shows that they were originally one people, or that they had emigrated from the same source. Many words in the language, and several of the traditions, customs, &c. of the Americans, so strongly resemble those of Asia, as to warrant the inference that they originally came from that part of the world. Whether some of the tribes who originally passed from Asia, along the Kurile or Aleutian Islands, across Behring's straits, to America, left part of their number, who were the progenitors of the present race inhabiting those islands; and that they, at some subsequent period, either attempting to follow the tide of emigration to the east, or steering to the south, were by the north-east trade-winds driven to the Sandwich Islands, whence they proceeded to the southern groups; or whether those who had traversed the north-west coast of America, sailed either from California or Mexico across the Pacific, under the favouring influence of the regular easterly winds, peopled Easter Island, and continued under the steady easterly or trade-winds advancing westward till they met the tide of emigration flowing from the larger groups or islands, in which the Malays form the majority of the population—it is not now easy to determine. But a variety of facts connected with the past and present circumstances of the inhabitants of these countries, authorize the conclusion, that, either part of the present inhabitants of the South Sea Islands came originally from America, or that tribes of the Polynesians have, at some remote period, found their way to the continent.

If the opinion of some American antiquaries be correct, that the skeletons found in the caverns of Kentucky and Tennessee are those of a Malay tribe, and some of the bodies were wrapped in feather cloaks, similar to those used "in the Sandwich and Figi islands," and "the best defined specimens of art among the antiquities of Ohio and Kentucky are clearly of a Polynesian character;" it would appear that the North Americans, Polynesians, and Malays were formerly the same people, or had one common origin. The difficulties in the passage of the first inhabitants from the American continent, to the most eastern islands of the Pacific, are not greater than must have attended the passage of the same tribe between the Society and Sandwich Islands; and yet the identity of the inhabitants of these is unequivocal. It is difficult to say which group was first peopled. Evidence of great-antiquity, compared with the peopling of smaller islands, may be adduced in favour of each; but I am, for various reasons, disposed to think the northern islands were first settled. Their genealogies extend much farther back. I am not aware that Tahiti, or the name of any of the southern islands, is given to any part of the Sandwich Islands; yet in some of their traditions, *Hawaii* is mentioned as the ancient name of Opoa; and Oro, who is by some described as both god and man, as having two bodies or forms, or being a kind of connecting link between the gods and men, is described as the first king of Hawaii, or Opoa in Raiatea. If it be supposed that any part of the American continent was settled by a maritime people, whether Malayan or Japanese, a portion of the same tribe who settled in Nootka, or whose remains are discovered in North America, might, in vessels corresponding with those in which they passed the straits, proceed southward to the Sandwich Islands, and thence spread over eastern Polynesia.

In the practice of tatauing, and in other respects, the Battas of Sumatra, and the tribes found in some of the islands to the south-west of Sumatra, who are regarded by Marsden as the descendants of the original inhabitants of this archipelago, especially the natives of the Poggi, or Nassau Islands, resemble the natives of Polynesia. Resemblances nearly, if not equally as strong, are found on the American continent.

La Perouse describes the inhabitants of the country in the neighbourhood of the Baie des Français, as remarkably fair; and in their features, complexion, &c. bearing a strong resemblance to the inhabitants of Mangeea, or, as the natives call it, Maonia, and the lighter coloured islanders of the Pacific. About lat. 36. N. the natives of the coast visited by Vancouver, are described as a people of pleasing and courteous deportment, and gentle expression of countenance, their features resembling those of Europeans; their complexion was of a light olive, and their skins tataued like those of the South Sea Islanders.*

The origin of the inhabitants of the Pacific is involved in great mystery, and the evidences are certainly strongest in favour of their derivation from the Malayan tribes inhabiting the Asiatic Islands; but, allowing this to be their source, the means by which they have arrived at the remote and isolated stations they now occupy, are still inexplicable. If they were peopled from the Malayan Islands, they must have possessed better vessels, and more accurate knowledge of navigation, than they now exhibit, to have made their way against the constant trade-winds prevailing within the tropics, and blowing regularly, with but transient and uncertain interruptions, from east to west. The nations at present inhabiting the islands of the Pacific, have undoubtedly been more extensively spread than they now are. In the most remote and solitary islands occasionally discovered in recent years, such as Pitcairn's, on which the mutineers of the Bounty settled, and on Fanning's Island near Christmas Island, midway between the Society and Sandwich Islands, although now desolate, relics of former inhabitants have been found. Pavements of floors, foundations of houses, and stone entrances, have been discovered; and stone adzes or hatchets have been found at some distance from the surface, exactly resembling those in use among the people of the North and South Pacific at the time of their discovery. These facts prove that the nations

* Pritchard's Physical Hist. of Mankind, vol. ii. p. 394.

now inhabiting these and other islands have been, in former times, more widely extended than they are at present. The monuments or vestiges of former population found in these islands are all exceedingly rude, and therefore warrant the inference that the people to whom they belonged were rude and uncivilized, and must have emigrated from a nation but little removed from a state of barbarism—a nation less civilized than those must have been, who could have constructed vessels, and traversed this ocean six or seven thousand miles against the regularly prevailing winds, which must have been the fact, if we conclude they were peopled only by the Malays.

On the other hand, it is easy to imagine how they could have proceeded from the east. The winds would favour their passage, and the incipient stages of civilization in which they were found, would resemble the condition of the aborigines of America, far more than that of the Asiatics. There are many well-authenticated accounts of long voyages performed in native vessels by the inhabitants of both the North and South Pacific. In 1696, two canoes were driven from Ancarso to one of the Philippine islands, a distance of 800 miles. "They had run before the wind for 70 days together, sailing from east to west." Thirty-five had embarked, but five had died from the effects of privation and fatigue during the voyage, and one shortly after their arrival. In 1720, two canoes were drifted from a remote distance to one of the Marian islands. Captain Cook found in the island of Wateo Atiu inhabitants of Tahiti, who had been drifted by contrary winds in a canoe, from some islands to the eastward, unknown to the natives. Several parties have, within the last few years, reached the Tahitian shores from islands to the eastward, of which the Society Islands had never before heard. In 1820, a canoe arrived at Maurua, about thirty miles west of Borabora, which had come from Rurutu, one of the Austral Islands. This vessel had been at sea between a fortnight and three weeks, and, considering its route, must have sailed seven or eight hundred miles. A more recent instance occurred in 1824: a boat belonging to Mr. Williams of Raiatea, left that island with a westerly wind for Tahiti. The wind changed after the boat was out of sight of land. They were driven to the island of Atiu, a distance of nearly 800 miles in a south-westerly direction, where they were discovered several months afterwards. Another boat, belonging to Mr. Barff of Huahine, was passing between that island and Tahiti about the same time, and has never since been heard of; and subsequent instances of equally distant and perilous voyages in canoes or open boats, might be cited. The traditions of the inhabitants of Rarotogna, one of the Harvey Islands, preserve the most satisfactory accounts, not only of single parties, at different periods for many generations back, having arrived there from the Society Islands, but also derive the origin of the population from the island of Raiatea. Their traditions according with those of the Raiateans on the leading points, afford the strongest evidence of these islands having been peopled from those to the eastward.

If we suppose the population of the South Sea Islands to have proceeded from east to west, these events illustrate the means by which it may have been accomplished; for it is a striking fact, that every such voyage related in the accounts of voyagers, preserved in the traditions of the natives, or of recent occurrence, has invariably been from east to west, directly opposite to that in which it must have been, had the population been altogether derived from the Malayan archipelago.

From whatever source, however, they have originated, the extent of geographical surface over which they have spread themselves, the variety, purity, and copiousness of their language, the ancient character of some of the best traditions, as of the deluge, &c. justify the supposition of their remote antiquity. Yet their ignorance of letters, of the use of iron till a short time prior to their discovery, and the rude character of all their implements, and of the monuments of their ancestry, seem opposed to the idea of their having been derived, as supposed by some eminent modern geographers, from an ancient, powerful nation, which cultivated maritime habits, but which has been frittered down into detached local communities unknown to each other.

CHAP. VI.

Habits of the Islanders—Unsocial in domestic life—Humiliating circumstances of the females—Irregular mode of life—Time of taking food—Cleanliness—Frequent bathing—Manner of wearing the hair, and removing the beard—Artificial flowers—Native toilet—Occupations—Agriculture—Implements, &c.—Fishing—Enclosures—Salmon and other nets—Use of the spear—Various kinds of hooks and lines—The vaa-tira—Fishing by torch light—Canoes used among the islands—Origin of the name—Skreened canoe and Maihi.

THE habits of the South Sea Islanders were in many respects interesting and commendable; yet in these, as in their moral character and dispositions, they often presented the most strange contradictions. Patriotism and public spirit were often strongly manifested. In their universal passion for public amusements they appear a social people, yet their domestic habits were unsocial and cheerless. This is probably to be attributed to the invidious distinction established by their superstition, and enforced by tabu between the sexes.

The father and the mother, with their children, never, as one social happy band, surrounded the domestic hearth, or, assembling under the grateful shade of the verdant grove, partook together, as a family, of the bounties of Providence. The nameless but delightful emotions, experienced on such occasions, were unknown to them, as well as all that we are accustomed to distinguish by the endearing appellation of domestic happiness. The institutes of Oro and Tane inexorably required, not only that the wife should not eat those kinds of food of which the husband partook, but that she should not eat in the same place, or prepare her food at the same fire. This restriction applied not only to the wife, with regard to her husband, but to all the individuals of the female sex, from their birth to their death. In sickness or pain, or whatever other circumstances, the mother, the wife, the sister, or the daughter, might be brought into, it was never relaxed. The men, especially those who occasionally attended on the services of idol worship in the temple, were considered *ra*, or sacred; while the female sex was considered *noa*, or common: the men were allowed to eat the flesh of the pig, and of fowls, and a variety of fish, cocoa-nuts, and plantains, and whatever was presented as an offering to the gods: these the females, on pain of death, were forbidden to touch; as it was supposed, they would pollute them. The fires at which the men's food was cooked, were also sacred, and were forbidden to be used by the females. The baskets in which their provision was kept, and the house in which the men ate, were also sacred, and prohibited to the females under the same cruel penalty. Hence the inferior food, both for wives, daughters, &c. was cooked at separate fires, deposited in distinct baskets, and eaten in lonely solitude by the females, in little huts erected for the purpose.

The most offensive and frequent imprecations which the men were accustomed to use towards each other, referred also to this degraded condition of the females. *E taha miti noa oe na to medua*, Mayest thou become a bottle, to hold salt water for thy mother; or another, Mayest thou be baked as food for thy mother; were imprecations they were accustomed to denounce upon each other: or, Take out your eye-ball, and give it to your mother to eat.

Their domestic habits were not only unsocial, but irregular, alike in their periods for refreshment and sleep, and their seasons of labour or amusement.

The natives of the South Sea Islands had no regular times for eating, but arranged their meals, in a great measure, according to their avocations, or the supply of their provision. They usually eat some time in the forenoon; but their principal meal is taken towards the evening. Their food being lighter, and of a less stimulating kind, than that of Europeans, is usually consumed by them in much larger quantities at a time. They do not appear ever to have been very temperate in their diet, excepting from necessity, and many seem to have made the gratification of their appetite the means of shortening their existence.

They had no stated periods for labour or rest. The morning they regard as the best part of the day: they rise early, generally with, and frequently before, day-break, though it is often late before they retire to rest, especially when the mild light of the moon illuminates their cool and pleasant evening hours. Much of their time, however, is passed in sleep, and unless urgent engagements forbid, all classes without hesitation resign themselves to slumber during the sultry hours of the middle of the day. A strong healthy man feels it no disgrace to lie stretched on his mat from morn-

BATHING IN RIVERS.

ing till evening, scarcely rising, except to eat, unless some amusement, or other call, urgently require it.

Although irregular, the people are cleanly; but to the influence of climate, the habit of frequent bathing, so prevalent among the South Sea Islanders, is probably to be attributed. This salutary custom is followed alike by all classes, without regard to sex or age. The infant immediately after its birth is with its mother taken to the sea; and the last effort often made by the aged and decrepit, is to crawl or totter to the water, and enjoy its refreshing influence. Their loose light mode of dressing, and the abundance of cool, clear, and secluded streams meandering through almost every valley in the islands, probably favour the frequency of the practice, and its grateful effects render it one of their greatest luxuries.

Contrary to the practice of those who are accustomed to resort to the sea-side for the purpose of bathing in salt-water, the natives of these islands, without exception, prefer on every account to bathe in the mountain streams. It is a principal remedy in many of their diseases; yet doubtless it often aggravates what they design to alleviate. It is, however, a practice of great benefit: for this, as well as every other purpose, they prefer the fresh water; and even those whose avocations lead them to frequent the sea for fishing, although they may have plunged beneath the wave fifty times in the day, yet invariably repair to the nearest stream to bathe, before they return to their houses. They say the sea-water produces an irritation which is peculiarly unpleasant. Children not more than three or four years of age, are often seen playing in groups along the margin of the sea, without the least apprehension of danger, and they as frequently resort for amusement to the rivers. It is probable that the people in general bathe less now than they were accustomed to do formerly, yet there are none, perhaps, who omit bathing once, and many who visit the river twice, in the course of the day. The universality and frequency of this custom is highly conducive to health, and produces a degree of personal cleanliness seldom met with among an uncivilized race.

Although some of their practices are offensive to every feeling of delicacy and propriety, yet they are certainly a remarkably cleanly people. This regards not only their repeated ablutions, but their care to remove every thing unsightly from their persons. No hair was allowed on their limbs; formerly it was plucked out by the roots, or shaved with a shell or a shark's tooth; and those who do not wear the European dress, are still very particular in removing the hair from their legs and arms. This is usually done with a knife, the razors they have among them being reserved for removing the beard.

The adults formerly wore their hair in a variety of forms; the heads of their children they always shaved with a shark's tooth. This operation was frequently repeated during their juvenile years. The females generally cut their hair short, but the men wore theirs in every diversity of form—sometimes half the head almost shaved, the hair being cut short, and the other half covered with long hair—sometimes the crown cut, and the edges left the original length. Frequently it was plaited in a broad kind of tail behind, or wound up in a knot on the crown of the head, or in two smaller ones above each ear. Since the introduction of Christianity it has been worn remarkably neat: the men's hair is usually short, the females the same, excepting in the front, though some wear it long, curled in front, and bound up on the crown.

Nothing at first sight produces a stronger impression on the most careless observer, in the difference between the inhabitants of an island where paganism prevails, and those of one where Christianity has been introduced, than the appearance of their hair. I have often seen one who was an idolater, or who had but recently embraced Christianity, and whose hair was uncut and his beard unshaven, standing in a group of Christians, and I have been struck with the contrast.

Sometimes the men plucked the beard out by the roots, shaved it off with a shark's tooth, or removed it with the edges of two shells, acting like the blades of a pair of scissors, by cutting against each other; while others allowed the beard to grow, sometimes twisting and braiding it together. These fashions, however, have all disappeared, and the beard is generally at least shaved once a week, and by the chiefs more frequently. These cut their whiskers rather singularly sometimes, and leave a narrow strip of their beard on the upper lip, resembling mustachios: the greater part, however, remove the beard altogether, which must often be no easy task. There are no barbers by profession, yet every man is not his own barber, but contrives to shave his neighbour, and is in return shaved by him. Some of the most ludicrous scenes ever exhibited in the islands occur while they are thus employed. Only a few of the chiefs are so far advanced in civilization as to use soap; the farmers cannot understand how it can help to remove the beard, they therefore dispense with it altogether.

When the edge of the razor or knife is adjusted, the person to undergo the operation, in order to be quite stationary, lies flat on his back on the ground, sometimes in his house, at other times under the shade of a tree, and his friend kneels down over him, and commences his labour. When he has finished, he lays himself down, and the man who is shaved gets up, and performs the same office for his friend. Sometimes the razor becomes rather dull, and something more than a little additional strength is necessary. A whetstone is then applied to the edge; but if this be not at hand, the man gets up half shaved, and both go together to the nearest grindstone; and I have beheld that the transition from the grindstone to the chin is sometimes direct, without any intermediate application to the edge of the razor. The hone and the strap, however, have been introduced, and ere long will probably supersede the use of the grindstone, and also of the whetstone.

The islanders appear to have paid at all times great attention, not only to cleanliness, but to personal ornaments. On public occasions, their appearance was in a high degree imposing. At their dances, and other places of amusement or festivity, they wore a profusion of ornament, and on ordinary occasions, with the exception of the aged and decrepit, devoted much time to the improvement of their appearance. The hair of the females, which was neatly dressed, and sometimes appeared in short loose curls, was an object of great attention; the eye-brows were also reduced, or shaped according to their ideas of beauty. The hair was ornamented with elegant native flowers, sometimes exhibited in great profusion and variety, at others with only one or two single jessamine blossoms, or a small wreath interwoven with their black and shining ringlets. They displayed great taste in the use of flowers, and the adorning of their hair. Frequently I have seen them with beautiful wreaths of yellow flowers, worn like fragrant necklaces on their bosoms, and garlands of the same around their brows, or small bunches of the brilliant scarlet *hibiscus rosæ chinensis* fastened in their hair. Though totally unacquainted with what we are accustomed to call artificial flowers, yet the brilliant and varied odoriferous plants, that grew spontaneously among their mountains or their valleys, did not suffice to gratify their wishes; they were therefore accustomed to manufacture a kind of artificial flowers, by extracting the petals and leaflets of the most fragrant plants and flowers, and fastening them with fine native thread, to the wiry stalk of the cocoa-nut leaf, which they saturated with monoi, or scented oil, and wore in each ear, or fixed in the native bonnet, made with the rich yellow cocoa-nut leaf. The men, though unaccustomed to adorn their hair with flowers, were careful of preserving and dressing it. They generally wore it long, and often fastened in a graceful braid on the crown, or on each side of the head, and spent not a small portion of their time in washing and perfuming it with scented oil, combing and adjusting it. When it was short, they sometimes dressed it with the gum of the bread-fruit tree, which gave it a shining appearance, and fixed it as straight as if it had been stiffened with rosin. The open air was the general dressing-place of both sexes; an a group of females might often be seen sitting under the shade of a clump of wide-spreading trees, or in the cool mountain-stream, employing themselves for hours together in arranging the curls of the hair, weaving the wreaths of flowers, and filling the air with their perfumes. Their comb was a rude invention of their own, formed by fixing together thin strips of the bamboo-cane. So important was the arrangement and adorning of the hair formerly considered, that there was a god of hair-dressers or combers, called To-toro-potaa, whose aid was invoked at the toilet. Their mirror was one supplied by nature, and consisted in the clear water of the stream, contained in a cocoa-nut shell.

The attention of the people to personal decoration rendered looking-glasses valuable articles of trade in their early intercourse with foreigners; and although the habit has very much declined, and their taste with regard to ornament, &c. is materially changed, looking-glasses are still, with many, desirable articles. Those, however, who have furnished them, have often made a mistake in sending, on account of their cheapness, an inferior kind, which, in consequence of a defect in the glass, exhibits the face in a distorted and ludicrous shape. Nothing will more offend a Tahitian than to ask him to look in one of these glasses. They call them *hio maamaa*, foolish glasses, and, instead of purchasing them, would sometimes hardly be induced to accept them as presents.

Since the introduction of Christianity, the use of flowers in the hair, and fragrant oil, has been in a great degree discontinued—partly from the connexion of those ornaments with the evil practices to which they were formerly addicted, and partly from the introduction of European caps and bonnets, the latter being now universally worn.

Like the semi-civilized inhabitants of most tropical countries, they are strongly inclined to indolence, which is probably increased, not only by the warmth of the climate, but by the abundance in which the fruits of the earth are spontaneously produced, and the facility with which the means of subsistence may be procured. For an uncivilized people, however, though there were no established trades, or regular divisions of labour, they may be considered as industrious, and their occupations, though few, considerably varied. The principal were agriculture, fishing, building, cloth-making, and cooking. Agriculture among them was but in its infancy; their implements were few and simple. The chief, and almost only implement used, was the *ó*, a stick sharpened at the point, and used in loosening and turning up the earth. Formerly they hardened the end with which they penetrated the soil, by charring it in the fire. An implement of this kind is still their greatest favourite. No ploughs or harrows have yet been introduced, for the want of oxen or horses. They are not very fond of English spades, hoes, &c. The spade, they say, takes up too much earth at once, and, besides the stooping required, is a heavier load than they like to lift repeatedly. The tool most frequently employed, is a long stick with a narrow sharp piece of iron, like a broad chisel, at the end; and, as much of the ground is stony, in such places it is found very convenient. The rudeness of the tool increases the labour of the person using it, while his singular position must render it exceedingly fatiguing. No use is made of the foot in thrusting the spade into the soil, but the person digging assumes a crouching attitude, pierces the ground, and breaks up the earth by the strength of the hands and arms. The making and repairing fences also occupies much of the time of those engaged in the cultivation of the soil. According to one of their legends, Matabu-fenua was the god of agriculturists.

The peculiar situation of the islanders, and their amphibious habits, lead them to seek a great part of their subsistence from the ocean that surrounds them. Many are fishermen by profession.

Their methods of fishing are numerous, some of them rude, others remarkably ingenious. In the shallow parts of their lakes they erect enclosures of stones for taking a number of small and middling-sized fish. This enclosure they call a *aua ia*, a fish fence.

A circular space, nine or twelve feet in diameter, is enclosed with a stone wall, built up from the bottom of the lake, to the edge of the water. An opening, four or six inches deep, and a foot or two wide, is left in the upper part of the wall. From each side of this opening, a wall of stone is raised to the edge of the water, extending fifty or a hundred yards, and diverging from the aperture, so that the wall leaves a space of water within, of the shape of a wedge, the point of which terminates in the circular enclosure. These walls diverge in a direction from the sea, so that the fish which enter the lake are intercepted only in their return. They are so numerous through the whole extent of the shallow parts of the lake, that it seems scarcely possible for a fish to escape. These enclosures are valuable; fish are usually found in them every morning, which furnish a means of subsistence to the proprietors, who have no other trouble than simply to take them out with a hand-net. They

METHOD OF FISHING.

are also excellent preserves, in which fish may be kept securely till wanted for use. Each enclosure has its distinct owner, whose right to the fish enclosed is always respected. Most of the fish from the lake are taken this way. The net and the spear are occasionally employed, but here the line is rarely used.

They have a singular mode of taking a remarkably timorous fish, which is called *au* or needle, on account of its long sharp head. The fishermen build a number of rafts, which they call *motoi;* each raft is about fifteen or twenty feet long, and six or eight wide, and it is made with the light branches of the hibiscus or purau. At one edge a kind of fence or skreen is raised four or five feet, by fixing the poles horizontally, one above the other, and fastening them to upright sticks, placed at short distances along the raft. Twenty or thirty of these rafts are often employed at the same time. The men on the raft go out at a distance from each other, enclosing a large space of water, having the raised part or frame on the outside. They gradually approach each other till the rafts join, and form a connected circle in some shallow part of the lake. One or two persons then go in a small canoe towards the centre of the enclosed space, with long white sticks, which they strike in the water with a great noise, and by this means drive the fish towards the rafts. On approaching these, the fish dart out of the water, and in attempting to spring over the raft, strike against the raised fence on the outer side, and fall on the surface of the horizontal part, when they are gathered into baskets, or canoes, on the outside. In this manner, great numbers of these and other kinds of fish, that are accustomed to spring out of the water when alarmed or pursued, are taken with facility.

Among the reefs, and near the shore, many fish are seized by preparing an intoxicating mixture from the nuts of the hutu, *betonica splendida*, or the hora, another native plant. When the water is impregnated with these preparations, the fish come from their retreats in great numbers, float on the surface, and are easily caught.

The favour of the gods was formerly considered essential to success in fishing. The gods of fishermen were numerous, though Tamai or Tahaura and Teraimateti were the principal. Matatine, or Autà, was the deity of those who manufactured nets.

Fishing nets were various; all were remarkably well made, and carefully preserved. Their light casting-nets were used with great dexterity, generally as they walked along the beach. When a shoal of small fish appeared, they would throw the net with the right-hand, and enclose sometimes the greater part of them. The nets used in taking operu, or herrings, were exceedingly large, and generally made of the twisted bark of the hibiscus. Several nets were used at the same time, the meshes of the outside net being very large, and those within smaller, for the purpose of detaining the fish. This kind of fish visit the coasts in shoals at one or two seasons of the year only, and as they do not design their nets to last longer than one season, they are not very carefully prepared.

Upea is the common name for net. The *upea ava*, or salmon net, is the most important, and is seldom possessed by any but the principal chiefs; it is sometimes forty fathoms long, and twelve or more feet deep. One of this kind was made by Hautia, the governor of Huahine, soon after our arrival. Although the former pagan ceremonies, and offerings at the marae, were discontinued, some of the ancient usages were observed, one of which appeared rather singular. As is customary on all occasions of public work, the proprietor of the net required the other chiefs to assist in its preparation. Before he began, two large pigs were killed and baked. When taken from the oven, they were cut up, and the governor's messenger sent with a piece to every chief; on delivery, the quantity was stated which each was desired to prepare towards the projected net. If the piece of pig was received, it was considered as an agreement to furnish it; but to return it, was, in effect, to refuse compliance with the requisition. At this time, however, no one returned the *tarahu*, or price, but all agreed to furnish one or two fathoms of the net. When any other chief wanted a net, he took the same course.

The cord was about a quarter of an inch in diameter, and made with the tough white bark of the mate, *ficus prolixa*, which, next to the romaha, or flax, is considered more durable than any other indigenous vegetable substance. The cord was twisted with the hand across the knee, in two or three strands or threads, and was even and firm. The meshes were about four inches square.

The servants of the chief furnished their quantity of netting, and the needle with which they wrought was not unlike that used by European workmen. As the other parties brought in their portions, the chief and his men joined them together. On entering the house of Hautia, I have found him in a profuse perspiration, toiling in the midst of his men at the manufacture of the net.

The floats were made with short pieces of dry,

light, buoyant hibiscus; and the bottom was hung with stones, generally circular and smooth, about three inches in diameter. These were not perforated, but enveloped in pieces of the matted fibre of the cocoa-nut husk, tied together at the ends, and attached to the lower border of the net.

The first wetting of a new net was formerly attended with a number of prayers, offerings, &c. at the temple, and on the beach. I recollect, at Afareaitu, when they were going to take out, for the first time, a large salmon-net, and had put it upon the canoe, the whole party, including the fishermen and chiefs of the district, kneeled down upon a pebbly beach, and offered a prayer to the true God, that they might be successful. This was about day-break; and as the sun rose above the waves, I saw them rowing cheerfully out to sea. Though these nets were called *upea ava,* salmon-nets, a variety of large fish was taken in them; a shark was not unfrequently enclosed, which sometimes made great havock among the fishermen, before they could transfix him with their spears.

This kind of fishing was followed not only as a means of procuring food, but as an amusement. The chiefs were exceedingly fond of it, and often strove to excel. Hautia was celebrated for his skill and strength in taking some kinds of fish. Their country was little adapted for hunting, and the only quadrupeds they ever pursued were the wild hogs in the mountains; but the smoothness and transparency of the sea within the reefs, was favourable to aquatic sports; and a chief and his men, furnished with their spears, &c. often set out on their fishing excursions with an exhilaration of spirits equal to that with which a European nobleman pursues the adventures of the chase

The more daring of the young chiefs were generally among the foremost in pursuing the shark, or other dauntless fish; while others, more advanced in years, remained in their canoes at a distance, gratified to behold the sport, and share in some degree the excitement it produced. When the *tautai* or fishing party returned, the nets were hung up on the branches of trees near the shore, as they appear in the view of Fa-re harbour. Besides the herring, hand, and salmon nets, they had a number of others, adapted to particular places, or kinds of fish.

Next to the net, the spear was most frequently used. It was variously formed, according to the purpose for which it was designed. Since their intercourse with foreigners, the best spears have been made with iron, barbed only on one side. Two or three small spear-heads were occasionally fastened to a single handle. Another kind of spear, in frequent use, was entirely of wood. Nine, ten, or twelve pointed pieces of hard wood, six or eight inches long, were fastened to a handle, from six to eight feet in length. When using this, they generally waded into the sea as high as the waist, and, standing near an opening between the rocks of coral, or near the shore, and watching the passage of the fish, darted the spear, sometimes with one hand, but more frequently with both, and often struck them with great precision.

Their aim with this spear, however, is much less certain than with one headed with iron; which some throw with great dexterity, though others are exceedingly awkward. When fishing on the reefs, they often wear a kind of sandal, made of closely netted cords of the bark of the native *auti*, or cloth-plant. This was designed to preserve their feet from the edges of the shells, the spikes of the echinus, &c. They use the angle or the spear in fishing at the edge of the reef, when the surf is low. I have often, when passing across the bay, stopped to gaze on a group of fishermen standing on a coral reef, or rock, amidst the roar of the billows and the dashing surf and foam, that broke in magnificent splendour around them. With unwavering glance, they have stood, with a little basket in one hand, and a pointed spear in the other, striking with unerring aim such fish as the violence of the wave might force within their reach.

They have a curious contrivance for taking several kinds of ray and cuttle-fish, which resort to the holes of the coral rocks, and protrude their arms or feet for the bait, but remain themselves firm within the retreat. The instrument employed consists of a straight piece of hard wood, a foot long, round and polished, and not half an inch in diameter. Near one end of this, a number of the most beautiful pieces of the cowrie or tiger-shell are fastened one over another, like the scales of a fish or the plates of a piece of armour, until it is about the size of a turkey's egg, and resembles the cowrie. It is suspended in an horizontal position, by a strong line, and lowered by the fisherman from a small canoe, until it nearly reaches the bottom. The fisherman then gently jerks the line, causing the shell to move as if inhabited by a fish. This jerking motion is called *tootoofe* the name of the singular contrivance.

The cuttle-fish, attracted, it is supposed, by the appearance of the cowrie, (for no bait is used,) darts out one of its arms or rays, which it winds round the shell, and fastens among the openings between the plates. The fisherman continues jerking the line, and the fish puts forth another and another arm or ray, till it has quite fastened itself to the shells, when it is drawn up into the canoe, and secured.

They use the hook and line both in the smooth water within the reef, and in the open sea; and in different modes display great skill. In this department they seldom have any bait, excepting a small kind of *oobu*, a black fresh-water fish, which they employ when catching albicores and bonitos. Their hooks usually answer the double purpose of hook and bait. Their lines are made with the tough elastic *romaha*, or flax, twisted by the hand.

In no part of the world, perhaps, are the inhabitants better fishermen; and, considering their former entire destitution of iron, their variety of fishing apparatus is astonishing. Their hooks were of every form and size, and made of wood, shell, or bone, frequently human bone. This was considered the most offensive use to which the bones of an enemy could be applied: and one of the most sanguinary modern wars in Tahiti originated in a declaration made by a fisherman of one party, that he had a hook made with the bone of a rival chief who had been slain in a former war.

The hooks made with wood were curious; some were exceedingly small, not more than two or three inches in length, but remarkably strong; others were large. The wooden hooks were never barbed, but simply pointed, usually curved inwards at the point, but sometimes standing out very wide, occasionally armed at the point with a piece of bone. The best were hooks ingeniously made with the small roots of the aito tree, casuarina, or iron wood. In selecting a root for this purpose, they chose one partially exposed, and growing by the side of a bank, preferring such as were free from knots and other excrescences. The root was twisted into the shape they wished the future hook to assume, and allowed to grow till it had reached a size large enough to allow of the outside or soft parts being removed, and a sufficiency remaining to make the hook. Some hooks thus prepared are not much thicker than a quill, and perhaps three or four inches in length. Those used in taking sharks are formidable looking weapons; I have seen some a foot or fifteen inches long, exclusive of the curvatures, and not less than an inch in diameter. They are such frightful things that no fish, less voracious than a shark, would approach them. In some, the marks of the shark's teeth are numerous and deep, and indicate the effect with which they have been used. I do not think the Tahitians take as many sharks as the Sandwich Islanders do: they, however, seldom spare them when they come in their way; and though sharks are not eaten now, the natives formerly feasted on them with great zest.

The shell, or shell and bone hooks, were curious and useful, and always answered the purpose of hook and bait; the small ones are made almost circular, and bent so as to resemble a worm, but the most common kind is the aviti, used in catching dolphins, albicores, and bonitos; the shank of the hook is made with a piece of the mother-of-pearl shell, five or six inches long, and three-quarters of an inch wide, carefully cut, and finely polished, so as to resemble the body of a fish. On the concave side, a barb is fastened by a firm bandage of finely twisted *romaha*, or flax; the barb is usually an inch and a half in length, and is of shell or bone. To the lower part of this, the end of the line is securely fastened, and being braided along the inner or concave side of the shell, is again attached to the upper end. Great care is taken in the manufacture of these pearl-shell hooks, and they are considered much better than any made in Europe.

The line is fastened to the hook in a curious manner, and, when taken to sea, is attached to a strong bamboo-cane, about twelve or fifteen feet long; light single canoes are preferred for catching dolphins, bonitos, or albicores. Two or three persons usually proceed to sea, and when they perceive a shoal of these fish, those who angle sit in the stern of the canoe, and hold the rod at such an elevation, as to allow the hook to touch the edge of the water, but not to sink. When the fish approach it, the rowers ply their paddles briskly, and the light bark moves rapidly along, while the fisherman keeps the hook near the surface of the water. The deception of the hook is increased by a number of hairs or bristles being attached to the end of the shell, so as to resemble the tail of a flying-fish. The bonito, &c. darting after, and grasping its prey, is itself secured. During the season, two men will sometimes take twenty or thirty large fish in this way in the course of the forenoon.

The most ingenious method, however, of taking these large fish is by means of what is termed a *tira*, or mast. A pair of ordinary sized canoes is usually selected for this purpose, and the lighter and swifter, the more suitable are they esteemed. Between the fore-part of the canoes, a broad deep oblong kind of basket is constructed, with the stalks of a strong kind of fern, interwoven with the tough fibres of the *ieie*, this is to contain the fish which may be taken, and thus secure them, without impeding the operations of the fishermen or rowers. To the fore-part of the canoes a long curved pole is fastened, branching in opposite directions at the outer end; the foot of this rests in a kind of socket, fixed between the two canoes.

Fishing Canoe.

From each of the projecting branches, lines with pearl-shell hooks are suspended, so adjusted as to be kept near the surface of the water. To that part of the pole which is divided into two branches, strong ropes are attached; these extend to the stern of the canoe, where they are held by persons watching the seizure of the hook. The tira, or mast, projects a considerable distance beyond the stem of the canoe, and bunches of feathers are fastened to its extremities. This is done to resemble the aquatic birds which follow the course of the small fish, and often pounce down and divide the prey which the large ones pursue. As it is supposed that the bonitos follow the course of the birds, as much as that of the fishes, when the fishermen perceive the birds, they proceed to the place, and usually find the fish. The undulation of the waves occasions the canoe to rise and sink as they proceed, and this produces a corresponding motion in the hook suspended from the mast; and so complete is the deception, that if the fish once perceives the pearl-shell hook, it seldom fails to dart after it; and if it misses the first time, is almost sure to be caught the second. As soon as the fish is fast, the men in the canoe, by drawing the cord, hoist up the tira, and drag in the fish, suspended as it were from a kind of crane. When the fish is removed, the crane is lowered; and as it projects over the stem of the canoe, the rowers hasten after the shoal with all possible celerity.

During the rainy season, or on the occurrence of a flood, when the rivers are swollen and rapid, discolouring the water of the sea to a great extent, a number of large fish approach the mouths of the rivers, for the purpose of preying on the eels and other fresh-water fish carried down in the torrent; at such seasons the fishermen are on the alert, and usually return from the sea richly laden

These, and a variety of other methods of fishing, are pursued by day-light; but many fish are taken by night: sometimes the fishery is carried on by moon light, occasionally in the dark, but fishing by torch-light is the most picturesque. The torches are bunches of dried reeds firmly tied together. Sometimes they pursue their nocturnal sport on the reef, and hunt the *totara*, or hedge-hog fish. Large parties often go out to the reef; and it is a beautiful sight to behold a long line of rocks illuminated by the flaring torches. These the fishermen hold in one hand, and stand with the poised spear in the other, ready to strike as soon as the fish appears.

In the rivers they also fish by torch-light, especially for eels; and though the circumstances are varied, the impression is not inferior. Few scenes present a more striking and singular effect than a band of natives walking along the shallow parts of the rocky sides of a river, elevating a torch with one hand, and a spear in the other; while the glare of their torches is thrown upon the overhanging boughs, and reflected from the agitated surface of the stream. Their own bronze-coloured and lightly clothed forms, partially illuminated, standing like figures in relief; while the whole scene appears in bright contrast with the dark and almost midnight gloom that envelops every other object.

Since their intercourse with Europeans, English-made steel hooks have been introduced. They like their sharpness at the point, but usually complain of them as too open or wide. For some kinds of fish they are preferred, but for most they find the mother-of-pearl hooks answer best. Every fisherman, I believe, would rather have a wrought-iron nail three or four inches long, or a piece of iron-wire of the size, and make a hook according to his own mind, than have the best European-made hook that could be given to him. Most of the nails which they formerly procured from the shipping were used for this purpose, and highly prized.

Their ideas of the nature of these valuable articles were very singular. Perceiving, in their shape and colour, a resemblance to the young shoots or scions that grow from the roots of the bread-fruit trees, they imagined that they were a hard kind of plant, and procured in the same way.

Anxious to secure a more abundant supply, they divided the first parcel of nails ever received, carried part to the temple, and deposited them on the altar; the rest they actually planted in their gardens, and awaited their growth with the highest anticipation. In the manufacture of hooks from nails, they manifested great patience and persevering labour: they had no files, but sharpened the points, and rounded the angles, by rubbing the nail on a stone; they also used a stone in bending it to the required shape. The use of files, however, has greatly facilitated their manufacture of fish-hooks.

In connexion with this subject, a striking instance of native simplicity and honesty occurred about the time of our arrival. Two Christian chiefs, Tati and Ahuriro, were walking together by the water-side, when they came to a place where a fisherman had been employed in making or sharpening hooks, and had left a large file, (a valuable article in Tahiti,) lying on the ground. The chiefs picked it up; and, as they were proceeding, one said to the other, "This is not ours. Is not our taking it a species of theft?" "Perhaps it is," replied the other. "Yet, as the true owner is not here, I do not know who has a greater right to it than ourselves." "It is not ours," said the former, "and we had better give it away." After further conversation, they agreed to give it to the first person they met, which they did; telling him they had found it, and requested that if he heard who had lost such a one, he would restore it.

The isolated situation of the islanders, and their dependence upon the sea for much of their subsistence, necessarily impart a maritime character to their habits, and render the building, fitting, and managing of the vessels one of the most general and important of their avocations. It also procures no small respect and endowment for the *Tahua tarai vaa,* builder of canoes. *Vaa waa,* or *vaka,* is the name of a canoe, in most of the islands of the Pacific; though by foreigners they are uniformly called canoes, a name first given to this sort of boat by the natives of the Caribbean Islands,* and adopted by Europeans ever since, to designate the rude boats used by the uncivilized natives in every part of the world.

The canoes of the Society Islanders are various, both in size and shape, and are double or single. Those belonging to the principal chiefs, and the public district canoes, were fifty, sixty, or nearly seventy feet long, and each about two feet wide, and three or four feet deep; the sterns remarkably high, sometimes fifteen or eighteen feet above the water, and frequently ornamented with rudely carved hollow cylinders, square pieces, or grotesque figures, called *tiis*. The rank or dignity of a chief was supposed, in some degree, to be indicated by the size of his canoe, the carving and ornaments with which it was embellished, and the number of its rowers.

Next in size to these was the pahi, or war canoe. I never saw but one of these: the stern was low, and covered, so as to afford a shelter from the stones and darts of the assailants; the bottom was round, the upper part of the sides narrower,

---

* After his first interview with the natives of the newly discovered islands, in the Caribbean sea, we are informed by Robertson, that Columbus returned to his ship, accompanied by many of the islanders in their boats, which they called *canoes;* and though rudely formed out of the trunk of a single tree, they rowed them with surprising dexterity.

and perpendicular; a rude imitation of the human head, or some other grotesque figure, was carved on the stern of each canoe. The stem, often elevated and curved like the neck of a swan, terminated in the carved figure of a bird's head, and the whole was more solid and compact than the other vessels. In some of their canoes, and in the pahi among the rest, a rude sort of grating, made with the light but tough wood of the bread-fruit tree, covered the hull of the vessels, the intervening space between them, and projected a foot or eigh-

teen inches over the outer edges. On this the rowers usually sat; and here the mariners, who attended to the sails, took their stations, and found it much more convenient and secure than standing on the narrow edges of the canoes, or the curved and circular beams that held them together. There was also a kind of platform in the front, or generally near the centre, on which the fighting men were stationed: these canoes were sometimes sixty feet long, between three and four feet deep, and, with their platforms in front or in the centre, were capable of holding fifty fighting men.* The vaatii, or sacred canoe, was always strong and large, more highly ornamented with carving and feathers than any of the others. Small houses were erected in each, and the image of the god, sometimes in the shape of a large bird, at other times resembling a hollow cylinder, ornamented with various coloured feathers, was kept in these houses. Here their prayers were preferred, and their sacrifices offered.

Their war canoes were strong, well-built, and highly ornamented. They formerly possessed large and magnificent fleets of these, and other large canoes; and, at their general public meetings, or festivals, no small portion of the entertainment was derived from the regattas, or naval reviews, in which the whole fleet, ornamented with carved images, and decorated with flags and streamers, of various native-coloured cloth, went through their different tactics with great precision. On these occasions the crews by which they were navigated, anxious to gain the plaudits of the king and chiefs, emulated each other in the exhibition of their seamanship. The vaati, or sacred canoes, formed part of every fleet, and were generally the most imposing in appearance, and attractive in their decorations.

The peculiar and almost classical shape of the large Tahitian canoes, the elevated prow and stern, the rude figures, carving, and other ornaments, the loose-flowing drapery of the natives on board, and the maritime aspect of their general places of abode, are all adapted to produce a singular effect

* In Cook's voyages a description is given of some, one hundred and eight feet long.

on the mind of the beholder. I have often thought, when I have seen a fleet of thirty or forty approaching the shore, that they exhibited no faint representation of the ships in which the Argonauts sailed, or the vessels that conveyed the heroes of Homer to the Trojan shores.

Every large canoe had a distinct name, always arbitrary, but frequently descriptive of some real or imaginary excellence in the canoe, or in memory of some event connected with it. Neither the names of any of their gods, or chiefs, were ever given to their vessels; such an act, instead of being considered an honour, would have been deemed the greatest insult that could have been offered. The names of canoes, in some instances, appear to have been perpetuated, as the king's state canoe was always called Anuanua, or the rainbow. The most general and useful kind of canoe is the tipairua, or common double canoe, usually from twenty to thirty feet long, strong and capacious, with a projection from the stem, and a low shield-shaped stern. These are very valuable, and usually form the mode of conveyance for every chief of respectability or influence, in the island. They are also used to transport provisions, or other goods, from one place to another.

One of these, in which we voyaged to Afareaitu soon after our arrival, was between thirty and forty feet in length, strong, and, as a piece of native workmanship, well built. The keel was formed with a number of pieces of tough tamanu wood, *inophyllum callophyllum*, twelve or sixteen inches broad, and two inches thick, hollowed on the inside, and rounded without, so as to form a convex angle along the bottom of the canoe; these were fastened together by lacings of tough elastic cord, made with the fibres of the cocoa-nut husk. On the front end of the keel, a solid piece, cut out of the trunk of a tree, so contrived as to constitute the forepart of the canoe; was fixed with the same lashing; and on the upper part of it, a thick board or plank projected horizontally, in a line parallel with the surface of the water. This front piece, usually five or six feet long, and twelve or eighteen inches wide, was called the *ihu vaa*, nose of the canoe, and without any joining, comprised the stem, bows, and bowsprit of the vessel.

The sides of the canoe were composed of two lines of short plank, an inch and a half or two inches thick. The lowest line was convex on the outside, and nine or twelve inches broad; the upper one straight. The stern was considerably elevated, the keel was inclined upwards, and the lower part of the stern was pointed, while the upper part was flat, and nine or ten feet above the level of the sides. The whole was fastened together with cinet, not continued along the seams, but by two, or, at most, three holes made in each board, within an inch of each other, and corresponding holes made in the opposite piece, and the lacing passed through from one to the other. A space of nine inches or a foot was left, and then a similar set of holes made. The joints or seams were not grooved together, but the edge of one simply laid on that of the other, and fitted with remarkable exactness by the adze of the workman, guided only by his eye: they never used line or rule. The edges of their planks were usually covered with a kind of pitch or gum from the bread-fruit tree, and a thin layer of cocoa-nut husk spread between them. The husk of the cocoa-nut swelling when in contact with water, fills any apertures that may exist, and, considering the manner in which they are put together, the canoes are often remarkably dry. The two canoes were fastened together by strong curved pieces of wood, placed horizontally across the upper edges of the canoes, to which they were fixed by strong lashings of thick coiar cordage.

Skreened Canoe.

The space between the two bowsprits, or broad planks projecting from the front of our canoe, was covered with boards, and furnished a platform of considerable extent; over this a kind of temporary awning of platted cocoa-nut leaves was spread, and under it the passengers sat during the voyage. The upper part of each of the canoes was not above twelve or fifteen inches wide; little projections were formed on the inner part of the sides, on which small moveable thwarts or seats were fixed, whereon the men sat who wrought with the paddle, while the luggage was placed in the bottom, piled up against the stern, or laid on the elevated stage between the two canoes. The heat of the sun was extreme, and the awning afforded a grateful shade.

The rowers appeared to labour hard. Their paddles, being made of the tough wood of the hibiscus, were not heavy; yet, having no pins in the sides of the canoe, against which the handles of the paddles could bear, but leaning the whole body over the canoe, first on one side, and then on the other, and working the paddle with one hand near the blade, and the other at the upper end of the handle, and shovelling as it were the water, appeared a great waste of strength. They often, however, paddle for a time with remarkable swiftness, keeping time with the greatest regularity. The steersman stands or sits in the stern, with a large paddle; the rowers sit in each canoe two or three feet apart; the leader sits next; the steersman gives the signal to start, by striking his paddle violently against the side of the canoe; every paddle is then put in and taken out of the water with every stroke at the same moment; and after they have thus continued on one side for five or six minutes, the leader strikes his paddle, and the rowers instantly and simultaneously turn to the other side, and thus alternately working on each side of the canoe, they advance at a considerable rate. There is generally a good deal of striking the paddle when a chief leaves or approaches the shore, and the effect resembles that of the smacking of the whip, or sounding of the horn, at the starting or arrival of a coach.

They have also a remarkably neat double canoe, called Maihi, or twins, each of which is made out of a single tree, and are both exactly alike. The stem and stern are usually sharp; although, occasionally, there is a small board projecting from each stem. These are light, safe, and swift, easily managed, and seldom used but by the chiefs. The late king Pomare was fond of this kind of conveyance.

The single canoes are built in the same manner, and with the same materials, as the double ones. Their usual name is *tipaihoe*, and they are more various in their kind than the others. The small *buhoe*, the literal name of which is single shell, is generally a trunk of a tree, seldom more than twenty feet in length, rounded on the outside, and hollow within; sometimes sharp at both ends, though generally only at the stem. It is used by fishermen among the reefs, and also along the shore, and in shallow water, seldom carrying more than two persons. The single maihi is only a neater kind of buhoe.

CHAP. VII.

Description of the vaa motu, or island-canoe—Methods of navigating native vessels—Danger from sharks—Affecting wreck—Accident in a single canoe—Tahitian architecture—Materials employed in building—Description of the various kinds of native houses—Dress of the Tahitians—Manufacture of native cloth—Variety of kinds—Durability and appearance—Methods of dyeing—Matting of Society and Paumotu islanders—Native pillow, seat, dishes, and other articles of household furniture.

The *vaa motu*, island-canoe, is generally a large, strong, single vessel, built for sailing, and principally used in distant voyages. In addition to the ordinary edge, or gunwale, of the canoe, planks, twelve or fifteen inches wide, are fastened along their sides, after the manner of wash-boards in a European boat. The same are also added to double canoes, when employed on long voyages. A single vaa is never used without an outrigger, varying in size with the vessel; it is usually formed with a light spar of the hibiscus, or of the erythrina, which was highly prized as an *ama*, or outrigger, on account of its being both light and strong. This is always placed on the left side, and fastened to the canoe by two horizontal poles, from five to eight feet long; the front one is straight and firm, the other curved and elastic; it is so fixed, that the canoe, when empty, does not float upright, being rather inclined to the left; but, when sunk into the water, on being laden, it is generally erect, while the outrigger, which is firmly and ingeniously fastened to the sides by repeated bands of cinet, floats on the surface. In addition to this, the island canoes have a strong plank, twelve or fourteen feet long, fastened horizontally across the centre, in an inclined position, one end attached to the outrigger, and the other extending five or six feet over the opposite side, and perhaps elevated four or five feet above the sea. A small railing of rods is fastened along the sides of this plank, and it is designed to assist the navigators in balancing the keel, as a native takes his station on the one side or the other, to counteract the inclination which the wind or sea might give to the vessel. Sometimes they approach the shore with a native standing or sitting on the extremity of the plank, and presenting a singular appearance, which it is impossible to behold without expecting every undulation of the sea will detach him from his apparently insecure situation, and precipitate him into the water.

Single, or Island Canoe.

This kind of canoe (*see next page,*) is principally employed in the voyages which the natives make to *Tetuaroa*, a cluster of islands, five in number, to the north of Tahiti.

In navigating their double canoes, the natives frequently use two sails, but in their single vessels only one. The masts are moveable, and are only raised when the sails are used. They are slightly fixed upon a step placed across the canoe, and fastened by strong ropes or braces extending to both sides, and to the stem and stern. The sails were made with the leaves of the pandanus split into thin strips, neatly woven into a kind of matting. The shape of the sails of the island-canoes is singular, the side attached to the mast is straight, the outer part resembling the section of an oval, cut in the longest direction. The other sails are commonly used in the same manner as sprit or lugger sails are used in European boats. The ropes from the corners of the sails are not usually fastened, but held in the hands of the natives. The rigging is neither varied nor complex; the cordage is made with the twisted bark of the hibiscus, or the fibres of the cocoa-nut husk—of which a very good *coiar* rope is manufactured.

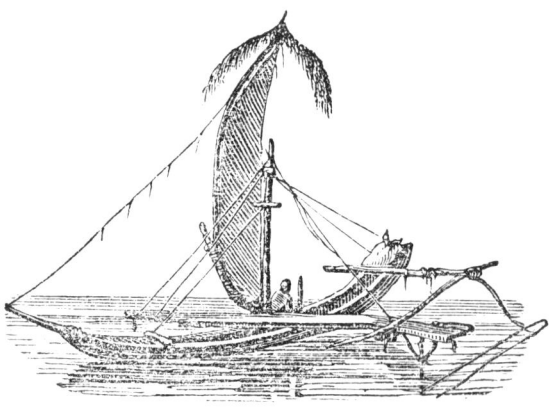

The paddles of the Tahitians are plain, having a smooth round handle, and an oblong-shaped blade. Their canoes having no rudder, are steered by a man in the stern, with a paddle generally longer than the rest. In long voyages, they have two or three steering paddles, including a very large one, which they employ in stormy weather, to prevent the vessel from drifting to leeward. Temariotuu, the god of mariners and pilots, was stated to have made his rudder, or steering-paddle, from the sacred aito of Ruaroroirai. The *tataa*, or scoop, with which they bale out the leakage, is generally a neat and convenient article, cut out of a solid piece of wood. Their canoes were formerly ornamented with streamers of various coloured cloths; and tufts of fringe and tassels of feathers were attached to the masts and sails, though they are now seldom used. A small kind of house or awning was erected in the centre, or attached to the stern, to skreen the passengers from the sun by day and the damp by night. The latter is still used, though the former is but seldom seen. They do not appear ever to have ornamented the body or hull of their vessels with carving or painting; but, notwithstanding this seeming deficiency, they had by no means an unfinished appearance.

In building their vessels, all the parts were first accurately fitted to each other, the whole was taken to pieces, and the outside of each plank smoothed by rubbing it with a piece of coral and sand moistened with water; it was then dried, and polished with fine dry coral. The wood was generally of a rich yellow colour, the *cinet* nearly the same, and a new well-built canoe is perhaps one of the best specimens of native skill, ingenuity, and perseverance, to be seen in the islands. Most of the natives can hollow out a buhoe, but it is only those who have been regularly trained to the work, that can build a large canoe, and in this there is a considerable division of labour,—some laying down the keel and building the hull, some making and fixing the sails, and others fastening the outriggers, or adding the ornaments. The principal chiefs usually kept canoe-builders attached to their establishments, but the inferior chiefs generally hire workmen, paying them a given number of pigs, or fathoms of cloth, for a canoe, and finding them in provision while they are employed. The trees that are cut down in the mountains, or the interior of the islands, are often hollowed out there, sometimes by burning, but generally by the adze, or cut into the shape designed, and then brought down to the shore.

Idolatry was interwoven with their naval architecture, as well as every other pursuit. The priest had certain ceremonies to perform, and numerous and costly offerings were made to the gods of the chief, and of the craft or profession, when the keel was laid, when the canoe was finished, and when it was launched. Valuable canoes were often among the national offerings presented to the gods, and afterwards sacred to the service of the idol.

The double canoes of the Society Islands were larger, and more imposing in appearance, than most of those used in New Zealand or the Sandwich Islands, but not so strong as the former, nor so neat and light as the latter. I have, however, made several voyages in them. In fine weather, and with a fair wind, they are tolerably safe and comfortable; but when the weather is rough, and the wind contrary, they are miserable sea-boats, and are tossed about completely at the mercy of the winds. Many of the natives that have set out on voyages from one island to another, have been carried from the group altogether, and have either perished at sea, or drifted to some distant island.

In long voyages, single canoes are considered safer than double ones, as the latter are sometimes broken asunder, and are then unmanageable; but, even though the former should fill or upset at sea, as the wood is specifically lighter than the water, there is no fear of their sinking. When a canoe is upset or fills, the natives on board jump into the sea, and all taking hold of one end, which they press down, so as to elevate the other end above the sea, a great part of the water runs out; they then suddenly loose their hold of the canoe, which falls upon the water, emptied in some degree of its contents. Swimming along by the side of it, they bale out the rest, and climbing into it pursue their voyage. This has frequently been the case; and, unless the canoe is broken by upsetting or filling, the detention is all the inconvenience it occasions. The only evil they fear in such circumstances, is that of being attacked by sharks, which have sometimes made sad havock among those who have been wrecked at sea.

An instance of this kind occurred a few years ago, when a number of chiefs and people, altogether thirty-two, were passing from one island to another, in a large double canoe. They were overtaken by a tempest, the violence of which tore their canoes from the horizontal spars by which they were united. It was in vain for them to endeavour to place them upright, or empty out the water, for they could not prevent their incessant overturning. As their only resource, they collected the scattered spars and boards, and constructed a raft, on which they hoped they might drift to land. The weight of the whole number, who were now collected on the raft, was so great as to sink it so far below the surface, that they sometimes stood above their knees in water. They made very little progress, and soon became exhausted by fatigue and hunger. In this condition they were attacked by a number of sharks. Destitute of a knife, or any other weapon of defence, they fell an easy prey to these rapacious monsters. One after another was seized and devoured, or carried away by them; and the survivors, who with dreadful anguish beheld their companions thus destroyed, saw the number of assailants apparently increasing, as each body was carried away, until only two or three remained. The raft, thus lightened of its load, rose to the surface of the water, and placed them beyond the reach of the voracious jaws of their relentless destroyers. The voyage on which they had set out, was only from one of the Society Islands to another, consequently they were not very far from land. The tide and the current now carried them to the shore, where they landed, to tell the melancholy fate of their fellow-voyagers.

But for the sharks, the South Sea Islanders would be in comparatively little danger from casualties in their voyages among the islands; and although when armed they have sometimes been known to attack a shark in the water, yet when destitute of a knife or other weapon, they become an easy prey, and are consequently much terrified at such merciless antagonists.

Another circumstance also, that added to this dread of sharks was, the superstitious ideas they entertained relative to some of the species. Although they would not only kill, but eat certain kinds of shark: the large blue sharks, *squalus glaucus*, were deified by them, and, rather than attempt to destroy them, they would endeavour to propitiate their favour by prayers and offerings. Temples were erected, in which priests officiated, and offerings were presented to the deified monsters, while fishermen and others, who were much at sea, sought their favour. In one of their fabulous legends, for which I am indebted to my friend Mr. Orsmond, the island of Tahiti is represented as having been a shark, originally from Raiatea: Matarafau, in the east, was the head; and a place near Faaa, on the west, was the tail; the large lake Vaihiria was the ventricles or gills; while the lofty Orohena, the highest mountain in the island, probably 6- or 7000 feet above the sea, was regarded as its dorsal fin; and its ventral fin was Matavai. Many ludicrous legends were formerly in circulation among the people, relative to the regard paid by the sharks at sea, to priests of their temples, whom they were always said to recognize, and never to injure. I received one from the mouth of a man, formerly a priest of an *akua mao*, shark god; but it is too absurd to be recorded. The principal motives, however, by which the people appear to have been influenced in their homage to these creatures, was the same that operated on their minds in reference to other acts of idolatry; it was the principle of fear, and a desire to avoid destruction, in the event of being exposed to their anger at sea.

The superstitious fears of the people have now entirely ceased. I was once in a boat, on a voyage to Borabora, when a ravenous shark approaching us, seized the blade of one of the oars, and on being shaken from it, darted at the keel of the boat, which he attempted to bite. While he was thus employed, the native whose oar he had seized, leaning over the side of the boat, grasped him by the tail, succeeded in lifting him out of the water, and, with the help of his companions, dragged him alive into the boat, where he began to flounder and strike his tail with rage and violence. Mr. Tyerman and myself, for we were sailing together, were climbing up on the seats out of his way, but the natives, giving him two or three blows on the nose with a small wooden mallet, quieted him, and then cut off his head. We landed the same evening, when I believe they baked and ate him.

The single canoes, though safer at sea, are yet liable to accident, notwithstanding the outrigger, which requires to be fixed with care, to prevent them from upsetting. To the natives this is a matter of slight inconvenience, but to a foreigner it is not always pleasant or safe. Mrs. Orsmond, Mrs. Barff, Mrs. Ellis, and myself, with our two children, and one or two natives, were once crossing the small harbour at Fa-re, in Huahine; a female servant was sitting in the fore part of the canoe, with our little girl in her arms, our infant boy was at his mother's breast, and a native, with a long light pole, was paddling or pushing the canoe along, when a small buhoe, with a native youth sitting in it, darted out from behind a bush that hung over the water, and before we could turn, or the youth could stop his canoe, it ran across our outrigger. This in an instant went down, our canoe was turned bottom upwards, and the whole party precipitated into the sea. The sun had set soon after we started from the opposite side, and, the twilight being very short, the shades of evening had already thickened around us, which prevented the natives on the shore from perceiving our situation.

The native woman held our little girl up with one hand, and swam with the other towards the shore, aiding, as well as she could, Mrs. Orsmond, who had caught hold of her long hair, which floated on the water behind her; Mrs. Barff, on rising to the surface, caught hold of the outrigger of the canoe that had occasioned our disaster, and, calling out for help, informed the people on the shore of our danger, and speedily brought them to our assistance.

Mr. Orsmond no sooner reached the beach, than he plunged into the sea; Mrs. O. leaving the native by whom she had been supported, caught hold of her husband, and not only prevented his swimming, but sunk him so deep in the water, that, but for the timely arrival of the natives, both would probably have found a watery grave. Mahine-vahine, the queen, sprang in, and conveyed Mrs. Barff to the shore. I came up on the side opposite to that on which the canoe had turned over, and found Mrs. Ellis struggling in the water, with the child still at her breast. I immediately climbed upon the canoe, and raised her so far out of the water, as to allow the little boy to breathe, till a small canoe came off to our assistance, into which she was taken, when I swam to the shore, grateful for the deliverance we had experienced.

It was not far from the beach where this occurred, yet the water was deep, and several articles which we had in the canoe, were seen the next day lying at the bottom, among coral and sand, seventeen or eighteen fathoms below the surface. Accidents of this kind, however, occur but seldom; and though we have made many voyages, this is the only occasion on which we have been in danger.

The natives of the eastern isles frequently come

down to the Society Islands in large double canoes, which the Tahitians dignify with the name of *pahi*, the term for a ship. They are built with much smaller pieces of wood than those employed in the structure of the Tahitian canoes, as the low coralline islands produce but very small kinds of timber, yet they are much superior both for strength, convenience, and sustaining a tempest at sea. They are always double, and one canoe has a permanent covered residence for the crew. The two masts are also stationary, and a kind of ladder, or wooden shroud, extends from the sides to the head of the mast. The sails are large, and made with fine matting. Several of the principal chiefs possess a pahi paumotu, which they use as a more safe and convenient mode of conveyance than their own canoes. One canoe, that brought over a chief from Rurutu, upwards of three hundred miles, was very large. It was somewhat in the shape of a crescent, the stem and stern high and pointed, and the sides broad; the depth from the upper edge of the middle to the keel, was not less than twelve feet. It was built with thick planks of the Barringtonia, some of which were four feet wide; they were sewn together with twisted or braided cocoa-nut husk, and although they brought the chief safely, probably more than six hundred miles, they must have been very ungovernable and unsafe in a storm or heavy sea.

The paumotu canoes, in their size, shape, and thatched cabins, resemble those used by the inhabitants of some of the islands to the west, and of the Caroline islanders, more than those of New Zealand, Tahiti, or the Sandwich Islands.

The building of their dwellings is another important occupation of the islanders. *Fa-re* is the term for house in most of the islands. The first abodes we occupied were native buildings, and an account of the erection of those prepared for us at Afareaitu, will convey a general idea of their plan and architecture. The timber being prepared, they planted the square posts which support the ridgepole about three feet deep. The piece forming the ridge was nearly triangular, flat underneath, but raised along the centre on the upper side, and about nine inches wide; the joints were accurately fitted, and square mortises were made, to receive tenons formed on the top of the posts. As soon as these were firmly secured, it was raised by ropes, and fixed in its place. The side-posts were next planted, about three or four feet apart; these were square, and nearly nine inches wide. In the top of each post, a groove, about six inches deep and an inch and a half wide, was cut; in this was fixed a strong board, eight or nine inches broad, bevelled on the upper edge, forming a kind of wall-plate along the side of the house. The rafters, which they call *aho*, were put on next; they are usually straight branches of the *purau*, an exceedingly useful tree, growing luxuriantly in every part of the islands. The poles used for rafters are about four inches in diameter at the largest end. As soon as they are cut, the bark is stripped off, and used in the manufacture of cordage, lines, &c. The rafters are then deposited in a stream of water for a number of days, in order to extract the juices with which they are impregnated, and which, the natives suppose, attract insects, that soon destroy them. When taken out, the poles are dried, and considered fit for use. The wood is remarkably light, its growth is rapid, and though the old parts of the tree are exceedingly tough, the young branches or poles, used for rafters and other purposes, are soft and brittle, resembling the texture and strength of branches of the English willow. The foot of the rafter is partially sharpened, and about eighteen inches from the end a deep notch is cut, which receives the bevelled edge of the *ra-pe*, or wall-plate, while the upper extremity rests upon the ridge. The rafters are generally ranged along on one side, three feet apart, with parallel rafters on the opposite side, which cross each other at the top of the ridge, where they are firmly tied together with cord, or the strong fibres of the *ieie*, a tough mountain plant. A pole is then fixed along, above the junction of the opposite rafters, and the whole tied down to pegs fastened in the piece of timber forming the ridge. The large wood used in building is of a fine yellow colour, the rafters are beautifully white; and as the house is often left some days in frame, its appearance is at once novel and agreeable.

The buildings are thatched with *rau fara*, (the leaves of the pandanus,) which are prepared with great care. When first gathered from the trees, they are soaked three or four days in the sea, or a stream of water. The sound leaves are then selected, and each leaf, after having been stretched singly on a stick fixed in the ground, is coiled up with the concave side outwards. In this state they remain till they are perfectly flat, when each leaf is doubled about one-third of the way from the stalk, over a strong reed or cane six feet long, and the folded leaf laced together with the stiff stalks of the cocoa-nut leaflets. The thatch, thus prepared, is taken to the building, and a number of lines of cinet are extended above the rafters, and in each of the spaces between, from the lower edge o the ridge. The thatchers now take a reed of leaves, and fasten it to the lower ends of the rafters at the left extremity of the roof, and, placing another reed about an inch above it, pierce the leaves with a long wooden needle, and sew it to the lines fixed on the outer side of the rafters, and in the space between them: when six or eight reeds are thus fixed, they pass the cord with which they are sewn two or three times round each of the three rafters over which the reed extends. Placing every successive reed about an inch above the last, they proceed until they reach the ridge. The workmen now descend, and carry up another course of thatch, in the same way inserting the ends of the reeds of the fresh course into the bent part of the leaves on the former. It is singular to see a number of men working underneath the rafters, in thatching a house.

When the roof is finished, the points only of the long palm-leaves are seen hanging on the outside; and the appearance within, from the shining brown colour of the leaves bent over the reeds, and the whiteness of the rafters, is exceedingly neat and ingenious. The inside of the rafters of the chiefs' houses, or public buildings, is frequently ornamented with braided cords of various colours, or finely-fringed white and chequered matting. These are bound or wrapped round the rafters, and the extremities sometimes hanging down twelve or thirteen inches, give to their roof or ceiling a light and elegant appearance. Most of the natives are able to thatch a house, but covering in the ridge is more difficult, and is only understood by those who have been regularly trained for the work. A quantity of large cocoa-nut or fern leaves is first laid on the upper part of the thatch, and afterwards a species of long grass, called *aretu*, is curiously fixed or woven from one end to the other, so as to remain attached to the thatch, and yet cover the ridge of the house.

The roof being finished, they generally level the ground within, and enclose the sides. In the erection of my house, this part was allotted to the king's servants. About thirty of them came one morning with a number of bundles of large white purau poles, from two to three inches in diameter. After levelling the floor, they dug a trench a foot deep round the outside, and then, cutting the poles to a proper length, planted them an inch and a half or two inches apart, until the building was completely enclosed, excepting the space left for a door in the front and opposite sides. In order to keep the poles in their proper place, two or three light sticks, called *tea*, were tied horizontally along the outside. Partitions were then erected in the same manner, as we were desirous, contrary to the native practice, to have more than one room. The house was now finished, and in structure resembled a large birdcage. In two of the rooms we laid down boards which we had brought from Port Jackson, and either paved the remainder of the floor with stones, or plastered it with lime. The outside was skreened with platted cocoa-nut leaves, lined with native cloth. This also constituted our curtains, and, hung up before the entrance to some of the apartments, answered the purpose of a door. Thus fitted up, our native house proved a comfortable dwelling during the months we remained at Afareaitu.

The houses of the natives, although varying in size and shape, were all built with the same kind of materials, and in a similar manner. Some of them were exceedingly large, capable of containing two or three thousand people. *Nanu*, a house belonging to the king, on the borders of Pare, was three hundred and ninety-seven feet in length. Others were a hundred or a hundred and forty feet long. These, however, were erected only for the leading chiefs. As the population has decreased, a diminution has also taken place in the size of the dwellings, yet, for some time after our arrival, several remained an hundred feet in length. The chiefs seem always to have been attended by a numerous retinue of dependants, or Areois, and other idlers. The unemployed inhabitants of the districts where they might be staying, were also accustomed to attend the entertainments given for the amusement of the chiefs, and this probably induced the people to erect capacious buildings for their accommodation.

Some of the houses were straight at each end, and resembled in shape an English dwelling; this was called *haupape:* but the most common form for the chiefs' houses was what they called *poté*, which was parallel along the sides, and circular at the ends. Houses of this kind have a very neat, light, and yet compact appearance. The above are the usual forms of their permanent habitations, and the durability of the house depends much upon the manner in which it is thatched; if there is much space between the reeds, it soon decays; but if they are placed close together, it will last five or seven years without admitting the rain. Occasionally two or three coverings of thatch are put on the same frame. The Tahitians are a social people, naturally fond of conversation, song, and dance; hence a number often resided under the same roof.

In addition to the oval and the oblong house, they often had the *fare pora*, the *fare rau*, and the *buhapa*, or other temporary dwellings, for encampments during the period of war, or when journeying among the mountains; and their *farau vaa*, or canoe houses, which were large, and built with care; a number of what they call *oa* were planted at unequal distances on both sides of the rafter and post, which being one piece of timber, tended to strengthen the building.

The floor of their dwellings was covered with long dried grass, which, although comfortable when first laid down, was not often changed, and, from the moisture occasioned by the water spilled at meals and other times, was frequently much worse than the naked sand or soil would have been. Their door was an ingenious contrivance, being usually a light trellis-frame of bamboo-cane, suspended by a number of braided thongs, and attached to a long cane in the upper part of the inside of the wall-plate—the thongs sliding backwards and forwards like the rings of a curtain, whenever it was opened or closed. Many of their houses are erected within their enclosures or plantations, but they generally stand on the shore, or by the wayside.

Every chief of rank, or person of what in Tahiti would be termed respectability, has an enclosure round his dwelling, leaving a space of ten or twenty feet width withinside. This court is often kept clean, sometimes spread over with dry grass, but generally covered with black basaltic pebbles, or *anaana*, beautifully white fragments of coral. The *aumoa* is a neat and durable fence, about four feet high; the upright pieces are tenoned into a polished rail along the top, or surrounded with the straight and peeled branches of the purau or tamanu.

Erected with such tools as are exhibited below, the size, structure, and conveniency of the Ta-

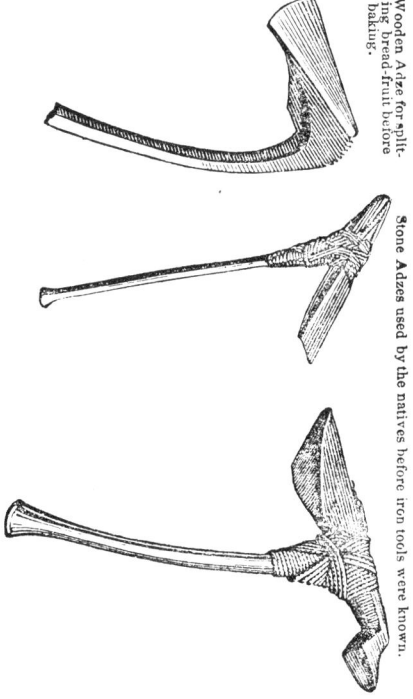

Wooden Adze for splitting bread-fruit before baking.

Stone Adzes used by the natives before iron tools were known.

hitian houses, such as Wallis found, and such as are here described, display no small degree of invention, skill, and attention to comfort, and show that the natives were even then far removed from a state of barbarism. They also warranted the inference that they were not deficient in capacity for improvement, and that, with better models and tuition, they would improve in the cultivation of every art of civilized life, especially when they should be put in possession of iron and iron tools, as those they had heretofore used were rude stone adzes, or chisels of bone.

It is, however, proper to remark, that although all were capable of building good native houses, and many erected comfortable dwellings, yet great numbers, from indolence or want of tools, reared only temporary and wretched huts, as unsightly in the midst of the beautiful landscape, as they were unwholesome and comfortless to their abject inhabitants.

The dress of the islanders was various as to its form, colour, and texture. It was neither cumbrous nor costly, but always light and loose; and though singular, often elegant. Wool, cotton, and silk were formerly unknown among them. The prince and the peasant, the warrior and the voluptuary, were clad in vestments of the same materials. The head was uncovered, excepting when adorned with flowers, and the brow was occasionally shaded by a light skreen of cocoa-nut leaves. The dress of the sexes differed but little; both wore the *pareu*, or folds of cloth, round the waist. The men, however, wore the *maro* or girdle, and the tiputa or poncho, while the females wore over their shoulders the light ahupu or ahutiapono, in the form of a vest, or loose scarf or shawl.

Next to those kinds of labour necessary to

obtain their subsistence, and construct their dwellings, their apparel claimed attention. This, though light, required, from the simple methods by which it was fabricated, a considerable portion of their time. Cloth made with the bark of a tree, constituted a principal article of native dress, prior to the introduction of foreign cloth. It is manufactured chiefly by females, and was one of their most frequent employments. The name for cloth, among the Tahitians, is *ahu*. The Sandwich Island word *tapa*, is, we believe, never used in this sense, but signifies a part of the human body. In the manufacture of their cloth, the natives of the South Sea Islands use a greater variety of materials than their neighbours in the northern group: the bark of the different varieties of *wauti*, or paper mulberry, being almost the only article used by the latter; while the former employ not only the bark of the paper mulberry, which they call *auti*, but also that of the aoa and of the bread-fruit.

The process of manufacture is much the same in all, though some kinds are sooner finished than others. When the bark from the branches of the bread-fruit or auti is used, the outer green or brown rind is scraped off with a shell; it is then slightly beaten, and allowed to ferment, or is macerated in water. A stout piece of wood, resembling a beam, twenty or thirty feet long, and from six to nine inches square, with a groove cut in the under side, is placed on the ground; across this, the bark is laid, and beaten with a heavy mallet of casuarina or iron-wood. The mallet is usually fifteen or eighteen inches long, about two inches square, and round at one end, for the purpose of being held firmly. The sides of the mallet are grooved; one side very coarse or large, the opposite side exceedingly fine. One of the remaining sides is generally cut in chequers or small squares, and the other is plain or ribbed. The bark is placed lengthwise across the long piece of wood, and beaten first with the rough side of the mallet, and then with those parts that are finer.

Cloth Mallet.

Vegetable gum is rarely employed; in general, the resinous matter in the bark is sufficiently adhesive. The fibres of the bark are completely interwoven by the frequent beating with the grooved or chequered side of the mallet; and when the piece is finished, the texture of the cloth is often fine and even; while the inequalities occasioned by the fine grooves, or small squares, give it the appearance of woven cloth. During the process of its manufacture, the cloth is kept saturated with moisture, and carefully wrapped in thick green leaves every time the workwomen leave off; but as soon as it is finished, they spread it to dry in the sun, and bleach it according to the purpose for which it is designed. The *ore* or cloth made with the bark of the aoa, is usually thin, and of a dark brown colour; that made with the bark of the bread-fruit and a mixture of the auti, is of a light brown, or fawn colour; but the finest and most valuable kind is called hobu.

It is made principally, and sometimes entirely, from the bark of the paper mulberry, and is bleached till beautifully white. This is chiefly worn by the females.

It is astonishing that they should be able, by a process so simple, to make bales, containing sometimes two hundred yards of cloth, four yards wide; the whole in one single piece, made with strips of bark seldom above four or five feet long, and, when spread open, not more than an inch and a half broad—joined together simply by beating them with the grooved mallet. When sufficiently bleached and dried, the cloth is folded along the whole length, rolled up into a bale, and covered with a piece of matting—this is called *ruru vehe*. The wealth of a chief is sometimes estimated by the number of these covered bales which he possesses. The more valuable kinds of cloth are rolled up in the same way, covered with matting or cloth of an inferior kind, and generally suspended from some part of the roof of the chief's house. The estimation in which it was held has been greatly diminished since they have become acquainted with European cloth, and large quantities are now seldom made. It is, however, still an article in general use among the lower classes of society, and the mother yet continues to beat her parure, or native pareu, for herself and children.

A number of smaller pieces are still made, among which the tiputa is one of the most valuable. It is prepared by beating a number of layers of cloth together, to render it thicker than the common cloth: for the outside layer, they select a stout branch of the auti, or bread-fruit, about an inch and a half in diameter: this they prepare with great attention, and, having beaten it to the usual width and length, which is about ten feet long and three feet wide, they fix it on the outside, and attach it to the others by rubbing a small portion of arrow-root on the inner side, before beating it together. The tiputa of the Tahitians corresponds exactly with the poncho of the South Americans. It is rather longer, but is worn in the same manner, having a hole cut in the centre, through which, when worn, the head is passed; while the garment hangs down over the shoulders, breast, and back, usually reaching, both before and behind, as low as the knees. Next to the tiputa, the ahufara is a general article of dress. These are either square like a shawl, or resemble a scarf. They are sometimes larger, and correspond with a counterpane more than a shawl, and are always exceedingly splendid and rich in their colours.

The natives of the Society Islands have a variety of vegetable dyes, and display more taste in the variations and patterns of the cloth, than in any other use of colours. Much of the common cloth is dyed either with the bark of the aito, *casuarina*, or tiari, *aleurites*. This gives it a kind of dark red or chocolate colour, and is supposed to add to its durability. The leaves of the arum are sometimes used, but brilliant red and yellow are their favourite hues. The former, which they call mati, is prepared by mixing the milky juice of the small berry of the mati, *ficus prolixa*, with the leaves of the tou, a species of *cordia*. When the dye is prepared by this combination, it is absorbed on the fibres of a kind of rush, and dried for use. It produces a most brilliant scarlet dye, which, when preserved with a varnish of gum, retains its brightness till the garment is worn out. The yellow is prepared from the inner bark of the root of the nono, *morinda citrifolia*, and though far more fugitive than the scarlet of the mati, is an exceedingly bright colour. The yellow dye is prepared by infusing the bark of the root in water, in which the cloth is allowed to remain till completely saturated, when it is dried in the sun. The mati, or scarlet dye, is moistened with water, and laid on the dry cloth. Their patterns are fixed with the scarlet dye on a yellow ground, and were formerly altogether devoid of uniformity or regularity, yet still exhibiting considerable taste. They now fix a border round the ahufara, and arrange the figures in different parts. Nature supplies the pattern. They select some of the most delicate and beautiful ferns, or the hibiscus flowers: when the dye is prepared, the leaf, or flower, is laid carefully on the dye; as soon as the surface is covered with the colouring matter, the stained leaf or flower, with its leaflets or petals correctly adjusted, is fixed on the cloth, and pressed gradually and regularly down. When it is removed, the impression is often beautiful and clear.

The scarf or shawl, and the tiputa, are the only dresses prepared in this way, and it is difficult to conceive of the dazzling and imposing appearance of such a dress, loosely folded round the person of a handsome chieftain of the South Sea Islands, who perfectly understands how to exhibit it to the best advantage. This kind of cloth is made better by the Tahitians than any other inhabitants of the Pacific. It is not, however, equal to the wairiirii of the Sandwich Islanders. Much of this cloth, beautifully painted, is now employed in their houses for bed and window curtains, &c. Several kinds of strong cloth are finished with a kind of gum or varnish, for the purpose of rendering them impervious.

But in the fabrication of glazed cloth, the natives of the Austral Islands, especially those of Rurutu, excel all with whom I am acquainted. Some of their pieces of cloth are thirty or forty yards square, exceedingly thick, and glazed on both sides, resembling the upper side of the English oil-cloth table-covers. It must have required immense labour to prepare it, yet it was abundant when they were first discovered. It is usually red on one side, and black on the other, the latter being highly varnished with a vegetable gum.

In the manufacture of cloth, the females of all ranks were employed; and the queen, and wives of the chiefs of the highest rank, strove to excel in some department—in the elegance of the pattern, or the brilliancy of the colour. They are fond of society, and worked in large parties, in open and temporary houses erected for the purpose. Visiting one of these houses at Eimeo, I saw sixteen or twenty females all employed. The queen sat in the midst, surrounded by several chief women, each with a mallet in her hand, beating the bark that was spread before her. The queen worked as diligently and cheerfully as any present.

The spar or square piece of wood on which the bark is beaten, being hollow on the under-side, every stroke produces a loud sound, and the noise occasioned by sixteen or twenty mallets going at one time, was to me almost deafening; while the queen and her friends seemed not only insensible to any inconvenience from it, but quite amused at its apparent effect on us. The sound of the cloth-beating mallet is not disagreeable, where heard at a distance, in some of the retired valleys, indicating the abode of industry and peace; but in the cloth-houses it is hardly possible to endure it.

As the wives and daughters of the chiefs take a pride in manufacturing superior cloth, the queen would often have felt it derogatory to her rank, if any other females in the island could have finished a piece of cloth better than herself. I remember, in the island of Huahine, when a native once passed by, wearing a beautiful ahufara, hearing one native woman remark to another—What a finely printed shawl that is! The figures on it are like the work, or the marking, of the queen! This desire, among persons in high stations, to excel in departments of labour, is what we have always admired. This feeling probably led Pomare to bestow so much attention on his hand-writing, and induced the king of the Sandwich Islands to request that we would not teach any of the people till we had fully instructed him in reading and writing.

The ahu, or cloth made with the bark of a tree, although exceedingly perishable when compared with European woven cloth, yet furnished, while it lasted, a light and loose dress, adapted to the climate, and the habits of the people. The duration of a Tahitian dress depended upon the materials with which it was made, the aoa being considered the strongest. Only the highly varnished kinds were proof against wet. The beauty of the various kinds of painted cloth was soon marred, and the texture destroyed, by the rain, as they were kept together simply by the adhesion of the interwoven fibres of the bark. Notwithstanding this, a tiputa, or a good strong pareu, when preserved from wet, would last several months.

Though the native cloth worn by the inhabitants was made by the women, there were some kinds used in the temples, in the service of the idols, which were made by men, and which it was necessary, according to the declarations of the priest, should be beaten during the night.

Although the manufacture of cloth was formerly the principal, it was not the only occupation of the females. Many of the people, especially the raateiras, or secondary chiefs, wore a kind of mat made with the bark of the hibiscus, which they call purau; and the preparation of this, as well as the beds or sleeping mats, occupied much of the time of the females. Great attention was paid to the manufacture of these fine mats. They chose for this purpose, the young shoots of the plant, and having peeled off the bark, and immersed it in water, placed it on a board, the outer rind being scraped off with a smooth shell. The strips of bark were an inch or an inch and a half wide, and about four feet long, and when spread out and dry, looked like so many white ribands. The bark was slit into narrow strips frequently less than the eighth of an inch wide. They were woven by the hand, and without any loom or machinery. They commenced the weaving at one corner, and having extended it to the proper width, which was usually three or four feet, continued the work till the mat was about nine or ten feet long, when the projecting ends of the bark were carefully removed, and a fine fringe worked round the edges.—Only half the pieces of bark used in weaving were split into narrow strips throughout their whole length. The others were slit five or six inches at the ends where they commenced, while the remaining part was rolled up like a riband. These they unrolled, and extended the slits as the weaving advanced, until the whole was complete. When first finished, they are of a beautifully white colour, and are worn only by the men, either bound round the loins as a pareu, or with an aperture in the centre as a tiputa or poncho, and sometimes as a mantle thrown loosely over the shoulder. Their appearance is light and elegant, and they are remarkably durable, though they become yellow from exposure to the weather.

The inhabitants of the Palliser Islands, to the eastward of Tahiti, exceed the Society Islanders in the quality of their mats, which are made of a tough white rush or grass, exceedingly fine and beautiful. They frequently manufacture a sort of girdle, called tiheri, six inches in width, and sometimes twenty yards in length, but remarkably fine and even, being woven by the hand, but with a degree of regularity rivalling the productions of the loom. They are highly valued by the Tahitians, and are a principal article of commerce between the inhabitants of the different islands.

The sails for their canoes, and beds on which they sleep, are a coarser kind of matting made with the leaves of different varieties of palm, or pandanus, found in the islands. Some kinds grow spontaneously others are cultivated for their leaves. The matting sails are much lighter than canvass, but less durable. The size and quality of the sleeping mats is regulated by the skill of the manufacturer, or the rank of the proprietor. Those who excel in making them, use very fine ones themselves. They are all woven by the hand, yet finished with remarkable regularity and neatness.

The ordinary mats are not more than six feet

wide, and nine or twelve feet long, but some are twelve feet wide, and sixty or eighty, or even a hundred yards long. Mats of this size, however, are only made for high chiefs, and in the preparation, perhaps, the females of several districts have been employed. They are kept rolled up, and suspended in some part of the chief's dwelling, more for the purpose of displaying his wealth, and the number of his dependents, than for actual use.

The kinds of leaf least liable to crack, are selected, and, for the purpose of sleeping upon, or even spreading on a floor, the use to which we generally applied them, the mats look neat, and last a considerable time. Several kinds of fine matting, ornamented with bright stained rushes interwoven with the others, were formerly made as articles of dress for the kings, or presents to the gods; but in this department of labour they were always inferior to the Sandwich Islanders, whose variegated mats are superior to any I have seen in the Pacific. Weaving of mats, with beating and staining of cloth, was the chief occupation of the females. A large portion of the property of the people consisted in mats and cloth, which also constituted part of their household furniture.

A variety of other articles were, however, necessary to the furnishing of their houses, but these were manufactured by the men. Next to a sleeping mat, a pillow was considered essential. This was of hard wood, and often exceedingly rude, though sometimes ingeniously wrought, resembling a short low stool, nine inches or a foot in length, and four or five inches high. The upper side was curved, to admit the head; the whole pillow, which they call tuaurua, is cut out of a single piece

Upon the bare wood they reclined their heads at night, and slept as soundly as the inhabitants of more civilized parts would do on the softest down.

Tahitian Pillow.

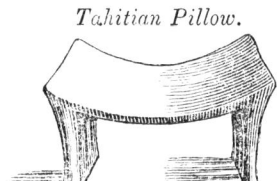

In general, they sat cross-legged on mats spread on the floor; but occasionally used a stool, which they called *iri* or *nohoraa*. This resembled the pillow in shape, and, though much larger, was made out of a single piece of wood. The tamanu, or *callophyllum*, was usually selected, and immense trees must have been cut down for this purpose. I have seen iris four or five feet long,

Tahitian Stool.

three feet wide, and each end three feet six inches high; yet the whole cut out of one solid piece of timber. The upper part was curved, and the extremes being highest, the seat resembled the concave side of a crescent, so that, however large it might be, only one sat on it at a time. The iri was finely polished, and the wood, in its grain and colour resembling the best kinds of mahogany, rendered it, although destitute of carving or other ornament, a handsome piece of furniture in a chieftain's dwelling. The rank of the host was often indicated by the size of this seat, which was used on public occasions, or for the accommodation of a distinguished guest. Those in more ordinary use were low, and less curved, but always made out of a single piece of wood.

Next to these, their weapons, drums, and other musical instruments, were their most important furniture; a great portion, however, of what might be called their household furniture, was appropriated to the preparation or preservation of their food.

The *umete*, or dish, was the principal. Sometimes it was exceedingly large, resembling a canoe or boat more than a dish for food. It was frequently made with the wood of the tamanu, exceedingly well polished; some were six or eight feet long, a foot and a half wide, and twelve inches deep, these belonged only to the chiefs, and were used for the preparation of arrow-root, cocoa-nut milk, &c. on occasions of public festivity. The umetes in ordinary use were oval, about two or three feet long, eighteen inches wide, and of varied depth. They are supported by four feet, cut out of the same piece of wood, and serve not only for the preparation of their food, but as dishes, upon which it is placed when taken from the oven.

The *papahia* is extensively used. It is a low solid block or stool, supported by four short legs, and smoothly polished on the top. It is cut out of one piece of wood, and is used instead of a mortar for pounding bread-fruit, plantains, or bruising taro; which is done by placing these upon the papahia, and beating them with a short stone pestle called a *penu*. This is usually made with a black sort of basalt, found chiefly in the island of Maurua, the most western of the group. The penu is sometimes constructed from a species of porous coral.*

The water used for washing their feet is kept in bottles called *aano*, made from the shells of large and full-grown cocoa-nuts. That which they drink is contained in calabashes, which are much larger than any I ever saw used for the same purpose in the Sandwich Islands, but destitute of ornament. They are kept in nets of cinet, and suspended from some part of the dwelling. It is customary with them to wash their hands both

Wooden Dish.

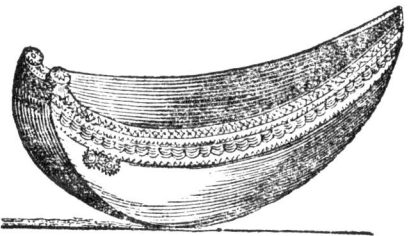

before and after eating. The dishes used for this purpose were often curiously carved. One I brought from the Austral Islands, of which the

* A fine specimen of that kind of *penu* which I procured at Rurutu, is deposited in the Missionary museum at Austin Friars.

accompanying wood-cut gives a correct representation, is neither inelegant nor rude.

The drinking cups are made with the cocoa-nut shell after it is full grown, but before it is perfectly ripe. The shell is then soft, and is scraped until much thinner than a saucer, and frequently transparent. They are of a yellow colour, and plain, though the cups formerly used for drinking ava were carved. These are the principal utensils in the preparation of their food; they are kept remarkably clean, and, when not in use, suspended from some part of the dwelling, or hung upon a stand.

The *fata*, or stand, is a single light post planted in the floor, with one or two projections, and a notch on the top, from which the calabashes of water, baskets of food, umetes, &c. are suspended. Great labour was formerly bestowed on this piece of furniture, and the fata pua was considered an ornament to the house in which it was erected. About a foot from the ground, a projection extended six or eight inches wide, completely round, flat on the top, but concave on the under side, in order to prevent rats or mice from ascending and gaining access to the food. Their only knife was a piece of bamboo-cane, with which they would cut up a pig, dog, or fish, with great facility.

The carriage of fruits and roots, from the garden to the dwelling-house, and the constructing of their ovens, in which much of their food is still prepared according to their former custom, is generally performed by the men, while the preparation for the meal within doors is made by the females.

CHAP. VIII.

Account of the music and amusements of the islanders—Description of the sacred drum—Heiva drum, &c. Occasions of their use—The bu or trumpet—Ihara—The vivo, or flute—General character of their songs—Elegiac singularly beautiful—Translation of a war song—Ballads, a kind of classical authority—Entertainments and amusements — Taupiti, or festival—Wrestling and boxing—Effects of victory and defeat—Foot-races — Martial games — Sham-fights — Naval reviews—Apai, bandy or cricket—Tuiraa, or foot-ball—The haruraa puu, a female game—Native dances—Heiva, &c.—The te-a, or archery—Bows and arrows—Religious ceremonies connected with the game—Never used by the Society Islanders except in their amusements—Discontinued since the introduction of Christianity.

As a people, the South Sea Islanders were peculiarly addicted to pleasure, and to their music, dances, and other amusements, nearly as much of their time was devoted as to all other avocations. Their music wanted almost every quality that could render it agreeable to an ear accustomed to harmony, and was deficient in all that constitutes excellence. It was generally boisterous and wild, and, with the exception of the soft and plaintive warblings of the native flute, was distinguished by nothing so much as its discordant, deafening sounds.

The principal musical instrument used by the South Sea Islanders, was the *pahu*, or drum. This varied in size and shape, according to the purpose for which it was designed. Their drums were all cut out of a solid piece of wood. The block out of which they were made, being hollowed out from one end, remaining solid at the other, and having the top covered with a piece of shark's skin, occasioned their frequently resembling, in construction and appearance, a kettle-drum. The pua and the reva, which are remarkably close-grained and durable, were esteemed the

Tahitian Drums.

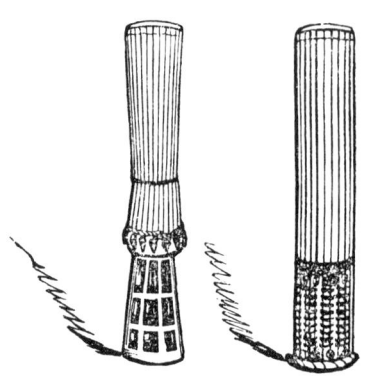

most suitable kinds of wood for the manufacture of their drums. The large drums were called *pahu*, and the smaller ones *toere*. The *pahu ra*, sacred drum, which was *rutu*, or beaten, on every occasion of extraordinary ceremony at the idol temple, was particularly large, standing sometimes eight feet high. The sides of one, that I saw in Tane's marae at Maeva, was not more than a foot in diameter, but many were much larger. In some of the islands, these instruments were very curiously carved. One which I brought from High Island, and have deposited in the Missionary Museum, is not inelegantly decorated; others, however, I have seen, exhibiting very superior workmanship.

The drums used in their heivas and dances were ingeniously made. Their construction resembled that of those employed in the temple, the skin forming the head was fastened to the open work at the bottom by strings of cinet, made with the fibres of the cocoa-nut husk. Drums were among the martial music of the Tahitians, and were used to animate the men when proceeding to battle. The drums beaten as accompaniments to the recital of their songs, were the same in shape, but smaller. They were all neatly made, and finely polished. The large drums were beaten with two heavy sticks, the smaller ones with the naked hand. When used, they were not suspended from the shoulders of the performers, but fixed upon the ground, and consequently produced no very musical effect. The sound of the large drum at the temple, which was sometimes beaten at midnight, and associations connected therewith, were most terrific. The inhabitants at Maeva, where my house stood within a few yards of the ruins of the temple, have frequently told me, that at the midnight hour, when the victim was probably to be offered on the following day, they have often been startled from their slumbers by the deep, thrilling sound of the sacred drum; and as its portentous sounds have reverberated among the rocks of the valley, every individual through the whole district has trembled with fear of the gods, or apprehension of being seized as the victim for sacrifice.

The sound of the trumpet, or shell, a species of murex, used in war to stimulate in action, by the priests in the temple, and also by the herald, and others on board their fleets, was more horrific than

The Trumpet Shell.

that of the drum. The largest shells were usually selected for this purpose, and were sometimes above a foot in length, and seven or eight inches in diameter at the mouth. In order to facilitate the blowing of this trumpet, they made a perforation, about an inch in diameter, near the apex of the shell. Into this they inserted a bamboo cane, about three feet in length, which was secured by binding it to the shell with fine braid; the aperture was rendered air-tight by cementing the outsides of it with a resinous gum from the breadfruit tree. These shells were blown when a procession walked to the temple, or their warriors marched to battle, at the inauguration of the king, during the worship at the temple, or when a tabu, or restriction, was imposed in the name of the gods. We have sometimes heard them blown. The sound is extremely loud, but the most monotonous and dismal that it is possible to imagine.

The *ihara* was another exceedingly noisy instrument. It was formed from the single joint of a large bamboo cane, cut off a short distance beyond the two ends or joints. In the centre, a long aperture was made from one joint towards the other. The ihara, when used, was placed horizontally on the ground, and beaten with sticks. It was not used in their worship, but simply as an amusement; its sounds were harsh and discordant. In its shape, &c. the ihara of the Polynesians appears to resemble the Toponaztli of the Mexicans, described by Claverigo. The huehuetl, or drum of the latter, appears also to be much the same as the drum of the Tahitians, and was used on similar occasions.

The *vivo*, or flute, was the most agreeable instrument used by the islanders. It was usually a bamboo cane, about an inch in diameter, and twelve or eighteen inches long. The joint in the cane formed one end of the flute; the aperture through which it was blown was close to the end;

it seldom had more than four other holes, three in the upper side covered with the fingers, and one beneath, against which the thumb was placed. Sometimes, however, there were four holes on the upper side. It was occasionally plain, but more frequently ornamented, by being partially scorched or burnt with a hot stone, or having fine and beautifully plaited strings of human hair wound round it alternately with rings of braided cinet. It was not blown from the mouth, but the nostril. The performer usually placed the thumb of the right hand upon the right nostril, applied the aperture of the flute, which he held with the fingers of his right hand, to the other nostril, and, moving his fingers on the holes, produced his music. The sound was soft, and not unpleasant, though the notes were few; it was generally played in a plaintive strain, though frequently used as an accompaniment to their *pehes*, or songs. These were closely identified both with the music and the dances. The *ihara*, the drum, and the flute, were generally accompanied by the song, as was also the native dance.

"In every nation it has been found that poetry is of much earlier date than any other production of the human mind," and I am disposed to ascribe the highest antiquity to the native ballads. Much of their mythology is probably to be ascribed to this source, and many of their legends were originally funeral or elegiac songs, in honour of departed kings or heroes. I have heard them recited, and have often been struck with their pathos and beauty; two lines of one, which Mr. Nott heard recited for the consolation of a mother and family, on the death of an only son, have always appeared exceedingly beautiful.

The grief generally felt was described in affecting strains, and then, in reference to sympathy of a higher order, it was added—

> *To rii rii te ua ite iriatae:*
> *Ere ra te ua, e roimata ïa no Oro.*

The literal rendering of which would be —

"Thickly falls the small rain on the face of the sea,
They are not drops of rain, but they are tears of Oro."

The sentiment of the second line is weakened by the introduction of the plural pronoun and the conjunction; but, preserving the idiom, as well as the sense, the line would be—

Not rain, but the *weeping* it (is) of Oro.

In the Tahitian, the word for tears, *roimata*, is the same in the singular and plural, and accords with the singular pronoun, it referring to the word *ua* or *rain*.

Their songs were generally historical ballads, which varied in their nature with the subjects to which they referred. They were exceedingly numerous, and adapted to every department of society, and every period of life. The children were early taught these *udes*, and took great delight in their recital. Many of their songs referred to the legends or achievements of their gods, some to the exploits of their distinguished heroes and chieftains; while others were of a more objectionable character. They were often, when recited on public occasions, accompanied with gestures and actions corresponding to the events described, and assumed a histrionic character. In some cases, and on public occasions, the action presented a kind of pantomime. They had one song for the fisherman, another for the cancebuilder, a song for cutting down the tree, a song for launching the canoe. But they were, with few exceptions, either idolatrous or impure; and were, consequently, abandoned when the people renounced their pagan worship. Occasionally, however, we heard parts of these songs recited, when events have occurred similar to those on which, in former times, they would have been used.

The following is one of their songs preparatory to war,—

> On the lifted club of Tane, great friend, I rely
> For defence from the storm (descending,) on the ship of peace, (or government,)
> To allay the raging deep, that it may rest,
> Let there be calm before the king,
> The king of the black purple deep,
> The king of the depths unknown,
> The king who fills with consternation;
> But Hiro is that warrior,
> Broad is the back of Hiro,
> A back of vast expanse,*
> His eyes are deep-fixed and dark,
> His ear hangs not down in fear,
> Like the pike-fish is the hair on his body,
> Let the slung stone fly,
> Make sacred the council of war,
> The collected clubs of the house of warriors,
> Soon I will reveal my council,
> The sacred and scarlet feathers, and blood,
> The slinger who stands,
> The beloved, the favourite of kings, who sits,
> The war-dress of Tu, warrior of the sky.

O Hiro, to whom shall I deliver the song of war!
Shall I declare it to Marama, the warrior born of Hiro
Who came forth with skill (to arrange the battle,)
With the savageness of the dog, the strength of the shark,
That shall sever the head where the skull joins the neck,
Causing the live bodies to run headless,
And shall pile dead bodies high as the temple walls,
In the cocoa-grove, at Taumau,† let us encamp,

---

* The name of one of their gods. † A small island whence the Huahine fleets sailed.

WAR-SONG.

That Uura king at Tarapati may behold it.
O Hiro, to whom shall I this war-song declare,
I declare it to the band of the keel,
The band of brave fighters who never fled,
The keel sustains the ship, warriors each other,
To the two pupils for whom the life of the stone battle-axe
    was created,
To the sky producer, or growing sky,
The clear sky, the spreading sky,
The sky above, sky even piled,
The treaty nursed in the lap,
Before the face of the armies of Rai and Roo.
And great Ru, who in Mauarahu lifted the heavens,
Gods shall enter, and there shall be darkness,
There shall be the blackness of darkness;
Our onset shall be as the rolling sea,
Our conflict the struggle of travail,
Let it be as the sea in a storm,
As the sea raised by sudden tempest,
Roo, the first-born god, shall cause destruction:
The heads of men shall be caught as fish in the net.
Shout the name of Ro on the right hand and the left,
Thus shall we the heads of men entangle.
Climb the rock half way to its summit, and return,
Climb the rock Fataufatau;
Enter the narrow cleft, whence it is high above, and deep
    below,
And weep as did the mother of Tafai,
She fled to the long mountain in Romaroma;*
Surrounded with war, she and her son fled,
The younger brother may climb the bread-fruit Maau,
Or fly to the elder brother.
The spear of Tuhorotua has been here:
Splendid his vestments,
As the east wind is the speech of the timorous,
Who would arrange for long and pleasant day,
Short be the darkness, a single night,
Let the toughness of the pia and teve†
And of the chosen warriors be shown.
At the root of the cocoa-tree I will wait,
Till a branch‡ shall spring forth,
To feed the visitors of divine Tumataroa in Ai-tupo,§

---

* A mountain near Borabora.   † Two native plants.   ‡ A good victim.   § A temple in Raiatea, to which the first taken or slain in battle was conveyed.

A small blow shall be a blow like the water-spout of the sea,
A blow to the rear of the army,
Shall be seen by thee before my face.
O god of earth, O god of ocean,
Let the armament be firm and true,
Only the worthless fly;
Let us (or may we) stand as the coral rock,
Move on terrific as the sea hedge-hog,
A corpulent and short-breathed fellow (is our opponent)
We shall obtain the passes;
Be as the large savage dog, turn not from blows.
Our defence (or steadiness) in battle shall be as that of the flock of birds,
Who sleep at sea in the midst of the storm.
Recite the song of battle,
Be courageous, be vigilant and strong;
Leave the dead among the dead,
Urge on the collected (or united) spears of bold warriors.

The annexed little fragment is from a song descriptive of one of the small islands near Maufiti, the westernmost of the Society Islands

Song of Tanatua.

A dwelling remote is the island Tiapa*,
A land whence appears well Maupiti,
Unequalled among the thousands of lands;
Easy is the access to Tuanai,†
Elevated is the (rock) Tauraura,
The eating-place of Oubuore;
Where the point of land meets the coral reef.
Cease to weep, great Ipo,
Here is beautiful Maupiti,
O the waters of Atimo,
Ane also at Maupiti.

Their traditionary ballads were a kind of standard, or classical authority, to which they referred, for the purpose of determining any disputed fact in their history. The fidelity of public recitals referring to former events, was sometimes

* A small island near Maupiti.   † An island.

questioned by the orators or chroniclers of the party opposed to that by whom the recital had been made. The disputes which followed, were often carried on with great pertinacity and determination. As they had no records to which they could at such times refer, they could only oppose one oral tradition to another, which unavoidably involved the parties in protracted, and often obstinate debates. At such times, a reference to some distich, in any of their popular and historic songs, often set the matter in dispute at rest. On a recent occasion, two parties were disputing in reference to an event which occurred in the bay of Papara during the time Captain Bligh remained there in the Bounty, in 1788 or 1789. The fact questioned was the loss of the buoy of his anchor: after disputing it for some time without convincing his opponent, the individual who had stated the fact, referred to the following lines in one of their ballads, relating that event:

> *O mea eiá e Tareu eiá*
> *Eiá te poito a Bligh.*

Such an one a thief, and Tareu a thief,
Thieved (or stole) the buoy of Bligh.

The song was one well known, and the existence of this fact, among the others that had taken place, and the remembrance of which the ballad was designed to preserve, was conclusive, and appeared to satisfy the parties by whom it had been questioned. Most of their historical events were thus preserved. These songs were exceedingly popular for a time. The facts on which they were grounded became thus generally known; and they were, undoubtedly, one of the most effectual means they had of preserving the knowledge of the leading events of former times.

Freed in a great degree, so far as the means of subsistence were concerned, from anxiety and labour, the islanders were greatly devoted to amusement, for which *heiva* was the general name, though voyagers have restricted that term to their dances. By the natives, *heiva* was applied to most of their amusements, hence they spoke of the *heiva-maona*, wrestling, *heiva-moto*, boxing, *heiva-vivo*, flute-playing, *heiva-ude*, singing, *heiva-haapee uo*, kite-flying, and *heiva-tea*, archery: war, pagan-worship, and pleasure, appear to have engaged their attention, and occupied the principal portion of their time. Their games were numerous and diversified, and were often affairs of national importance. They do not appear ever to have been gamblers, or to have accompanied any of their sports with betting, or staking property upon success, as the Sandwich Islanders have done from the earliest periods of their history, but seem to have followed their games simply for amusement.

The Taupıti, or Oroa, was generally a season of public festivity, when thousands of both sexes, arrayed in splendid garments, assembled to witness the games. These festivals were usually connected with some religious ceremony, or cause of national rejoicing. The return of the king from a tour, or the arrival of a distinguished visitor, were among the most ordinary occasions of these games. Wrestling was the favourite, and perhaps most frequent sport; hence the taupiti, or assembly, was often called the taupiti maona, assembly for wrestling. A large quantity of food was always prepared, and generally served out to the different parties, at the commencement of the festival, whereby the banquet was concluded before the games began. The wrestlers of one district sometimes challenged those of another, but the trial of strength and skill often took place between the inhabitants of different islands; the servants of the king of the island forming one band, and those in the train of his guest the other.

In this, as in most of their public proceedings, the gods presided. Before wrestling commenced, each party repaired to the marae of the idols of which they were the devotees. Here they presented a young plantain-tree, which was frequently a substitute for a more valuable offering, and having invoked aid of the tutelar deity of the game, they repaired to the spot where the multitude had assembled. A space covered with a grassy turf, or the level sands of the sea-beach, was usually selected for these exhibitions. Here a ring was formed, perhaps thirty feet in diameter, the aufenua, people of the country, being on one side, the visitors on the other. The inner rank sat down, the others stood behind them; each party had their instruments of music with them, but all remained quiet until the games began. Six or ten, perhaps, from each side, entered the ring at once, wearing nothing but the maro or girdle, and having their limbs sometimes anointed with oil.

The fame of a celebrated wrestler was usually spread throughout the islands, and those who were considered good wrestlers, priding themselves upon their strength or skill, were desirous of engaging only with those they regarded as their equals. Hence, when a chief was expected, in whose train were any distinguished wrestlers, those among the adherents of the chief, by whom the party was to be entertained, who wished to engage, were accustomed to send a challenge previous to their arrival. If this, which was called tipaopao, had been the case when they entered the ring, they closed at once, without ceremony. But if no such arrangement had been made, the wrestlers of one party, or perhaps their champion, walked around and across the ring, having the left arm bent, with the hand on the breast; and gave the challenge by striking the right hand violently against the left, and the left against the side, which produced a loud hollow sound. The strokes on the arm were sometimes so violent, as not only to bruise the flesh, but to cause the blood to gush out.

When the challenge was accepted, the antagonists closed, and the most intense interest was manifested by the parties to which they respectively belonged. Several were sometimes engaged at once, but more frequently only two. They grasped each other by the shoulders, and exerted all their strength and art, each to throw his rival; this was all that was requisite; and although they generally grappled with each other, this was not necessary according to the rules of the game. Mape, a stout, and rather active, though not a large man, who was often in my house at Eimeo, was a famous wrestler. He was seen in the ring once, with a remarkably tall heavy man, who was his antagonist; they had grappled and separated, when Mape walked carelessly towards his rival, and on approaching him, instead of stretching out his arms as was expected, he ran the crown of his head with all his might against the temple of his antagonist, and laid him flat on the earth.

Unbroken silence and deep attention was manifested during the struggle; but as soon as one was thrown, the scene was instantly changed; the vanquished was scarcely stretched on the sand, when a shout of exultation burst from the victor's friends. Their drums struck up; the women rose, and danced in triumph over the fallen wrestler, and sung in defiance to the opposite party. These were neither silent nor unmoved spectators, but immediately commenced a most deafening noise, partly in honour of their own clan or tribe, but principally to mar and neutralize the triumph of the victors. It is not easy to imagine the scenes that must often have been presented at one of their taupitis, or great wrestling matches, when not less than four or five thousand persons, dressed in their best apparel, and exhibiting every variety of costume and brillancy of colour, were under the influence of excitement. One party were drumming, dancing, and singing, in the pride of victory, and the menace of defiance; while, to increase the din and confusion, the other party were equally vociferous in reciting the achievements of the vanquished, or predicting the shortness of his rival's triumph.

However great the clamour might be, as soon as the wrestlers who remained in the ring engaged again, the drums ceased, the song was discontinued, and the dancers sat down. All was perfectly silent, and the issue of the second struggle was awaited with as great an intensity of interest as the first. If the vanquished man had a friend or taio in the ring, he usually arose, and challenged the victor, who having gained one triumph, either left the ring, which it was considered honourable for him to do, or remained and awaited a fresh challenge. If he had retired, two fresh combatants engaged, and when one was thrown, exhibitions of feeling, corresponding with those that had attended the conclusion of the first struggle, were renewed, and followed every successive engagement. When the contest was over the men repaired again to the temple, and presented their offering of acknowledgment, usually young plantain trees, to the idols of the game.

There are a number of men still living, who, under the system of idolatry, were celebrated as wrestlers through the whole of the islands. Among these, Fenuapeho, the hardy chieftain of Tahaa, is perhaps the most distinguished. He is not a large man, but broad, strong, sinewy, and remarkably firm-built. In person he appears to have been adapted to excel in such kinds of savage sports.

Although wrestling was practised principally by the men, it was not confined to them. Often, when they had done, the women contended, sometimes with each other, and occasionally with men, who were not perhaps reputed wrestlers. Persons in the highest rank sometimes engaged in the sport; and the sister of the queen has been seen wearing nearly the same clothing as the wrestlers wore, covered all over with sand, and wrestling with a young chief, in the midst of a ring, around which thousands of the people were assembled.

On all great festivals, wrestling was succeeded by the Moto-raa, or Boxing. This does not appear to have been so favourite an amusement with the Tahitians as wrestling; and there was generally a smaller number to engage. It was mostly practised by the lower orders and servants of the Areois, and was with them, as boxing is every where, savage work; though, considering the rude and barbarous state of the people, who had little idea of influence or power, but as connected with their gods, or with mere brute strength, we are not surprised that it should have existed. The challenge was given in the same way as in wrestling; but when the combatants engaged, the combat was much sooner ended, and no time was spent in sparring or parrying the blows. These were generally straight-forward, severe, and heavy; usually aimed at the head. They fought with the naked fist, and the whole skin of the forehead has been at times torn or driven off at a blow. No one interfered with the combatants while engaged; but as soon as either of them fell, or stooped, or shunned his antagonist, he was considered vanquished, the battle closed, and was instantly succeeded by the shouts and dances of triumph.

These barbarous sports, though generally followed by the common people, were not confined to them; other classes sometimes engaged; chiefs and priests were often among the most famous boxers and wrestlers. These games were not only dreadfully barbarous, but demoralizing in their influence on the people, who would set up a shriek of exultation when the blood started, or the vanquished fell senseless on the sand. They were also often fatal. *Metia, a taura no Oro,* priest of Oro, who resided at Matavai, was celebrated for his prowess, and slew two antagonists, a father and a son, at one of these festivals, in Taiarapu. Considering the brutalizing tendency and the fatal results of boxing and wrestling, we cannot but rejoice that they have ceased with that system of barbarism, licentiousness, and cruelty with which they were associated, and by which they were supported.

Connected with these athletic sports was another, less objectionable than either. This was the *faatitiaihe-mo raa*, or foot-race, in which the young men of the opposite parties engaged. Great preparation was made for this trial of strength and agility. The bodies of the runners were anointed with oil; the *maro*, or girdle, the only garment they wore, was bound tight round the loins. A wreath of flowers adorned the brows, and a light white or coloured bandage of native cloth was sometimes bound like a turban round the head. A smooth line of sandy beach was usually selected for the course. Sometimes they returned to the place from which they had started, but in general they ran the prescribed distance in a straight line. One of these races took place at Afareaitu while we resided there. It was between one of the king's servants, and a young man recently arrived from the Pearl Islands. The stranger was a tall, thin, handsome young man; and, as they walked past my house to the course, the people in general seemed to think his rival had but little prospect of equalling the swiftness of his speed, and it was thought he had already secured the *re*, or prize. The result, however, disappointed their expectations; and, as the spectators returned, I learned that, although on the first effort it was impossible to determine to whom the prize belonged, after repeated trials it was adjudged to Pomare's domestic. The *faatitiaihe-mo raa vaa*, or canoe-race, was occasionally practised on the smooth waters of the ocean, within the reefs, and appeared to afford a high degree of satisfaction.

Their martial games were numerous; and to these preparatory sports, the youth paid great attention. The *moto*, or boxing, and the *maona*, or wrestling, were regarded as a sort of military drilling; but the *vero patia*, throwing the spear or javelin, and the practice of throwing stones from a sling, were the principal military games. In the latter, the Tahitians excelled most of the nations of the Pacific; devoting to its practice a considerable portion of their time, and being able to cast the stone with great accuracy.

Throwing the spear, or darting the javelin, was an amusement in which they passed many of their juvenile hours. It was not a mere exercise of strength, like that exhibited in shooting with the bow and arrow, but a trial of skill. The stalk, or stem, of a plantain tree was their usual mark or target. This they fixed perpendicularly in the ground; and, retiring to a spot a number of yards distant, endeavoured to strike the mark with their missiles. These, thrown with precision and force, readily penetrated its soft and yielding substance. Although this was with some a favourite amusement, the Tahitians do not appear to have followed it with such avidity as the Sandwich Islanders were accustomed to do, nor to have made such proficiency in the art. In order to avoid accidents while practising with the sling, the boys generally employed the fruit of the nono, *morinda citrifolia*, instead of a stone. The mark at which they threw was a thin cane, or small white stick, fixed erect in the ground; and the force and precision with which it was repeatedly struck, were truly astonishing.

Besides these games, they often had what might be termed reviews of their land and naval forces.

In these, all the appendages of battle were exhibited on land, and the fleets were equipped as in maritime war. The fighting men, in both exhibitions, wore the dress and bore the arms employed in actual combat. They also performed their different evolutions, in attack and defence, advance and retreat. Sham-fights were connected with these displays of naval or military parade. In their mock engagements, they threw the spear, thrust the lance, parried the club, and at length, with deafening shouts, mingled in general and promiscuous struggle. Some of the combatants were thrown, others captured, and the respective parties retreated to renew the contest.

Their naval reviews often exhibited a spectacle, which to them was remarkably imposing. Ninety or a hundred canoes were, on these occasions, ranged in a line along the beach, ready to be launched in a moment. Their elevated and often curiously carved stems, their unwieldy bulk, the raised and guarded platform for the fighting men, the motley group assembled there, bearing their singularly and sometimes fantastically shaped weapons, the numerous folds of native cloth that formed their cumbrous dress, their high, broad turbans, the lofty sterns of their vessels, grotesque and rudely carved, together with the broad streamers floating in the breeze, combined to inspire them with the most elevated ideas of their naval prowess. The effect thus produced was heightened by the appearance of the sacred canoes, bearing the images or the emblems of the gods, the flag of the gods, and the officiating or attending priests. Often, while the vessels were thus ranged along the beach, the king stood in a small one, drawn by a number of his men, who walked in the sea.

In front of each canoe he paused, and addressed a short harangue to the warriors, and an *ubu*, or invocation, to the gods. After this was ended, at a signal given, the whole fleet was in a moment launched upon the ocean, and pulled with rapidity and dexterity to a considerable distance from the shore, where the several varieties of their naval tactics were exhibited; after which, they returned in regular order, with precision, to the shore.

Many of their games were most laborious. One at which the men played, called *apai*, or *paipai*, resembled a sport in some parts denominated "bandy." A similar game, called *palican*, was formerly a frequent amusement among the aborigines of South America, and those inhabiting the northern parts of the same continent, even as far as Canada. A ball is provided, and the players are furnished with sticks about three or four feet long, bent at one end; with these they strike the ball, each party endeavouring to send it beyond the boundary mark of their opponents. The ball is made with tough shreds of native cloth, tightly knotted together. The sticks used by the Tahitians were rude and unpolished, just as they were cut from the tree; but those used by the inhabitants of the Southern Islands are made with the *aito*, or iron-wood, the handle wrought with great care, and sometimes curiously carved, while a round protuberance is formed at the lower end, which, being slightly curved, augments the force with which they strike the ball.

The *tuiraa*, or foot-ball, is also a frequent game, followed more by the women than the men. Whole districts engaged in this amusement. In the former, they only struck the ball with a stick; in this, they employed the foot, and each party endeavoured to send it beyond the opposite boundary line, which had been marked out before they began. When either party succeeded in this, the air was rent with their shouts of success.

The *haru raa puu*, seizing of the ball, was however the favourite game of this kind. The females alone engaged in the seizing of the ball; in projecting which, neither sticks nor feet were allowed to be applied. An open place was necessary for all their sports, and the sea-beach was usually selected. The boundary mark of each party was fixed by a stone on the beach, or some other object on the shore, having a space of fifty or a hundred yards between. The ball was a large roll or bundle of the tough stalks of the plantain leaves twisted closely and firmly together. They began in the centre of the space. One party, seizing the ball, endeavoured to throw it over the boundary mark of the other. As soon as it was thrown, both parties started after it, and, in stooping to seize it, a scramble often ensued among those who first reached the ball; the numbers increased as the others came up, and they frequently fell one over the other in the greatest confusion. Amidst the shouts, and din, and disorder that followed, arms or legs were sometimes broken before the ball was secured. As the pastime was usually followed on the beach, the ball was often thrown to the sea; here it was fearlessly followed, and, with all the noise and cheering of the different parties, forty or fifty women might sometimes be seen, up to their knees or their waists in the water, splashing and plunging amid the foam and spray, after the object of their pursuit. These are only some of the games that were followed by the adults, at their great meetings or national festivals. In these, and in feasting, the hours of the day were spent.

Their dances were numerous and diversified; and were performed by men and women—in many the parties did not dance together. Their movements were generally slow, but regular and exact; the arms, during their dances, were exercised as much as their feet. The drum and the flute were the music by which they were led; and the dance was usually accompanied by songs and ballads. Ori is the native word for dance, but each kind of dance had a distinct name. The least objectionable was the *hura*, which appears to have been the kind of dance witnessed by Captain Cook in Huahine. The hura was sometimes a pantomimic exhibition, with dancing at intervals during the performance; but the most decent and respectable was that which consisted principally of dancing. It was practised from a motive which many will think manifested a decisive elevation above savage life. The families of the distinguished chiefs in the neighbourhood were always invited to witness the hura. They usually came arrayed in their best apparel, followed by numbers of their attendants. It was generally designed to bring into notice the daughters of the chiefs, and recommend them to young men of rank and station equal or superior to their own, who, it was hoped, might be so charmed by their dancing, as to become their future husbands.

The daughters of the chiefs, who were the dancers on these occasions, at times amounted to five or six, though occasionally only one exhibited her symmetry of figure, and gracefulness of action. Their dress was singular, but elegant.

The head was ornamented with tamau, a fine and beautiful braid of human hair, wound round the head in the form of a turban.* A triple wreath of scarlet, white, and yellow flowers, composed of the aute, the fragrant gardenia, or Cape jessamine, and the beslaria laurifolia, tastefully interwoven, adorned the curious head-dress. The tahema, a loose vest of spotted cloth, covered the lower part of the bosom. The tihi, of fine white stiffened cloth, frequently edged with a scarlet border, gathered like a large frill, passed under the arms, and reached below the waist; while the araitihi, a handsome fine cloth, fastened round the waist with a band or sash, covered the feet. The breasts were ornamented with rainbow-coloured mother-of-pearl shells, or the pii, which was a covering of curiously wrought net-work and feathers.

The music of the hura was the large and small drum, and occasionally the flute. Besides the musicians, the haapii, teacher or prompter, was an important personage. He was attired in three or four finely fringed mats, fastened round his waist, and stood or sat near the mat on which the dancers stood. His business was, by the expression of his countenance and the action of his hands, to direct the performers. Their dancing was not lively and nimble, and seldom could those engaged be said to trip

On the light fantastic toe.

Their movements were generally slow, but always easy and natural, and no exertion, on the part of the performers, was wanting, to render them graceful

* Mr. Barff, to whom I am indebted for the principal part of this account, procured a head-dress of this kind, containing one hundred fathoms of the finest braided human hair.

and attractive. Besides the distinguished females who performed the hura, there were others who were regarded as appendages to the exhibition. These were the faata, who were men, generally four in number, who were arrayed in fringed mats, fastened round the waist, and each was a sort of clown or harlequin. Their business was, during the intervals between the different parts of the hura, to dance in the most comic and ludicrous manner, for the mirth of the spectators. They were called *ei ataraa na te mataitai*—cause of laughter to the lookers on. The heva tiaraau was another dance, inferior to the hura, and not more objectionable. There were many others, but they were all too indelicate or obscene to be noticed. These were sometimes held in the open air, but more frequently performed under the cover of the houses, erected in most of the districts for public entertainments. These structures were frequently spacious, and well built; consisting of a roof supported by pillars, without any shelter for the sides. A low fence, called *aumoa*, surrounded the house; and the inside was covered with mats, on which the company sat and the dancers performed. The *patau,* or prompter, sat by the drum, and regulated the several parts of the performance. After the athletic exercises of the day, the dances ensued in the evening, and were often continued till the dawn of the following morning. There were gods supposed to preside over their dances, whose sanction patronized the debasing immoralities connected with them.

The *te-a*, or archery, was also a sacred game, more so, perhaps, than any other; it was also called heiva te-a, play, or amusement of archery. The bows, arrows, quiver, and cloth in which they were kept together, with the dresses worn by the archers, were all sacred, and under the special care of persons appointed to keep them. It was usually practised as a most honourable recreation, between the residents of a place and their guests The sport was generally followed either at the foot of a mountain, or on the sea-shore. My house, in the valley of Haamene at Huahine, stood very near an ancient *vahi te-a*, a place of archery. Before commencing the game, the parties repaired to the marae, and performed several ceremonies; after which, they put on the archers' dress, and proceeded to the place appointed. They did not shoot at a mark; it was therefore only a trial of strength. In a place to which they shot the arrows, two small white flags were displayed, between which the arrows were directed.

The bows were made of the light, tough wood of the *purau;* and were, when unstrung, perfectly straight, about five feet long; an inch, or an inch and a quarter, in diameter in the centre, but smaller at the ends. They were neatly polished, and sometimes ornamented with finely braided human hair, or cord of the fibres of cocoa-nut husk, wound round the ends of the bow in alternate rings. The string was of *romaha*, or native flax; the arrows were small bamboo reeds, exceedingly light and durable. They were pointed with a piece of *aito*, or iron-wood, but were not barbed. Their arrows were not feathered; but, in order to their being firmly held while the string was drawn, the lower end was covered with a resinous gum from the bread-fruit tree. The length of the arrows varied from two feet six inches to three feet. The spot from which they were shot was considered sacred; there was one of these within my garden at Huahine. It was a stone pile, about three or four feet high, of a triangular form, one side of the angle being convex.

When the preparations were completed, the archer ascended this platform, and, kneeling on one knee, drew the string of the bow with the right hand, till the head of the arrow touched the centre of the bow, when it was discharged with great force. It was an effort of much strength in this position to draw the bowstring so far. The line often broke, and the bow fell from the archer's hand when the arrow was discharged. The distance to which it was shot, though various, was frequently three hundred yards. A number of men, from three to twelve, with small white flags in their hands, were stationed, to watch the arrows in their fall. When those of one party went farther than those of the other, they waved the flags as a signal to the party below. When they fell short, they held down their flags, but lifted up their foot, exclaiming *uau pau*, beaten.

This was a sport in the highest esteem, the king and chiefs usually attending to witness the exercise. As soon as the game was finished, the bow, with the quiver of arrows, was delivered to the charge of a proper person: the archers repaired to the marae, and were obliged to exchange their dress, and bathe their persons, before they could take refreshment, or enter their dwellings. It is astonishing to notice how intimately their system of religion was interwoven with every pursuit of their lives. Their wars, their labours, and their amusements, were all under the control of their gods. Paruatetavae was the god of archers.

The arrows they employed were sometimes beautifully stained and variegated. The bows were plain, but the quivers were often elegant in shape and appearance. They were made with the single joint of a bamboo cane, three feet six or nine inches long, and about two inches in diameter. The outside was sometimes handsomely stained, and finely polished at the top and the bottom they were adorned with braided cord, and plaited human hair. The cap or cover of the quiver was a small, handsome, well-formed cocoa-nut, of a dark brown chocolate colour, highly polished, and attached to the quiver by a cord passing up the inner side of the quiver, and fastened near the bottom.

The bow and arrow were never used by the Society Islanders excepting in their amusements; hence, perhaps, their arrows, though pointed, were not barbed, and they did not shoot at a mark. In throwing the spear, and the stone from the sling, both of which they used in battle, they were accustomed to set up a mark; and practised, that they might throw with precision, as well as force. In the Sandwich Islands, they are used also as an amusement, especially in shooting rats, but are not included in their accoutrements for battle; while in the Friendly Islands, the bow was not only employed on occasions of festivity, but also used in war; this, however, may have arisen from their proximity to the Feejee Islands, where it is a general weapon. In the Society and Sandwich Islands, it is now altogether laid aside, in consequence of its connexion with their former idolatry. I do not think the Missionaries ever inculcated its discontinuance, but the adults do not appear to have thought of following this, or any other game, since Christianity has been introduced among them.

CHAP. IX.

Cockfighting—Aquatic sports—Swimming in the surf—Danger from sharks—Juvenile amusements—Account of the Areois, the institution peculiar to the inhabitants of the Pacific—Antiquity of the Areoi society—Tradition of its origin—Account of its founders—Infanticide enjoined with its establishment—General character of the Areois—Their voyages—Public dances—Buildings for their accommodation—Marine exhibitions—Oppression and injury occasioned by their visits—Distinction of rank among them—Estimation in which they are held—Mode of admission—Ceremonies attending advancement to the higher orders—Demoralizing nature of their usages—Singular rites at their death and interment—Description of Rohutunoanoa, the Areois heaven—Reflections on the baneful tendency of the Areoi society, and its dissolution.

The most ancient, but certainly not the most innocent game among the Tahitians, was the *faatitoraamoa*, literally, the causing fighting among fowls, or cock-fighting. The traditions of the people state, that fowls have existed in the islands as long as the people, that they came with the first colonists by whom the islands were peopled, or that they were made by Taaroa at the same time that men were made. The traditions and songs of the islanders, connected with their amusements, are as ancient as any in existence among them. The Tahitians do not appear to have staked any property, or laid any bets, on their favourite birds, but to have trained and fought them for the sake of the gratification they derived from beholding them destroy each other. Long before the first foreign vessel was seen off their shores, they were accustomed to train and to fight their birds. The fowls designed for fighting were fed with great care; a finely carved *fatapua*, or stand, was made as a perch for the birds. This was planted in the house, and the bird fastened to it by a piece of cinet, braided flat that it might not injure the leg. No other substance would have been secure against the attacks of his beak. Their food was chiefly *poe*, or bruised bread-fruit, rolled up in the hand like paste, and given in small pieces. The fowl was taught to open his mouth to receive his food and his water, which was poured from his master's hand. It was also customary to sprinkle water over these birds to refresh them.

The natives were universally addicted to this sport. The inhabitants of one district often matched their birds against those of another, or those of one division of a district against those of another. They do not appear to have entertained any predilection for particular colour in the fowls, but seem to have esteemed all alike. They never trimmed any of the feathers, but were proud to see them with heavy wings, full-feathered necks, and long tails. They also accustomed them to fight without artificial spurs, or other means of injury. In order that the birds might be as fresh as possible, they fought them early in the morning, soon after day-break, while the air was cool, and before they became languid from heat. More than two were seldom engaged at once, and so soon as one bird avoided the other, he was considered as *vi*, or beaten. Victory was declared in favour of his opponent, and they were immediately parted. This amusement was sometimes continued for several days successively, and, as well as the other recreations, was patronized by their idols. Ruaifaatoa, the god of cockfighters, appears among the earliest of their inferior divinities.

Like the inhabitants of most of the islands of the Pacific, the Tahitians are fond of the water, and lose all dread of it before they are old enough to know the danger to which we should consider them exposed. They are among the best divers in the world, and spend much of their time in the sea, not only when engaged in acts of labour, but when following their amusements. One of their favourite sports is the *horue* or *faahee*, swimming in the surf, when the waves are high, and the billows break in foam and spray among the reefs. Individuals of all ranks and ages, and both sexes, follow this pastime with the greatest avidity. They usually selected the openings in the reefs, or entrances of some of the bays, for their sport; where the long heavy billows of the ocean rolled in unbroken majesty upon the reef or the shore. They used a small board, which they called *papa fahee*—swam from the beach to a considerable distance, sometimes nearly a mile, watched the swell of the wave, and when it reached them, resting their bosom on the short flat pointed board, they mounted on its summit, and, amid the foam and spray, rode on the crest of the wave to the shore: sometimes they halted among the coral rocks, over which the waves broke in splendid confusion. When they approached the shore, they slid off the board which they grasped with the hand, and either fell behind the wave, or plunged toward the deep, and allowed it to pass over their heads. Sometimes they were thrown with violence upon the beach, or among the rocks on the edges of the reef. So much at home, however, do they feel in the water, that it is seldom any accident occurs.

I have often seen, along the border of the reef forming the boundary line to the harbour of Fa-re, in Huahine, from fifty to a hundred persons, of all ages, sporting like so many porpoises in the surf, sometimes mounted on the top of the wave, and almost enveloped in spray; at other times plunging beneath the mass of water that has swept in mountains over them, cheering and animating each other; and, by the noise and shouting they made, rendering the roaring of the sea, and the dashing of the surf, comparatively imperceptible. Their surf-boards are inferior to those of the Sandwich Islanders, and I do not think swimming in the sea as an amusement, whatever it might have been formerly, is now practised so much by the natives in the south, as by those in the north Pacific. Both were exposed in this sport to one common cause of interruption; and this was, the intrusion of the shark. The cry of a *mao* among the former, and a *manò* among the latter, is one of the most terrific they ever hear; and I am not surprised that such should be the effect of the approach of one of these voracious monsters. The great shouting and clamour which they make, is principally designed to frighten away such as may approach. Notwithstanding this, they are often disturbed and sometimes meet their death from these formidable enemies.

A most affecting instance of this kind occurred very recently in the Sandwich Islands, of which the following account is given by Mr. Richards, and published in the American Missionary Herald:

"At nine o'clock in the morning of June 14th, 1826, while sitting at my writing-desk, I heard a simultaneous scream from multitudes of people, *Pau i ka mano! Pau i ka mano!* "Destroyed by the shark! Destroyed by the shark!" The beach was instantly lined by hundreds of persons, and a few of the most resolute threw a large canoe into the water, and, alike regardless of the shark and the high rolling surf, sprang to the relief of their companion. It was too late. The shark had already seized his prey. The affecting sight was only a few yards from my door, and while I stood watching, a large wave almost filled the canoe, and at the same instant a part of the mangled body was seen at the bow of the canoe, and the shark swimming towards it at her stern. When the swell had rolled by, the water was too shallow for the shark to swim. The remains, therefore, were taken into the canoe, and brought ashore. The water was so much stained by the blood, that we discovered a red tinge in all the foaming billows, as they approached the beach.

"The unhappy sufferer was an active lad about fourteen years old, who left my door only about half an hour previous to the fatal accident. I saw his mother, in the extremity of her anguish, plunge into the water, and swim towards the bloody spot, entirely forgetful of the power of her former god.

"A number of people, perhaps a hundred, were at this time playing in the surf, which was higher than usual. Those who were nearest to the victim heard him shriek, perceived him to strike with his right hand, and at the same instant saw a shark seize his arm. Then followed the cry which I heard, which echoed from one end of Lahaina to the other. All who were playing in the water made the utmost speed to the shore, and those who were standing on the beach saw the surf-board of the unhappy sufferer floating on the water, without any one to guide it. When the canoe reached the spot, they saw nothing but the blood with which the water was stained for a considerable distance, and by which they traced the remains, whither they had been carried by the shark, or driven by the swell. The body was cut in two by the shark, just above the hips; and the lower part, together with the right arm, were gone.

"Many of the people connect this death with their old system of religion; for they have still a superstitious veneration for the shark, and this veneration is increased rather than diminished by such occurrences as these.

"It is only about four months since a man was killed in the same manner at Waihee, on the eastern part of this island. It is said, however, that there are much fewer deaths by the sharks than formerly. This, perhaps, may be owing to their not being so much fed by the people, and therefore they do not visit the shores so frequently."

Besides the *faahee*, or surf-swimming, of which Huaouri was the presiding god, and in which the adults principally engaged, there were a number of aquatic pastimes peculiar to the children, among these, the principal was erecting a kind of stage near the margin of a deep part of the sea or river, leaping from the highest elevation into the sea, and chasing each other in the water, diving to an almost incredible depth, or skimming along the surface. Large companies of children, from nine or ten to fifteen or sixteen years of age, have often been seen, the greater part of the forenoon, eagerly following this apparently dangerous game, with the most perfect confidence of safety. Another amusement, which appears to afford high satisfaction to the children of the islanders, is the construction of small canoes, boats, or ships, and floating them in the sea. Although they are rude in appearance, and soon destroyed, many of the boys display uncommon ingenuity in constructing this kind of toy. The hull is usually made with a piece of light wood of the hibiscus, the cordage of bark, and the sails are either of the leaflets of the cocoa-nut, or the native cloth. The owners of these little vessels frequently go in small parties, and, taking their small-craft in their hands, wade up to their waist or arm-pits in the sea, and sometimes swim still further out; and then, launching their miniature fleets, consisting of ships, brigs, sloops, boats, canoes, &c. return towards the shore. They usually fix a piece of stone at the bottom of the little barks, which keeps them upright; and as the wind wafts them along the bay, their owners run along up to their knees in the sea, splashing and shouting as they watch their progress.

Such were some of the amusements of the natives in the South Sea Islands. In these, when not engaged in war, they spent much of their time. There were also others, of a less athletic kind, and of less universal prevalence. Among these, the *aperea* was one of the most prevalent; it consisted in jerking a reed, two feet and a half or three feet in length, along the ground. The men seldom played at it, but it was a common diversion for the women and children. *Timo*, or *timotimo*, was another game with the same class. The parties sat on the ground, with a heap of stones by their side, held a small round stone in the right hand, which they threw several feet up into the air, and, before it fell, took up one of the stones from the heap, which they held in the right hand till they caught that which they had thrown up, when they threw down the stone they had taken up, tossed the round stone again, and continued taking up a fresh stone every time they threw the small round one into the air, until the whole heap was removed. The *teatea mata* was a singular play among the children, who stretched open their eyelids by fixing a piece of straw, or stiff grass, perpendicularly across the eye, so as to force open the lids in a most frightful manner. Tupaurupauru, a kind of blind-man's-buff, was also a favourite juvenile sport.

They were very fond of the *tahoro*, or swing, and frequently suspended a rope from the branch of a lofty tree, and spent hours in swinging backwards and forwards. They used the rope singly, and at the lower end fastened a short stick, which was thus suspended in a horizontal position; upon this stick they sat, and, holding by the rope, were drawn or pushed backwards and forwards by their companions. Walking in stilts was also a favourite amusement with the youth of both sexes. The stilts were formed by nature, and generally consisted of the straight branches of a tree, with a smaller branch projecting on one side. Their naked feet were placed on this short branch, and thus elevated about three feet from the ground, they pursued their pastime.

The boys were very fond of the *uo*, or kite, which they raised to a great height. The Tahitian kite was different in shape from the kites of the English boys. It was made of light native cloth instead of paper, and formed in shape according to the fancy of its owner.

These are only some of the principal games or amusements of the natives; others might be added, but these are sufficient to shew that they were not destitute of sources of entertainment, either in their juvenile or more advanced periods of life. With the exception of one or two, they have all, however, been discontinued, especially among the adults; and the number of those followed by the children is greatly diminished. This is, on no account, matter of regret. Many were in themselves repulsive to every feeling of common decency, and all were intimately connected with practices inimical to individual chastity, domestic peace, and public virtue. When we consider the debasing tendency of many, and the inutility of others, we shall rather rejoice that much of the time of the adults is passed in more rational and beneficial pursuits. The practice of useful mechanic arts, of agriculture, and of fishing, are better adapted to preserve the robustness and vigour of their constitutions, and at the same time to exempt them from the moral evils of their games. Few, if any of them, are so sedentary in their habits, as to need these amusements for exercise; and they are not accustomed to apply so closely to any of their avocations, as to require them merely for relaxation.

The greatest source of amusement to the people, as a nation, was most probably the existence of a society, peculiar to the Islands of the Pacific, if not to the inhabitants of the southern groups. This was an institution called the Areoi society. Many of the regulations of this body, and the practices to which they were addicted, cannot be made public, without violence to every feeling of propriety; but, so far as it can be consistently done, it seems desirable to give some particulars respecting this most singular institution. Although I never met with an account of any institution analogous to this, among the barbarous nations in any parts of the world, I have reason to believe it was not confined to the Society group, and neighbouring islands. It does not appear to have existed in the Marquesas or Sandwich Islands; but the Jesuit Missionaries found an institution, bearing a striking resemblance to it, among the inhabitants of the Caroline or Ladrone Islands; a privileged fraternity, whose practices were, in many respects, similar to those of the Areois of the southern islands. They were called *uritoy;* which, omitting the *t*, would not be much unlike *areoi:* a greater difference exists in the pronunciation of words known to be radically the same.

How long this association has existed in the South Sea Islands, we have no means of ascertaining with correctness. According to the traditions of the people, its antiquity is equal to that of the system of pollution and error with which it was so intimately allied; and, by the same authority, we are informed that there have been Areois almost as long as there have been men. These, however, were all so fabulous, that we can only infer from them that the institution is of ancient origin According to the traditions of the people, Taaroa created, and, by means of Hina, brought forth when full grown, Orotetefa and Urutetefa. They were not his sons; *oriori* is the term employed by the people, which seems to mean *create.* They were called the brothers of Oro, and were numbered among the inferior divinities. They remained in a state of celibacy; and hence the devotees were required to destroy their offspring. The origin of the Areois institution is as follows.

Oro, the son of Taaroa, desired a wife from the daughters of Taata, the first man; he sent two of his brothers, Tufarapainuu and Tufarapairai, to seek among the daughters of man a suitable companion for him; they searched through the whole of the islands, from Tahiti to Borabora, but saw no one that they supposed fit to become the wife of Oro, till they came to Borabora. Here, residing near the foot of Mouatahuhuura, *red-ridged mountain,* they saw Vairaumati. When they beheld her, they said one to the other, This is the excellent woman for our brother. Returning to the skies, they hastened to Oro, and informed him of their success; told him they had found among the daughters of man a wife for him, described the place of her abode, and represented her as a *vahine purotu aiai,* a female possessed of every charm. The god fixed the rainbow in the heavens, one end of it resting in the valley at the foot of the red-ridged mountain, the other penetrating the skies, and thus formed his pathway to the earth.

When he emerged from the vapour, which, like a cloud, had encircled the rainbow, he discovered the dwelling of Vairaumati, the fair mistress of the cottage, who became his wife. Every evening he descended on the rainbow, and returned by the same pathway on the following morning to the heavenly regions. His wife bore a son, whom he called *Hoa-tabu-i-te-rai,* friend, sacred to the heavens. This son became a powerful ruler among men.

The absence of Oro from his celestial companions, during the frequent visits he made to the cottage of Vairaumati in the valley of Borabora, induced two of his younger brothers, Orotetefa and Urutetefa, to leave their abode in the skies, and commence a search after him. Descending by the rainbow in the position in which he had placed it, they alighted on the earth near the base of the red-ridged mountains, and soon perceived their brother and his wife in their terrestrial habitation. Ashamed to offer their salutations to him and his bride without a present, one of them was transformed on the spot into a pig, and a bunch of *uru,* or red feathers. These acceptable presents the other offered to the inmates of the dwelling, as a gift of congratulation. Oro and his wife expressed their satisfaction at the present; the pig and the feathers remained the same, but the brother of the god assumed his original form.

Such a mark of attention, on such an occasion, was considered by Oro to require some expression of his commendation. He accordingly made them gods, and constituted them Areois, saying, *Ei Areoi orua i te ao, nei, ia noaa ta orua tuhaa:* "Be you two Areois in this world, that you may have your portion, (in the government," &c.) In the commemoration of this ludicrous fable of the pig and the feathers, the Areois, in all the taupiti, and public festivals, carried a young pig to the temple; strangled it, bound it in the *ahu haio,* (a loose open kind of cloth,) and placed it on the altar. They also offered the red feathers, which they called the *uru maru no te Areoi,* "the shadowy uru of the Areoi," or the red feathers of the party of the Areoi.

It has been already stated that the brothers, who were made gods and kings of the Areois lived in celibacy; consequently they had no descendants. On this account, although they did not enjoin celibacy upon their devotees, they prohibited their having any offspring. Hence, one of the standing regulations of this institution was, the murder of their children. The first company, the legend states, were nominated, according to the Oro's direction, by Urutetefa and Orotetefa, and comprised the following individuals: Huatua, of Tahiti; Tauraatua, of Moorea, or Eimeo; Temaiatea, of Sir Charles Sanders' Island; Tetoa and Atae, of Huahine; Taramanini and Airipa, of Raiatea; Mutahaa, of Tahaa; Bunaruu, of Borabora; and Marore, of Maurua. These individuals, selected from the different islands, constituted the first Areoi society. To them, also, the gods whom Oro had placed over them delegated authority, to admit to their order all such as were desirous to unite with them, and consented to murder their infants.* These were always the names of the principal Areois in each of the islands; and were borne by them in the several islands at the time of their renouncing idolatry; when the Areois name, and Areois customs, were simultaneously discontinued.

It is a most gratifying fact, that some of those who bore these names, and were ringleaders in all the vice and cruelty connected with the system, have since been distinguished for their active benevolence, and moral and exemplary lives. Auna, one of the first deacons in the church at Huahine, one of the first native teachers sent out

* The above is one of the most regular accounts of the origin of the Areoi institution, extant among the people. Mr. Barff, to whom I am indebted for it, received it from Auna, and Mahine the king of Huahine.

by that church to the heathen, and who has been the minister of the church in Sir Charles Sanders Island, an indefatigable, upright, intelligent, and useful man, as a Christian Missionary in the South Sea Islands, was the principal Areoi of Raiatea. He was the Taramanini of that island, until he embraced Christianity.

They were a sort of strolling players, and privileged libertines, who spent their days in travelling from island to island, and from one district to another, exhibiting their pantomimes, and spreading a moral contagion throughout society. Great preparation was necessary before the *mareva*, or company, set out. Numbers of pigs were killed, and presented to Oro; large quantities of plantains and bananas, with other fruits, were also offered upon his altars. Several weeks were necessary to complete the preliminary ceremonies. The concluding parts of these consisted in erecting, on board their canoes, two temporary maraes, or temples, for the worship of Orotetefa and his brother, the tutelar deities of the society. This was merely a symbol of the presence of the gods; and consisted principally in a stone for each, from Oro's marae, and a few red feathers from the inside of the sacred image. Into these symbols the gods were supposed to enter when the priest pronounced a short *ubu*, or prayer, immediately before the sailing of the fleet. The numbers connected with this fraternity, and the magnitude of some of their expeditions, will appear from the fact of Cook's witnessing, on one occasion, in Huahine, the departure of seventy canoes filled with Areois.

On landing at the place of destination, they proceeded to the residence of the king or chief, and presented their *marotai*, or present; a similar offering was also sent to the temple and to the gods, as an acknowledgment for the preservation they had experienced at sea. If they remained in the neighbourhood, preparations were made for their dances and other performances.

On public occasions, their appearance was, in some respects, such as it is not proper to describe. Their bodies were painted with charcoal, and their faces, especially, stained with the *mati*, or scarlet dye. Sometimes they wore a girdle of the yellow *ti* leaves; which, in appearance, resembled the feather girdles of the Peruvians, or other South American tribes. At other times they wore a vest of ripe yellow plantain leaves, and ornamented their heads with wreaths of the bright yellow and scarlet leaves of the hutu, or *Barringtonia;* but, in general, their appearance was far more repulsive than when they wore these partial coverings.

Upaupa was the name of many of their exhibitions. In performing these, they sometimes sat in a circle on the ground, and recited, in concert, a legend or song in honour of their gods, or some distinguished Areoi. The leader of the party stood in the centre, and introduced the recitation with a sort of prologue, when, with a number of fantastic movements and attitudes, those that sat around began their song in a low and measured tone and voice; which increased as they proceeded, till it became vociferous and unintelligibly rapid. It was also accompanied by movements of the arms and hands, in exact keeping with the tones of the voice, until they were wrought to the highest pitch of excitement. This they continued, until, becoming breathless and exhausted, they were obliged to suspend the performance.

Their public entertainments frequently consisted

in delivering speeches, accompanied by every variety of gesture and action; and their representations, on these occasions, assumed something of the histrionic character. The priests, and others, were fearlessly ridiculed in these performances, in which allusion was ludicrously made to public events. In the taupiti, or oroa, they sometimes engaged in wrestling, but never in boxing; that would have been considered too degrading for them. Dancing, however, appears to have been their favourite and most frequent performance. In this they were always led by the manager or chief. Their bodies, blackened with charcoal, and stained with mati, rendered the exhibition of their persons on these occasions most disgusting. They often maintained their dance through the greater part of the night, accompanied by their voices, and the music of the flute and the drum. These amusements frequently continued for a number of days and nights successively at the same place. The upaupa was then *hui*, or closed, and they journeyed to the next district, or principal chieftain's abode, where the same train of dances, wrestlings, and pantomimic exhibitions, was repeated.

Several other gods were supposed to preside over the upaupa, as well as the two brothers who were the guardian deities of the Areois. The gods of these diversions, according to the ideas of the people, were monsters in vice, and of course patronized every evil practice perpetrated during such seasons of public festivity.

Substantial, spacious, and sometimes highly ornamented houses, were erected in several districts throughout most of the islands, principally for their accommodation, and the exhibition of their performances. The house erected for this purpose, which we saw at Tiataepuaa, was one of the best in Eimeo. Sometimes they performed in their canoes, as they approached the shore; especially if they had the king of the island, or any principal chief, on board their fleet. When one of these companies thus advanced towards the land, with their streamers floating in the wind, their drums and flutes sounding, and the Areois, attended by their chief, who acted as their prompter, appeared on a stage erected for the purpose, with their wild distortions of person, antic gestures, painted bodies, and vociferated songs, mingling with the sound of the drum and the flute, the dashing of the sea, and the rolling and breaking of the surf, on the adjacent reef; the whole must have presented a ludicrous imposing spectacle, accompanied with a confusion of sight and sound, of which it is not very easy to form an adequate idea.

The above were the principal occupations of the Areois; and in the constant repetition of these, often obscene exhibitions, they passed their lives, strolling from the habitation of one chief to that of another, or sailing among the different islands of the group. The farmers did not in general much respect them; but the chiefs, and those addicted to pleasure, held them in high estimation, furnishing them with liberal entertainment, and sparing no property to gratify them. This often proved the cause of most unjust and cruel oppression to the poor cultivators. When a party of Areois arrived in a district, in order to provide daily a sumptuous entertainment for them, the chief would send his servants to the best plantations in the neighbourhood; and these grounds, without any ceremony, they plundered of whatever was fit for use. Such lawless acts of robbery were repeated every day, so long as the Areois continued in the district; and when they departed, the gardens often exhibited a scene of desolation and ruin, that, but for the influence of the chiefs, would have brought fearful vengeance upon those who had occasioned it.

A number of distinct classes prevailed among the Areois, each of which was distinguished by the kind or situation of the tatauing on their bodies. The first or highest class was called *Avae parai*, painted leg; the leg being completely blackened from the foot to the knee. The second class was called *Otiore*, both arms being marked, from the fingers to the shoulders. The third class was denominated *Harotea*, both sides of the body, from the arm-pits downwards, being marked with tatau. The fourth class, called *Hua*, had only two or three small figures, impressed with the same material, on each shoulder. The fifth class, called *Atoro*, had one small stripe, tataued on the left side. Every individual in the sixth class, designated *Ohemara*, had a small circle marked round each ankle. The seventh class, or *Poo*, which included all who were in their noviciate, was usually denominated the *Poo faarearea*, or pleasure-making class, and by them the most laborious part of the pantomimes, dances, &c. was performed; the principal or higher orders of Areois, though plastered over with charcoal, and stained with scarlet dye, were generally careful not to exhaust themselves by physical effort, for the amusement of others.

In addition to the seven regular classes of Areois, there were a number of individuals, of both sexes, who attached themselves to this dissipated and wandering fraternity, prepared their food and their dresses, performed a variety of servile occupations, and attended them on their journeys, for the purpose of witnessing their dances, or sharing in their banquets. These were called Fanaunau, because they did not destroy their offspring, which was indispensable with the regular members.

Although addicted to every kind of licentiousness themselves, each Areoi had his own wife, who was also a member of the society; and so jealous were they in this respect, that improper conduct towards the wife of one of their own number, was sometimes punished with death. This summary and fatal punishment was not confined to their society, but was sometimes inflicted, for the same crime, among other classes of the community.

Singular as it may appear, the Areoi institution was held in the greatest repute by the chiefs and higher classes; and, monsters of iniquity as they were, the grand masters, or members of the first order, were regarded as a sort of superhuman beings, and treated with a corresponding degree of veneration by many of the vulgar and ignorant. The fraternity was not confined to any particular rank or grade in society, but was composed of individuals from every class. But although thus accessible to all, the admission was attended with a variety of ceremonies; a protracted noviciate followed; and it was only by progressive advancement, that any were admitted to the superior distinctions.

It was imagined that those who became Areois were generally prompted or inspired to adopt this course by the gods. When any individual therefore wished to be admitted to their society, he repaired to some public exhibition, in a state of apparent *neneva*, or derangement. He generally wore a girdle of yellow plantain or *ti* leaves round his loins; his face was stained with *mati*, or scarlet dye; his brow decorated with a shade of curiously platted yellow cocoa-nut leaves; his hair perfumed with powerfully scented oil, and ornamented with a profusion of fragrant flowers. Thus arrayed, disfigured, and adorned, he rushed through the crowd assembled round the house in which the actors or dancers were performing, and, leaping into the circle, joined with seeming frantic wildness in the dance or pantomime. He continued in the midst of the performers until the exhibition closed. This was considered an indication of his desire to join their company; and if approved, he was appointed to wait, as a servant, on the principal Areois. After a considerable trial of his natural disposition, docility, and devotednesss in this occupation, if he persevered in his determination to join himself with them, he was inaugurated with all the attendant rites and observances.

This ceremony took place at some taupiti, or other great meeting of the body, when the principal Areoi brought him forth arrayed in the *ahu haio*, a curiously stained sort of native cloth, the badge of their order, and presented him to the members who were convened in full assembly. The Areois, as such, had distinct names, and, at his introduction, the candidate received from the chief of the body, the name by which in future he was to be known among them. He was now directed, in the first instance, to murder his children; a deed of horrid barbarity, which he was in general too ready to perpetrate. He was then instructed to bend his left arm, and strike his right hand upon the bend of the left elbow, which at the same time he struck against his side, whilst he repeated the song or invocation for the occasion; of which the following is a translation.

"The mountain above, *moua tabu*,* sacred mountain. The floor beneath *Tamapua*,† projecting point of the sea. *Manunu*, of majestic or kingly bearing forehead. *Teariitaria*,‡ the splendour of the sky. I am such a one, (pronouncing his new Areoi name,) of the mountain huruhuru." He was then commanded to seize the cloth worn by the chief woman present, and by this act he completed his initiation, and became a member, or one of the seventh class.

The lowest members of the society were the principal actors in all their exhibitions, and on them chiefly devolved the labour and drudgery of dancing and performing, for the amusement of the spectators. The superior classes led a life of dissipation and luxurious indolence. On this account, those who were novices continued a long time in the lower class; and were only admitted to the higher order, at the discretion of the leaders or grand masters.

The advancement of an Areoi from the lower classes, took place also at some public festival, when all the members of the fraternity in the island were expected to be present. Each individual appointed to receive this high honour, attended in the full costume of the order. The ceremonies

---

* The conical mountain near the lake of Maeva.

† The central district on the borders of the lake, lying at the foot of the mountain.

‡ The hereditary name of the king or highest chief of Huahine.

were commenced by the principal Areoi, who arose, and uttered an invocation to *Te buaa ra*, (which, I presume, must mean the sacred pig,) to the sacred company of *Tabutabuatea*, (the name of a principal national temple in Raiatea,) belonging to Taramanini, the chief Areoi of that island. He then paused, and another exclaimed, Give us such an individual, or individuals, mentioning the names of the party nominated for the intended elevation.

When the gods had been thus required to sanction their advancement, they were taken to the temple. Here, in the presence of the gods, they were solemnly anointed, the forehead of each person being sprinkled with fragrant oil. The sacred pig, clothed or wrapped in the *haio* or cloth of the order, was next put into his hand, and offered to the god. Each individual was then declared, by the person officiating on the occasion, to be an Areoi of the order to which he was thus raised. If the pig wrapped in the sacred cloth was killed, which was sometimes done, it was buried in the temple; but if alive, its ears were ornamented with the *orooro*, or sacred braid and tassel, of cocoa-nut fibre. It was then liberated, and being regarded as sacred, or belonging to the god to whom it had been offered, was allowed to range the district uncontrolled till it died.

The artist or priest of the tatau was now employed to imprint, with unfading marks, the distinctive badges of the rank or class to which the individuals had been raised. As this operation was attended with considerable suffering to the parties invested with these insignia of rank, it was usually deferred till the termination of the festival which followed the ceremony. This was generally furnished with an extravagant profusion: every kind of food was prepared, and large bales of native cloth were also provided, as presents to the Areois, among whom it was divided. The greatest peculiarity, however, connected with this entertainment was, that the restrictions of tabu, which prohibited females, on pain of death, from eating the flesh of the animals offered in sacrifice to the gods, were removed, and they partook, with the men, of the pigs, and other kinds of food considered sacred, which had been provided for the occasion. Music, dancing, and pantomime exhibitions, followed, and were sometimes continued for several days.

These, though the general amusements of the Areois, were not the only purposes for which they assembled. They included

'All monstrous, all prodigious things;'

and these were 'abominable, unutterable.' In some of their meetings, they appear to have placed their invention on the rack, to discover the worst pollutions of which it was possible for man to be guilty, and to have striven to outdo each other in the most revolting practices. The mysteries of iniquity, and acts of more than bestial degradation, to which they were at times addicted, must remain in the darkness in which even they felt it sometimes expedient to conceal them. I will not do violence to my own feelings, or offend those of my readers, by details of conduct, which the mind cannot contemplate without pollution and pain. I should not have alluded to them, but for the purpose of shewing the affecting debasement, and humiliating demoralization, to which ignorance, idolatry, and the evil propensities of the human heart, when uncontrolled or unrestrained by the institutions and relations of civilized society and sacred truth, are capable of reducing mankind, even under circumstances highly favourable to the culture of virtue, purity, and happiness.

In these pastimes, in their accompanying abominations, and the often-repeated practices of the most unrelenting, murderous cruelty, these wandering Areois passed their lives, esteemed by the people as a superior order of beings, closely allied to the gods, and deriving from them direct sanction, not only for their abominations, but even for their heartless murders. Free from labour or care, they roved from island to island, supported by the chiefs and the priests; and often feasted on plunder from the gardens of the industrious husbandman, while his own family was not unfrequently deprived thereby, for a time, of the means of subsistence. Such was their life of luxurious and licentious indolence and crime. And such was the character of their delusive system of superstition, that, for them, too, was reserved the Elysium which their fabulous mythology taught them to believe was provided, in a future state of existence, for those so preeminently favoured by the gods.

A number of singular ceremonies were, on this account, performed at the death of an Areoi. The *otohaa*, or general lamentation, was continued for two or three days. During this time the body remained at the place of its decease, surrounded by the relatives and friends of the departed. It was then taken by the Areois to the grand temple, where the bones of the kings were deposited. Soon after the body had been brought within the precincts of the marae, the priest of Oro came and, standing over the corpse, offered a long prayer to his god. This prayer, and the ceremonies connected therewith, were designed to divest the body of all the sacred and mysterious influence the individual was supposed to have received from the god, when, in the presence of the idol, the perfumed oil had been sprinkled upon him, and he had been raised to the order or rank in which he died. By this act it was imagined they were all returned to Oro, by whom they had been originally imparted. The body was then buried as the body of a common man, within the precincts of the temple, in which the bodies of chiefs were interred. This ceremony was not much unlike certain portions of the degrading rites performed on the person of a heretic, in connexion with an auto de fé, in the Romish church.

The resources of the Areois were ample. They were, therefore, always enabled to employ the priest of Romatane, who was supposed to have the keys of Rohutu noanoa, the Tahitian's paradise. This priest consequently succeeded the priest of Oro, in the funeral ceremonies: he stood by the dead body, and offered his petitions to Urutaetae, who was not altogether the Charon of their mythology, but the god whose office it was to conduct the spirits of Areois and others, for whom the priest of Romatane was employed, to the place of happiness.

This Rohutu noanoa, literally, (perfumed or fragrant Rohutu,) was altogether a Mahomedan paradise. It was supposed to be near a lofty and stupendous mountain in Raiatea, situated in the vicinity of Hamaniino harbour, and called *Temehani unauna*, splendid or glorious Temehani. It was, however, said to be invisible to mortal eyes, being in the *reva*, or aerial regions. The country was described as most lovely and enchanting in appearance, adorned with flowers of every form and hue, and perfumed with odours of every fragrance. The air was free from every noxious vapour, pure, and salubrious. Every species of enjoyment, to which the Areois and other favoured classes had been accustomed on earth, was to be participated there; while rich viands and delicious fruits were supposed to be furnished in abundance, for the celebration of their sumptuous festivals. Handsome youths and women, *purotu anae*, all perfection, thronged the place. These honours and gratifications were only for the privileged orders, the Areois and the chiefs, who could afford to pay the priests for the passport thither: the charges were so great, that the common people seldom or never thought of attempting to procure it for their relatives; besides, it is probable that the high distinction kept up between the chiefs and people here, would be expected to exist in a future state, and to exclude every individual of the lower ranks, from the society of his superiors.

Those who had been kings of Areois in this world, were the same there for ever. They were supposed to be employed in a succession of amusements and indulgences similar to those to which they had been addicted on earth, often perpetrating the most unnatural crimes, which their tutelar gods were represented as sanctioning by their own example.

These are some of the principal traditions and particulars relative to this singular and demoralizing institution, which, if not confined to the Georgian and Society Islands, appears to have been patronized and carried to a greater extent there than among any other islands of the Pacific. Considering the imagined source in which it originated, the express appointment of Oro, their powerful god, the antiquity it claimed, its remarkable adaptation to the indolent habits and depraved uncontrolled passions of the people, the sanction it received here, and the prospect it presented to its members, of the perpetuity, in a future state, of gratifications most congenial to those to whom they were exhibited, the Areoi institution appears a master-piece of satanic delusion and deadly infatuation, exerting an influence over the minds of an ignorant, indolent, and demoralized people, which no human power, and nothing less than a Divine agency, could counteract or destroy

CHAP. X.

Customs of the islanders—Infanticide—Numbers destroyed—Universality of the crime—Mode of its perpetration—Reasons assigned for its continuance—Disproportion it occasioned between the sexes—Former treatment of children—Ceremonies performed at the temple on the birth of chiefs—Manner of carrying their children—Evils of neglecting parental discipline—Practice of tatauing—Tradition of its origin—Account of the dye instruments and process of tatauing—Variety of figures or patterns—The operation painful, and frequently fatal—Marriage contracts—Betrothment—Ancient usages—Ceremonies in the temple—Conduct of the relatives—Prevalence of polygamy.

NEXT to the occupations and amusements of the islanders, such of their customs and observances as were peculiar or striking require to be briefly noticed. Many of their usages were singular, some remarkably interesting, and others horribly cruel. Among the latter kind, the murder of their children, violating the closest and tenderest sympathies of human nature, and seizing its victims with their first consciousness of existence, stands prominently forward.

Infanticide, the most revolting and unnatural crime that prevails, even amongst the habitations of cruelty which fill the dark places of the earth, was intimately connected with the execrable Areoi institution. This affecting species of murder was not peculiar to the inhabitants of the Pacific. It has prevailed in different parts of the world, in ancient and modern times, among civilized as well as barbarous nations: but, until the introduction of Christianity, it was probably practised to a greater extent, and with more heartless barbarity, by the South Sea Islanders, than by any other people with whose history we are acquainted. Although we have been unable accurately to ascertain the date of its introduction to Tahiti and the adjacent isles, the traditions of the people warrant the inference, that it is of no very recent origin. I am, however, inclined to think it was practised less extensively in former times than during the fifty years immediately preceding the subversion of their ancient system of idolatry. There is every reason to suppose that, had the inhabitants murdered their infants during the early periods of their history, in any great degree, much less to the extent to which they have carried this crime in subsequent years, the population would never have become so numerous, as it evidently was, not many generations prior to their discovery.

It is difficult to learn to what extent infanticide was practised at the time Wallis discovered Tahiti, or the subsequent visits the islanders received from Cook; but its frequency and avowed perpetration was such as to attract the attention of the latter. Captain Cook's general conduct among the natives, notwithstanding the harsh measures he deemed it expedient to pursue towards the inhabitants of Eimeo, was humane; he took every opportunity of remonstrating with the king and chiefs, against a usage so merciless and savage.

When the Missionaries arrived in the Duff, this was one of the first and most affecting appendages of idolatry that awakened their sympathies, and called forth their expostulation and interference. Adult murder sometimes occurred; many were slain in war; and during the first years of their residence in Tahiti, human victims were frequently immolated. Yet the amount of all these and other murders did not equal that of infanticide alone. No sense of irresolution or horror appeared to exist in the bosoms of those parents who deliberately resolved on the deed before the child was born. They often visited the dwellings of the foreigners, and spoke with perfect complacency of their cruel purpose. On these occasions, the Missionaries employed every inducement to dissuade them from executing their intention, warning them, in the name of the living God, urging them also by every consideration of maternal tenderness, and always offering to provide the little stranger with a home, and the means of education. The only answer they generally received was, that it was the custom of the country; and the only result of their efforts, was the distressing conviction of the inefficacy of their humane endeavours. The murderous parents often came to their houses almost before their hands were cleansed from their children's blood, and spoke of the deed with worse than brutal insensibility, or with vaunting satisfaction at the triumph of their customs over the persuasions of their teachers.

In their earliest public negociations with the king and the chiefs, who constituted the government of the island, the Missionaries had enjoined, from motives of policy, as well as humanity and a regard to the law of God, the abolition of this cruel practice. The king Pomare acknowledged that he believed it was not right; that Captain

Cook, for whom they entertained the highest respect, had told him it ought not to be allowed; and that for his part he was willing to discontinue it. These, however, were bare professions; for his own children were afterwards murdered, as well as those of his subjects.

In point of number, the disproportion between the infants spared and those destroyed, was truly distressing. It was not easy to learn exactly what this disproportion was; but the first Missionaries have published it as their opinion, that not less than two-thirds of the children were murdered by their own parents. Subsequent intercourse with the people, and the affecting details many have given since their reception of Christianity, authorize the adoption of the opinion as correct. The first three infants, they observed, were frequently killed; and in the event of twins being born, both were rarely permitted to live. In the largest families more than two or three children were seldom spared, while the numbers that were killed were incredible. The very circumstance of their destroying, instead of nursing their children, rendered their offspring more numerous than it would otherwise have been. We have been acquainted with a number of parents, who, according to their own confessions, or the united testimony of their friends and neighbours, had inhumanly consigned to an untimely grave, four, or six, or eight, or ten children, and some even a greater number. I feel hence, the painful and humiliating conviction which I have ever been reluctant to admit, forced upon me from the testimony of the natives themselves, the proportion of children found by the first Missionaries, and existing in the population at the time of our arrival—that during the generations immediately preceding the subversion of paganism, not less than two-thirds of the children were massacred. A female, who was frequently accustomed to wash the linen for our family, had thus cruelly destroyed five or six. Another, who resided very near us, had been the mother of eight, of which only one had been spared. But I will not multiply instances, which are numerous in every island, and of the accounts of which the recollection is most distinct. I am desirous to establish beyond doubt the belief of the practice, as it is one which, from every consideration, is adapted to awaken in the Christian mind liveliest gratitude to the Father of mercies, strongest convictions of the miseries inseparable from idolatry, tenderest commiseration for the heathen, and vigorous efforts for the amelioration of their wretchedness.

The universality of the crime was no less painful and astonishing than its repeated perpetration by the same individuals. It does not appear to have been confined to any rank or class in the community; and though it was one of the indispensable regulations of the Areoi society, enforced on the authority of those gods whom they were accustomed to consider as the founders of their order, it was not peculiar to them. It was perhaps less practised by the raatiras, or farmers, than any other class, yet they were not innocent. I do not recollect having met with a female in the islands, during the whole period of my residence there, who had been a mother while idolatry prevailed, who had not imbrued her hands in the blood of her offspring. I conversed more than once on the subject with Mr. Nott, during his recent visit to his native country. On one occasion, in answer to my inquiry, he stated, that he did not recollect having, in the course of the thirty years he had spent in the South Sea Islands, known a female, who was a mother under the former system of superstition, who had not been guilty of this unnatural crime. Startling and affecting as the inference is, it is perhaps not too much to suppose, that few, if any, became mothers, in those later periods of the existence of idolatry, who did not also commit infanticide. Recent facts confirm this melancholy supposition. During the year 1829, Mr. Williams was conversing with some friends in his own house in the island of Raiatea, on this subject. Three native females were sitting in the room at the time, the eldest not more than forty years of age. In the course of conversation he observed, "Perhaps some of these females have been guilty of this crime." The question was proposed, and it was found that no one was guiltless; and the astonishment of the parties was increased, when it was reluctantly confessed, that these three females had destroyed not fewer than one-and-twenty infants. One had destroyed nine, another seven, and the third five. These individuals were not questioned as having been more addicted to the practice of this crime than others, but simply because they happened to be in the room when the conversation took place. Without reference to other deeds of barbarism, they were in this respect a nation of murderers; and, in connexion with the Areoi institution, murder was sanctioned by their laws.

The various methods by which infanticide was effected are most of them of such a nature as to prohibit their publication. It does not appear that they ever buried them alive, as the Sandwich Islanders were accustomed to do, by digging a hole, sometimes in the floor of the dwelling, laying a piece of native cloth upon the infant's mouth, and treading down the earth upon the helpless child. Neither were the children as liable to be destroyed, after having been suffered to live for any length of time. The horrid deed was always perpetrated before the victim had seen the light, or in a hurried manner, and immediately after birth. The infants, thus disposed of, were called *tamarii huihia*, *uumihea*, or *tahihia*, children stabbed or pierced with a sharp-pointed strip of bamboo cane, strangled by placing the thumbs on the throat, or *tahihia*, trodden or stamped upon. These were the mildest methods; others, sometimes employed, were too barbarous to be mentioned.

The parents themselves, or their nearest relatives, who often attended on the occasion for this express purpose, were the executioners. Often, almost before the new-born babe could breathe the vital air, gaze upon the light of heaven, or experience the sensations of its new existence, that existence has been extinguished by its cruel mother's hand; and the " felon sire," instead of welcoming, with all a father's joy, a daughter or a son, has dug its grave upon the spot, or among the thick-grown bushes a few yards distant. On receiving the warm palpitating body from its mother's hand, he has, with awful unconcern, deposited the precious charge, not in a father's arms, but in its early sepulchre; and instead of gazing, with all that thrilling rapture which a father only knows, upon the tender babe, has concealed it from his view, by covering its mangled form with the unconscious earth; and, to obliterate all traces of the deed, has trodden down the yielding soil, and strewed it over with green boughs, or covered it with verdant turf. This is not an exaggerated description, but the narrative of actual fact; other details, more touching and acute, have been repeatedly given to me in the islands, by individuals who had been themselves employed in these unnatural deeds.

The horrid act, if not committed at the time the infant entered the world, was not perpetrated at any subsequent period. Whether this was a kind of law among the people, or whether it was the power of maternal affection, by which they were influenced, it is not necessary now to inquire; but the fact is consolatory. If the little stranger was, from irresolution, the mingled emotions that struggled for mastery in its mother's bosom, or any other cause, suffered to live ten minutes or half an hour, it was safe; instead of a monster's grasp, it received a mother's caress and a mother's smile, and was afterwards nursed with solicitude and tenderness. The cruel act was indeed often committed by the mother's hand; but there were times when a mother's love, a mother's feelings, overcame the iron force of pagan custom, and all the mother's influence and endeavours have been used to preserve her child. Most affecting instances, which I forbear reciting, have been detailed by some, who now perhaps are childless, of the struggles between the mother to preserve, and the father and relatives to destroy, the infant. This has arisen from the motives of false pride by which they were on some occasions influenced.

The reasons assigned for this practice, though varied, were uniformly shameful and criminal. The first is the regulation of the Areoi institution, in order to be a member of which it was necessary, in obedience to the express injunction of the tutelar gods of the order, that no child should be permitted to live. Another cause was the weakness and transient duration of the conjugal bond, whereby, although the marriage contract was formed by individuals in the higher ranks of society, with persons of corresponding rank, fidelity was seldom maintained.

The marriage tie was dissolved whenever either of the parties desired it; and though amongst their principal chiefs it was allowed nominally to remain, the husband took other wives, and the wife other husbands. These were mostly individuals of personal attractions, but of inferior rank in society. The progeny of such a union was almost invariably destroyed, if not by the parents themselves, by the relatives of those superior in rank, lest the dignity of the family, or their standing in society, should be injured by being blended with those of an inferior class. More infant murders have probably been committed under these circumstances, from barbarous notions of family pride, than from any other cause. One of my Missionary companions[*] states, that by the murder of such children, the party of inferior birth has been progressively elevated in rank, and that the degree of distinction attained, was according to the number of children destroyed,—that by this means, parties, before unequal, were considered as corresponding in rank, and their offspring allowed to live.

The *raatiras*, or secondary class of chiefs, and others by whom it was practised, appear to have been influenced by the example of their superiors, or the shameless love of idleness. The spontaneous productions of the soil were so abundant, that little care or labour was necessary to provide

[*] Mr. Williams.

the means of subsistence: the climate was so warm, that the clothing required, as well as the food, could be procured with the greatest facility; yet they considered the little trouble required as an irksome task. A man with three or four children, and this was a rare occurrence, was said to be a *taata taubuubuu*, a man with an unwieldy or cumbrous burden; and there is reason to believe that, simply to avoid the trifling care and effort necessary to provide for their offspring during the helpless periods of infancy and childhood, multitudes were consigned to an untimely grave. A Malthusian motive has sometimes been adduced, and they have been heard to say, that if all the children born were allowed to live, there would not be food enough produced in the islands to support them. This, however, has only been resorted to when other methods of defending the practice have failed.

During the whole of their lives, the females were subject to the most abasing degradation; and their sex was often, at their birth, the cause of their destruction: if the purpose of the unnatural parents had not been fully matured before, the circumstance of its being a female child, was often sufficient to fix their determination on its death. Whenever we have asked them, what could induce them to make a distinction so invidious, they have generally answered,—that the fisheries, the service of the temple, and especially war, were the only purposes for which they thought it desirable to rear children; that in these pursuits women were comparatively useless; and therefore female children were frequently not suffered to live. Facts fully confirm these statements.

In the adult population of the islands at the time

of our arrival, the disproportion between the sexes was very great. There were, probably four or five men to one woman. In all the schools established on the first reception of Christianity, the same disproportion prevailed. In more recent years the sexes are nearly equal. In addition to this cruel practice, others, equally unnatural, prevailed, for which the people had not only the sanction of their priests, but the direct example of their respective deities.

Without pursuing this painful subject any further, or inquiring into its antiquity or its origin, which is probably co-eval with that of the monstrous Areoi institution; these details are of a kind that must impress every mind, susceptible of the common sympathies of humanity, with the greatest abhorrence of paganism, under the sanction of which such cruelties were perpetrated. They are also adapted to convey a most powerful conviction of the true character of heathenism, and the miseries which its votaries endure.

The abolition of this practice, with the subversion of idolatry, of which an account will be found in the succeeding pages, is a grateful reward to those who have sent the mild and humanizing principles of true religion to those islands. This single fact demands the gratitude of every Christian parent, especially of every Christian female, and affords the most cheering encouragement to those engaged in spreading the gospel throughout the world.

The child of a king, or chief of high rank, soon after its birth, was taken to the temple, and delivered to the *paia*, or priest, whose office it was to perform the required rites. The sacred implements of war, which were regarded as emblems of greatness, were placed in prescribed order on the pavement. Over them a large leaf of the *arum costatum* was laid, and filled with water, in which he bathed the infant, laying upon it the sacred knife, or sting-ray bone. *Tiarai*, and the other priests who officiated, now offered over the infant an *ubu*, called the prayer of life, which was preferred to the tutelar god of the island. A surgical operation was now performed, and the infant was removed to the *fare apaa*, a kind of tent, made by bending four pliant sticks or canes over a small mat; each end of the sticks being fixed in the ground, they formed a circular arch over the little bed. Upon the sticks the sacred cloth of the god was spread, to indicate that the child was admitted to the society of the gods, and exalted above ordinary men. Another temporary building, within the precincts of the temple, was prepared, to receive the infant, as soon as this ceremony terminated. In this building, called *farehua*, it remained five or six days, when it was taken to its parents' dwelling. During the time the infant remained at the marae, the kindling of fire, launching of a canoe, or beating of cloth, was prohibited, on pain of death.

From these ceremonies, and the privileges they were supposed to confer, all female children, except those of the king or highest chiefs, were excluded.

The raatiras, or inferior chiefs, imitating the example of their superiors, endeavoured to secure renown for their children, by performing corresponding ceremonies at their family maraes, but no attention was paid to it, except by the members of the relatives and dependents.

In the treatment of those children belonging to this class, formerly spared, a number of singular customs were observed, and several ceremonies performed. The mother bathed in the sea immediately after a profuse perspiration had been induced, and the infant was taken to the water almost as soon as it entered the world. It was also taken to the marae, where a variety of ceremonies were celebrated. In some of the islands, a number of these were attended to before its birth. When the mother repaired to the temple, the priest, after presenting costly and numerous offerings, caught the god in a kind of snare or loop, made with human hair, and also offered up his prayer that the child might be an honour to his family, a benefit to the nation, and be more famous than any of his ancestors had been. This usage prevailed in the Hervey Islands. A number of ceremonies were performed in the Society Islands. The child was, soon after its birth, invested with the name and office of its father, who was henceforward considered its inferior. This, however, during the minority of the child, was merely nominal: the father exercised all authority, though in the name of the child. The children were frequently nursed at the breast till they were able to walk, although they were fed with other food.

As soon as the child was able to eat, a basket was provided, and its food was kept distinct from that of the parent. During the period of infancy, the children were seldom clothed, and were generally laid or carried in a horizontal position. They were never confined in bandages, or wrapped in tight clothing, but though remarkably plump and healthy in appearance, they were generally very weak until nearly twelve months old. As soon as able to sit up, the child was not, when taken out, carried in the arms, so as to rest on the bosom, but nursed or carried at the side, seated on the hip of the person by whom it was borne.

The Tahitian parents and nurses were careful in observing the features of the countenance, and the shape of the child's head, during the period of infancy, and often pressed or spread out the nostrils of the females, as a flat nose was considered by them a mark of beauty. The forehead and the back of the head, of the boys, were pressed upwards, so that the upper part of the skull appeared in the shape of a wedge. This, they said, was done, to add to the terror of their aspect, when they should become warriors. They were then careful to *haune*, or shave, the child's head with a shark's tooth. This must have been a tedious, and sometimes a painful operation, yet it was frequently repeated; and although every idolatrous ceremony, connected with the treatment of their children, has been discontinued for a number of years, the mothers are still very fond of shaving the heads, or cutting the hair of their infants as close as possible. This often gives them a very singular appearance. The children are in general large, and finely formed; and, but for the prevalence of the disease which produces such a distortion of the spine, there is reason to believe that a deformed person would be very rarely seen among the inhabitants of the South Sea Islands.

No regular parental discipline was maintained in the native families. As soon as the child was able to will or act for itself, it was generally exempt from all control, and given up to the influence of its own inclinations. If ever control was attempted, it was only by the father, the mother was always disregarded, and the father has often encouraged the insult and violence, while all interference of the mother has been resisted by the child. Their years of childhood and youth were passed in indolence, irregularity, and the unrestrained indulgence in whatever afforded gratification. One of the earliest and singular usages to which they attended was that of tatauing or marking the skin. This was generally commenced at the age of eight or ten years, and continued at intervals, perhaps, till the individual was between twenty and thirty.

Tatauing, usually called tatooing, is not confined to them, but pervades the principal groups, and is extensively practised by the Marquesians and New Zealanders. Although practised by all classes, I have not been able to trace its origin. It is by some adopted as a badge of mourning, or memorial of a departed friend; and from the figures we have sometimes seen upon the persons of the natives, and the conversation we have had, we should be induced to think it was designed as a kind of historical record of the principal actions of their lives. But it was adopted by the greater number of the people merely as a personal adornment; and tradition informs us, that to this it owes its existence.

The following is the native account of the origin of tatauing. Hina, the daughter of the god Taaroa, bore to her father a daughter, who was called Apouvaru, and who also became the wife of Taaroa. Taaroa and Apouvaru looked stedfastly at each other, and Apouvaru, in consequence, afterwards brought forth her first-born, who was called Matamataaru. Again the husband and the wife looked at each other, and she became the mother of a second son, who was called Tiitiipo. After a repetition of this visual intercourse, a daughter was born, who was called Hinaereeremonoi. As she grew up, in order to preserve her chastity, she was made pahio, or kept in a kind of enclosure, and constantly attended by her mother. Intent on her seduction, the brothers invented tatauing, and marked each other with the figure called Taomaro. Thus ornamented, they appeared before their sister, who admired the figures, and, in order to be tataued herself, eluding the care of her mother, broke the enclosure that had been erected for her preservation, was tataued, and became also the victim to the designs of her brothers. Tatauing thus originated among the gods, and was first practised by the children of Taaroa, their principal deity. In imitation of their example, and for the accomplishment of the same purposes, it was practised among men. Idolatry not only disclosed the origin, but sanctioned the practice. The two sons of Taaroa and Apouvaru were the gods of tatauing. Their images were kept in the temples of those who practised the art professionally, and every application of their skill was preceded by a prayer addressed to them, that the operation might not occasion death, that the wounds might soon heal, that the figures might be handsome, attract admirers, and answer the ends of wickedness designed.

Tatauing, which must have been a painful operation, was seldom applied to any extent at the same time. There were *tahua*, professors of the art of tatauing, who were regularly employed to perform it, and received a liberal remuneration.

The colouring matter was the kernel of the candle-nut, *aleurites triloba*, called by the natives *tiairi*. This was first baked, then reduced to charcoal, afterwards pulverized, and mixed with oil. The instruments were rude, though ingenious, and consisted of the bones of birds or fishes, fastened with fine thread to a small stick. Another stick, somewhat heavier, was also used, to strike the above when the skin was perforated. The figure, or pattern to be tataued, was portrayed upon the skin with a piece of charcoal, though at times the operation was guided only by the eye.

When the idolatrous ceremonies attending its commencement were finished, the performer, immersing the points of the sharp bone instrument in the colouring matter, which was a beautiful jet, applied it to the surface of the skin, and, striking it smartly with the elastic stick which he held in his right hand, punctured the skin, and injected the dye at the same time, with as much facility as an adder would bite, and deposit her poison.

So long as the person could endure the pain, the operator continued his work, but it was seldom that a whole figure was completed at once. Hence it proved a tedious process, especially with those who had a variety of patterns, or stained the greater part of their bodies. Both sexes were tataued.

The tatauing of the Sandwich and Palliser Islanders, though sometimes abundant, is the rudest I have seen; that of the New Zealanders and the Marquesians is very ingenious, though different in its kind. The former consists principally in narrow, circular, or curved lines, on different parts of the face; the lines in the latter were broad and straight, interspersed with animals, and sometimes covered the body so as nearly to conceal the original colour of the skin, and almost even to warrant the description given by Schouten of the inhabitants of Dog Island, who, he observes, " were marked with snakes and dragons, and such like reptiles, which are very significant emblems of their own mischievous nature."

The Tahitian tatauing is more simple, and displays greater taste and elegance than either of the others. Though some of the figures are arbitrary, such as stars, circles, lozenges, &c.; the patterns are usually taken from nature, and are often some of the most graceful. A cocoa-nut tree is a favourite object; and I have often admired the taste displayed in the marking of a chiefs' legs, when I have seen a cocoa-nut tree correctly and distinctly drawn, its root spreading at the heel, its elastic stalk pencilled as it were along the tendon, and its waving plume gracefully spread out on the broad part of the calf. Sometimes a couple of stems would be twined up from the heel, and divided on the calf, each bearing a plume of leaves.

The ornaments round the ankle, and upon the instep, make them often appear as if they bore the elegant eastern sandal. The sides of the legs are sometimes tataued from the ankle upward, which gives the appearance of wearing pantaloons with ornamented seams. From the lower part of the back, a number of straight, waved, or zigzag lines, rise in the direction of the spine, and branch off regularly towards the shoulders. But, of the upper part of the body, the chest is the most tataued. Every variety of figure is to be seen here: cocoanut and bread-fruit trees, with convolvolus wreaths hanging round them, boys gathering the fruit, men engaged in battle, in the manual exercise, triumphing over a fallen foe; or, as I have frequently seen it, they are represented as carrying a human sacrifice to the temple. Every kind of animal—goats, dogs, fowls, and fish—may at times be seen on this part of the body; muskets, swords, pistols, clubs, spears, and other weapons of war, are also stamped upon their arms or chest.

They are not all crowded upon the same person, but each one makes a selection according to his fancy; and I have frequently thought the tatauing on a man's person might serve as an index to his disposition and his character. The neck and throat were sometimes singularly marked. The head and the ears were also tataued, though among the Tahitians this ornament was seldom applied to the face.

The females used the tatau more sparingly than the men, and with greater taste. It was always the custom of the natives to go barefooted, and the feet, to an inch above the ankles, of the chief women, were often neatly tataued; appearing as if they wore a loose sandal, or elegant open-worked boot. The arms were frequently marked with circles, their fingers with rings, and their wrists with bracelets. The thin transparent skin over the black dye, often gave to the tatau a tinge of blue.

The females seldom, if ever, marked their faces; the figures on their feet and hands were all the ornaments they exhibited. Many suffered much from the pain occasioned by the operation, and from the swelling and inflammation that followed, which often continued for a long time, and ultimately proved fatal. This, however, seldom deterred others from attempting to secure this badge of distinction or embellishment of person.

On account of the immoral practices invariably connected with the process of tatauing, the chiefs prohibited it altogether, and, excepting a few foreign seamen, who often evinced as great a desire to have some figure tataued on their arms or hands.

as the natives themselves, the practice was discontinued for some years.

The celebration of marriage frequently took place among the Tahitians at an early age, with females at twelve or thirteen, and with males when two or three years older. Betrothment was the frequent method by which marriage contracts were made among the chiefs, or higher ranks in society. The parties themselves were not often sufficiently advanced in years to form any judgment of their own, yet, on arriving at maturity, they rarely objected to the engagements their friends had made.

The period of courtship was seldom protracted among any class of the people; yet all the incident and romantic adventure that was to be expected in a community in which a high degree of sentimentality prevailed, was occasionally exhibited, and the unsuccessful suitor, perhaps, led to the commission of suicide, under the influence of revenge and despair. Unaccustomed to disguise either their motives or their wishes, they generally spoke and acted without hesitation; hence, whatever barriers might oppose the union of the parties, whether it was the reluctance of either of the individuals, or of their respective families, the means used for their removal were adopted with much less ceremony than is usually observed in civilized society. Several instances of this kind occurred during our residence in Huahine: one regarded a chief of Eimeo, who had followed Taaroarii the king's son. His figure was tall and gigantic, his countenance and manners not unpleasing, and his disposition mild. He was upwards of twenty years of age. Some time after our arrival in Huahine, he became attached to the niece of the principal raatira in the island, and tendered proposals of marriage. Her family admitted his visits, and favoured his design, but the object of his choice declined every proposal he made. No means to gain her consent were left untried, but all proved unavailing. He discontinued his ordinary occupations, left the establishment of the young chief who had selected him for his friend, and repaired to the habitation of the individual whose favour he was so anxious to obtain. Here he appeared subject to the deepest melancholy, and, leaving the other members of the family to follow their regular pursuits, from morning to night, day after day, he attended his mistress, performing humiliating offices with apparent satisfaction, and constantly following in her train whenever she appeared abroad.

His friends interested themselves in his behalf, and the disappointment, of which he was the subject, became for a time the topic of general conversation in the settlement. At length the object of his attachment was induced to accept his offer; they were publicly married, and lived very comfortably together. Their happiness, however, was but of short duration, for his wife, for whom he appeared to cherish the most ardent affection, died a few months afterwards.

Another instance of rather a different kind, subsequently occurred. A party of five or six persons arrived in a canoe from Tahiti, on a visit to their friends in the Leeward Islands. Though Borabora was their destination, they remained several weeks at Huahine, the guests of Taraimano. During this period, a young woman, one of the belles of the island belonging to the household of their hostess, became exceedingly fond of the society of one of the young men, and it was soon intimated to him that she wished to become his companion for life. The intimation, however, was disregarded by the young man, who expressed his intention to prosecute his voyage. The young woman became unhappy, and made no secret of the cause of her distress. She was assiduous in redoubling her efforts to please the individual whose affection she was desirous to obtain. At this period I never saw him either in the house of his friend, or walking abroad, without the young woman by his side.

Finding the object of her attachment, who was probably about eighteen years of age, unmoved by her attentions, she not only became exceedingly unhappy, but declared, that if she continued to receive the same indifference and neglect, she would either strangle or drown herself. Her friends endeavoured to dissuade her from her purpose; but, as she declared her determination was unaltered, they used their endeavours with the stranger, who afterwards returned the attentions he had received, and the parties were married at Huahine. His companions pursued their voyage to Borabora, and afterwards returned to Tahiti, while the new-married couple continued to reside with Taraimano. Their happiness was of short duration; not that death dissolved their union, but that attachment, which had been so ardent in the bosom of the young woman before marriage, was superseded by a dislike as powerful; and although I never heard the slightest charge of unkindness preferred against the husband, his wife not only treated him with insult, but finally left him. Instances of such unhappy marriages, though not unusual formerly, are now of rare occurrence.

It is only among the middle and lower ranks of society, that the contract is made by the parties themselves. I am not aware that the husband received any dowry with his wife, unless the rank of her family was inferior to that of his own. The suitor often made presents to the parents of the individual whom he wished to marry, in order to gain their consent.

Among the higher ranks, the individuals themselves were usually passive, and the arrangements were made by their respective friends. They were often betrothed to each other during childhood, and the female thus betrothed was called a *vahine pahio*. As she grew up, for the preservation of her chastity, a small platform, of considerable elevation, was erected for her abode, within the dwelling of her parents. Here she slept, and spent the whole of the time she passed within doors. Her parents, or some member of the family, attended her by night and by day, supplied her with every necessary, and accompanied her whenever she left the house. Some of their traditions warrant the inference that this mode of life, in early years, was observed by other females besides those who were betrothed.

When the time fixed for the marriage arrived, and the parties themselves agreed to the union, great preparations were made for the dances, amusements, and festive entertainment, usual on such occasions. A company of Areois generally attended, and, on the day preceding the nuptials, commenced their *upaupa*, or dance, and pantomimic exhibitions.

On the morning of the marriage-day, a temporary altar was erected in the house of the bride. The relics of her ancestors, perhaps their skulls or bones, were placed upon it, and covered with fine white native cloth; presents of white cloth were also given by her parents, and those relatives of the family who attended.

The sanction of the gods they considered essential to the marriage contract, and these preliminaries being adjusted, the parties repaired to the *marae*, or temple. The ceremony was generally performed in the family marae, excepting when the parties were connected with the reigning family, which rendered it necessary that it should be solemnized in the temple of Oro or of Tane, the two principal national idols. On entering the temple, the bride and bridegroom changed their dresses, and arrayed themselves in their wedding garments, which were afterwards considered sacred; they took their stations in the place appointed for them, the bride on one side of the area, and the bridegroom on the other, five or six yards apart.

The priest now came forward, clad in the habiliments of his office, and, standing before them, addressed the bridegroom usually in the following terms: *Eita anei oe a faarue i ta oe vahine?* "Will you not cast away your wife?" to which the bridegroom answered, *Eita;* "No." Turning to the bride, he proposed to her the same question, and received a similar answer. The priest then addressed them both, saying, "Happy will it be, if thus with ye two." He then offered a prayer to the gods in their behalf, imploring for them that they might live in affection, and realize the happiness marriage was designed to secure.

The relatives now brought a large piece of white cloth, which they call *ahu vauvau*, spreading cloth: it was spread out on the pavement of the marae. The bridegroom and bride took their station upon this cloth, and clasped each other by the hand. The skulls of their ancestors, which were kept carefully preserved by survivors, who considered the spirits of the proprietors of these skulls as the guardian spirits of the family, were sometimes brought out and placed before them.

The relatives of the bride then took a piece of sugar-cane, and, wrapping it in a branch of the sacred miro, placed it on the head of the bridegroom, while the new-married pair stood holding each other's hands. Having placed the sacred branch on the bridegroom's head, they laid it down between them. The husband's relatives then performed the same ceremony towards the bride. On some occasions, the female relatives cut their faces and brows with the instrument set with shark's teeth, received the flowing blood on a piece of native cloth, and deposited the cloth, sprinkled with the mingled blood of the mothers of the married pair, at the feet of the bride.

By the latter parts of the ceremony, any inferiority of rank that might have existed was removed, and they were considered as equal. The two families, also, to which they respectively belonged, were ever afterwards regarded as one. Another large piece of cloth, called the *tapoi*, covering, was now brought, and the ceremony concluded by the relatives throwing it over the bridegroom and bride.

The cloth used on these occasions, as well as the dress, was considered sacred, and was taken to the king, or appropriated to the use of the Areois. The parties returned to their habitation, where sumptuous feasting followed, the duration of which was according to the rank or means of the families thus united.

Such were the marriage ceremonies formerly observed among the inhabitants of the South Sea Islands. They exhibited much that was curious and affecting, especially in the blood of their parents, and the skulls of their ancestors, presented before the parties. The one, perhaps, as the emblem of their union, and the other as an intimation that the inhabitants of the world of spirits were witnesses of the agreement. Considering these, and other significant usages, it is surprising how a people, so uncivilized and rude as in many respects they certainly were, should ever have instituted observances so singular and impressive, in connexion with the marriage contract.

Notwithstanding all this ceremony and form in entering into the engagement, the marriage tie was probably one of the weakest and most brittle that existed among them; neither party felt themselves bound to abide by it any longer than it suited their inclinations and their convenience. The slightest cause was often sufficient to occasion or to justify their separation, though among the higher classes the relation was nominally continued long after it had actually ceased.

Polygamy was practised more extensively by the Tahitians than by the inhabitants of the Sandwich Islands, and probably prevailed to as great an extent among them as among any of the Polynesian tribes. Many of the raatiras, or inferior chiefs, had two or three wives, who appeared to receive an equal degree of respect and support. With the higher chiefs, however, it was different; although they might, like Hamanemane, keep a number of females, it was rather a system of concubinage, than a plurality of wives, that prevailed among them. The individual to whom the chief was first united in marriage, or whose rank was nearest his own, was generally considered as his wife, and, so long as she lived with her husband, the other females were regarded as inferior. When the rank of the parties was equal, they often separated; the husband took other wives, and the wife other husbands; and if the rank of the wife was in any degree superior to that of her husband, she was at liberty to take as many other husbands as she pleased, although still nominally regarded as the wife of the individual to whom **she had** been first married.

CHAP. XI.

Frequency of war in the South Sea Islands—Polynesian war-god—Religious ceremonies and human sacrifices, prior to the commencement of hostilities—National councils—Mustering of forces—Emblems of the gods taken to the war—Strength of their fleets or armies—The battle of Hooroto—Women engaging in battle—Tahitian banners—Martial music—Modes of attack—Single combats, challenges, &c.—The rauti, or orators of battle—Sacrifice of the first prisoner—Manifestation of affection, and motives to revenge—Auguries of the war—Use of the sling—Singular custom of the chiefs in marching to battle—Sanguinary and exterminating character of their engagements—Desolation of the country.

War among uncivilized nations is often an object of the highest ambition, the road to most envied distinction, and the source of most ardent delight. It was so among the South Sea Islanders. They appear to have been greatly addicted to it from the earliest periods of their history. It occurred very frequently, prior to the introduction of Christianity. During the fifteen years Mr. Nott spent in the islands, while the people were pagans, the island of Tahiti was involved in actual war ten different times. The Missionaries were painfully familiar with it. It surrounded their dwelling; and the wounded in battle have often, with their wounds fresh and bleeding, sought their houses for relief.

Oro was the principal war-god, but he was not the only deity whose influence was important on these occasions. Tairi, Maahiti, Tetuahuruhuru, Tane, and Rimaroa, "long hand, or arm," the ancient gods of war, were all deities of the first rank, having been created by Taaroa, according to their fabulous traditions, before Oro existed.

In modern times, however, Oro's influence has been principally sought in war. This they imagined was the chief object of his attention; and when it proceeded in its bloodiest forms, it was supposed to afford him the highest satisfaction. Somewhat of his imagined character may be inferred from the fact of his priest requiring every victim offered in sacrifice, to be covered with its own blood, in order to his acceptance. The influence ascribed to the gods in war may be in a measure inferred from the frequent and sanguinary appeals made to them at its commencement, and during every period of its progress.

When war was in agitation, a human sacrifice was offered to Oro, and was denominated the Matea: the ceremony connected with it was called—fetching the god to preside over the *nuu* or army. The image of the god was brought out; when the victim was offered, a red feather was taken from his person, and given to the party, who bore it to their companions, and considered it as the symbol of Oro's presence and sanction, during their subsequent preparations. The commencement of war, the violating of a treaty, was called the *aoti a pito*, the cutting of the cord of union; whenever this took place, a human victim was offered by the offending party, to prevent the gods from being angry at their treachery. A human victim, called the *Amoatabu*, was also offered by the party assailed, to secure protection from the gods, and punishment on their enemies. Another human sacrifice was now taken, called the Maui faatere, and was equivalent to the public declaration of war, and such it was also considered by the opposing party. In 1808, when the late Pomare heard that Taute, his former chief minister, and the most celebrated warrior in the nation, had joined the rebel chiefs, and that the Maui faatere had been offered, and the sanction of the gods thus implored, he was so affected that he wept; and it was in vain that one of his orators, in alluding to this event subsequently, exclaimed, Who is Taute? He is a man, and not a god, his head reaches not to the skies. Who is Taute? The king's spirits and courage never revived.

If it was a naval expedition, canoes were now collected and equipped, and the weapons put in order, the spears and clubs cleaned with a boar's tusk, pointed with bones of the sting-ray, and having been carefully polished, the handle of every weapon was covered with the resinous gum of the bread-fruit, that it might adhere to the warrior's hand, and render his grasp firm.

When the implements of destruction were ready, and this seldom occupied many days, another human sacrifice was offered, called the *haea mati*—the tearing of the mati in the presence of the gods, as the fibres of mati were torn at the temple, before being twisted into cord for the sacred net. This was immediately before the expedition started; and if accepted, Oro generally inspired one of his prophets, who declared that the fleet or army should be victorious. On all these occasions, human sacrifices, covered with their own blood, were offered to Oro, in numbers proportioned to the magnitude of the undertaking, or the force of the parties confederated.

While these ceremonies were proceeding, national councils were held. Peace, or war, was usually determined by a few leading individuals, including the king, priests, and the principal chiefs. The prayers and sacrifices offered, oracles consulted, responses received, and councils held, were only parts of the external machinery by which, as it regarded the mass of the population, these movements were directed. This, however, was not always the case, and peace or war was often the result of the impressions produced by the popular orators on the general assemblies. These harangues were specimens of the most impassioned natural eloquence, bold and varied in its figures, and impressive in its effects.

I never had an opportunity of attending one of their national councils when the question of war was debated, under the imposing influence imparted by their mythology, whereby they imagined the contention between the gods of the rivals was as great as that sustained by the parties themselves. A number of the figures and expressions used on these occasions are familiar; but, detached and translated, they lose their force. From what I have beheld in their public speeches, in force of sentiment, beauty of metaphor, and effect of action, I can imagine that the impression of an eloquent harangue, delivered by an ardent warrior, armed perhaps for combat, and aided by the influence of highly excited feeling, could produce no ordinary effect; and I have repeatedly heard Mr. Nott declare, (and no one can better appreciate native eloquence,) he would at any time go thirty miles to listen to an address impassioned as those he has sometimes heard on these occasions.

When war was determined, the king's *vea*, or herald, was sent round the island, or through the districts dependent on the parties, and all were required to arm, and repair to the appointed rendezvous. Sometimes the king's flag was carried round. The women, the children, and the aged, called the *ohua*, were either left in the villages, or lodged in some place of security, while the men hastened to the field.

Their arms were kept with great care, in high preservation. In some of the houses, on our arrival in the Leeward Islands, especially in the dwelling of Fenuapeho, the chief of Tahaa, every kind of weapon was in such order, and so carefully fixed against the sides of the house, that the dwelling appeared more like an armoury than a domestic abode. Many a one, whom the summons from the chief has found destitute in the morning, has been known to cut down or rive a tall cocoa-nut tree, finish his lance or his spear, and join the warriors at the close of the same day. The chief of each district led his own tenantry to the war—reported, on his arrival, the number of men he had brought —and then formed his *buhapa*, or encampment, with the rest of the forces.

A number of ceremonies still remained to be observed. The priests were important personages in every expedition; their influence with the gods was considered the means of victory, and they received a proportionate share of consideration. The first service of this kind was called the *taamu raa ra*—the binding of the sacredness or supernatural influence; and while the chiefs and warriors had been employed in the preliminaries of war, the priests had been unremitting in their prayers that the *ra atua*, &c. the influence of the gods, &c. might be turned against their enemies, or that the gods would leave them defenceless. When their prayers were successful, it was supposed that the gods of their enemies left them, and came to the party by whom they were thus implored, and, entering the canoes, clubs, spears, and other weapons of their army, insured its triumph. As a compensation for this important service, the chiefs assembled; a quantity of cloth, mats, and perhaps a canoe, was spread before them, surmounted by a branch of the sacred *miro*, and a few red feathers, emblematical of the tutelar gods. The priests were then sent for, and the whole presented to them from the heads of the army by an orator, the burden of whose address was—"This is the recompense for your fatigue in imploring the aid of the gods by night and by day."

A second ceremony followed, called *fairaro*: a large quantity of cloth, mats, &c. were given to the priests, that they might persevere in their labours. This was succeeded by a third, of the same kind, called the *haameii*, in which, in addition to the other kinds of property, a number of fine pigs, each distinguished by a distinct name, were given to the priests, that they might redouble their vigilance to induce their own gods to keep with them, and the gods of their enemies to forsake those enemies, and, by means of the weapons of those who now sought their favour, to exert their power against the parties they had formerly aided.

The *atoa fare ia Manaha*—the building of the house of Manaha, or *hosts* of gods—was a singular ceremony. It was designed for the abode of the gods and spirits, who they supposed fought with them, and whose favour they desired. In order to propitiate the gods, a human sacrifice was offered. The work was begun, and the house must be finished in one day, on which day every individual must abstain from all kinds of food, no canoe must be launched, no fire lighted, while the work was in progress, and at the foot of the central pillar the body of a man offered in sacrifice was deposited. Into this house the *toos*, or images of the spirits, were sometimes taken; but although the priest always offered his prayer here, the gods were usually left in their sacred temples, and only a feather was taken from their images, which they supposed to be endowed with all their power.

The last religious ceremony, prior to the commencement of conflict, was the *haumanava*. Slight temples were erected in the sacred canoes of Oro, and the other gods. In these, the red feathers taken from the idols were deposited; they were called *manutahi no Tane*, &c. or single bird of Tane; all the gods were supposed to be present, having been brought from their elysian abodes by the prayers of the priests. There was a kind of intermediate race of beings, between men and gods, who were employed as messengers, to fetch the latter in cases of emergency; each god had his own messenger, hovering about the habitations of men, in the shape of a bird or a shark. When the priest by prayers sought the aid of these gods, they imagined that the messenger set off to the place of the god's abode, somewhere in *fare papa*, near "the foundation of the world," and made the usual declaration—*Mai haere i te ao, e tamae ti te ao*, "Come to the world, or state of light, there is war in the world."

The sacred feathers being deposited in the temporary maraes erected in the canoes, a large number of the finest hogs they could procure were killed, and baked in the temple on shore, the heads cut off, and placed on a small altar in the canoe, before the symbol of the idols' presence. The remaining part of the body was eaten by the priests, and those who feasted on the sacrifices. Whether they fought by sea or by land, as their principal engagements were near the shore, a fleet usually accompanied the army, and on board the canoes the principal idols were generally kept. The arrangements being now completed, with the emblems of their gods, and the offerings they made, they speedily set out for the combat, confident of victory.

Nuu and *papaupea* were the terms usually employed to designate an army, though it is probable the former was applied principally to an army, or fleet, filled with fighting men, and the latter to an army on shore, together with the multitude that followed for the purposes of plunder, &c. Their armies must formerly have been large: when Captain Cook was there in 1774, he supposed the fleet to consist of not fewer than 1700 canoes, each carrying forty men; making altogether 6000 fighting men. I think, however, there must have been some mistake in his calculation. In the last war but one, in which the people of Huahine were engaged with those of Raiatea, at the battle of Hooroto, in the latter island, according to the testimony of Mahine, the present king of Huahine, who was there, and whose father was the general of the forces, the fleet consisted of ninety ships, or war-canoes, each about one hundred feet long, filled with men, who, besides their ordinary arms, possessed the two guns left with Mai by Captain

SANGUINARY BATTLE OF HOOROTO. 283

Cook, from the use of which they expected an easy victory. This was one of the most sanguinary conflicts that had occurred for many years. Tenana, the king of Huahine, went down to avenge the cause of Ohunehaapaa, whose son is still living in Raiatea. Ohunehaapaa had been banished by the Raiatean chiefs, and the chiefs and people of Huahine undertook to reinstate him. The Windward fleet anchored at Tipaemau, when the Raiateans fled to Tahaa. The Huahinean chief sent to demand from Tapoa the surrender of the land. This was refused, and both parties prepared for battle. Next day the hostile fleets met near Hooroto, and a most bloody and obstinate engagement ensued; both parties lost so many, that when piled up, on the day after the battle, the dead bodies are said to have formed a heap as high as the young cocoa-nut trees. They still determined to persevere till one party should be destroyed; but Mauai, a native of Borabora, inspired by Oro, intimated the will of the god that they should desist. An armistice was concluded; the warriors of two districts of Huahine, Faretou, and Fareihi, being comparatively uninjured, sailed over to Tahaa, for the purpose of plunder. They, however, met with a more determined resistance than they had expected, and were not only repulsed, but almost cut off. Mato, the father of the present king of Huahine, and general of the army, was slain. The survivors were glad to return to their own island, and the Raiateans were too much enfeebled to endeavour to prevent them.

In this war, the greater part of the chiefs and warriors of the Leeward or Society Islands were destroyed. The island of Huahine never recovered from the shock of this murderous conflict.

Tamai or tuua is the general term for war, in all its diversified forms; the same word is also used to denote quarrelling; *aro* is the term for battle. The modes of attack and defence were various, and regulated by circumstances. Among the principal, were the *fatatia*, where two armies, led on by their respective sovereigns, advanced face to face; the *duu mata,* in which none turn back; the *maiva*, in which a select band, joining hands, rushed into the fiercest part of the conflict, and endeavoured to spread confusion and terror among the enemy; the *aro nee*, where only a small front was shown, and the main force concealed; the *moohono*, jointless backbone, and the *aro ro*, (ant-fight) in which the army is formed in lines, and the front line, when hard pressed, retires, while those immediately behind advance to sustain the conflict. Besides these there were a number of others, such as the *butoa*, coral rock, in which the army stood and repelled every assailant; the *rapatahi*, in which the assailants singled out the chiefs and leaders; but the most desperate was the *uura tama faarere*, when the warriors forsook land, house, wife, and children, and, determining to refuse quarter, went forth to conquer or die. The divisions of the army were: 1. The *viro aro,* front line, or advanced guard; 2. the *apoa viri,* second rank; 3. the *tapono viri,* shoulder viri, or third rank; 4. the *hotuai,* or fourth line; and 5. the *hoe haabua,* or last division, including the wives, children, baggage, and property of the warriors. The rank immediately in front of the king or principal chief, always contained the bravest men.

The forces were marshalled for the fight by the principal leader, who was said to *tarai te aro,* shape or form the battle; when this was accomplished, the signal was given, and uniting in the *umera ia Ra*, song of battle to the god of war, or in deafening shouts and imprecations, they rushed with bold and menacing impetuosity to *u*, or join in combat. Sometimes their attacks were made by night, but then they generally bore a *rama*, or torch. To ambuscades they seldom had recourse, though they occasionally adopted what was called the *aro nee*, or attack by stealth, surprising their enemies by an unexpected onset.

The flags of the gods, or the emblems of the idols, were carried to the battle, to inspire the combatants with confidence, and the martial banners they employed were formerly hoisted on board the different fleets, but more recently carried by the bravest of the warriors in the centre of their armies. Their flags were red, white, or black. Rude and harsh kinds of music animated the warriors in their fleets, and since the reign of Oro the combatants have marched to the battle, inspired by the sounds of the trumpet and the drum. Before this time, during the celestial supremacy of Tane and Ra, these gods were accustomed in action to advance before those bands of warriors whom they were disposed to aid, and to spread dismay through the ranks of their enemies by waving their tails, which the natives supposed resembled the tails of comets, or the luminous appearance called a falling or shooting star.

It is a singular fact, that although they left their images in their respective temples, no offerings were presented after the haumanava had been performed, and no sacrifice was deposited on the altars of any of the temples, lest the gods should hereby be induced to forsake the army, or remain behind.

When their modes of attack were deliberate, the celebrated warriors of each army occasionally marched forward beyond the first line of the body to which they belonged, and, on approaching the ranks of the enemy, sat down on the sand or the grass. Two or three from one of these parties would then rise, and, advancing a few yards towards their opponents, boastfully challenge them to the combat. When the challenge was accepted, which it often was with the utmost promptitude, the combatants advanced with intimidating menaces.

These often addressed each other by recounting their names, the names and deeds of their ancestors, their own achievements in combat, the prowess of their arms, and the augmented fame they should acquire by the addition of their present foes to the number of those they had already slain; in conclusion, inviting them to advance, that they might be devoted to their god, who was hovering by to receive the sacrifice. With taunting scorn the antagonist would reply much in the same strain, sometimes mingling affected pity with his denunciations. When they had finished their harangue, the *omoreaa*, club of insult, or insulting spear, was raised, and the onset commenced. Sometimes it was a single combat, fought in the space between the two armies, and in sight of both.

At other times, several men engaged on both sides, when those not engaged, though fully armed and equipped, kept their seat on the ground. If a single combat, when one was disabled or slain, the victor would challenge another; and seldom thought of retreating, so long as one remained. When a number were engaged, and one fell, a warrior from his own party rose, and maintained the struggle; when either party retreated, the ranks of the army to which it belonged rushed forward to sustain it; this brought the opposing army on, and, from a single combat or a skirmish, it became a general engagement. The conflict was carried on with the most savage fury, such as might be expected in barbarous warriors, who imagined the gods, on whom their destinies depended, had actually entered into their weapons, giving precision and force to their blows, direction to their missiles, and imparting to the whole a supernatural fatality.

The din and clamour of the deadly fray were greatly augmented by the efforts of the Rauti. These were, as the Druids among the ancient Britons, the orators of battle. They were usually men of commanding person and military prowess, arrayed only in a girdle of the leaves of the ti-plant round their waist; sometimes carrying a light spear in the left, but always a small bunch of green ti-leaves in the right hand. In this bunch of leaves the principal weapon, a small, sharp, serrated, and barbed *airo fai*, (bone of the stingray,) was concealed, which they were reported to use dexterously when in contact with the enemy. The principal object of these Rautis was, to animate the troops by recounting the deeds of their forefathers, the fame of their tribe or island, the martial powers of their favouring gods, and the interests involved in the contest. In the discharge of their duties they were indefatigable, and by night and day went through the camp rousing the ardour of the warriors. On the day of battle they marched with the army to the onset, mingled in the fray, and hurried to and fro among the combatants, cheering them with the recital of heroic deeds, or stimulating them to achievements of daring and valour.

Any attempt at translating their expressions would convey so inadequate an idea of their original force, as to destroy their effect. "Roll onward like the billows—break on them with *te haruru o te tai*, the ocean's foam and roar when bursting on the reefs—hang on them as *te uira mau tai*, the forked lightning plays above the frothing surf—give out the vigilance, give out the strength, give out the anger, the anger of the devouring wild dog,—till their line is broken, till they flow back like the receding tide." These were the expressions sometimes used, and the impression of their spirit-stirring harangues is still vivid in the recollection of many, who, when any thing is forcibly urged upon them, often involuntarily exclaim, "*Tini Rauti teie*," equal to a Rauti this.

If the battle continued for several successive days, the labours of the Rautis were so incessant by night through the camp, and by day amid the ranks in the field, that they have been known to expire from exhaustion and fatigue. The priests were not exempted from the battle; they bore arms, and marched with the warriors to the combat.

The combatants did not use much science in the action, nor scarcely aim to parry their enemy's weapons; they used no shield or target, and, believing the gods directed and sped their weapons with more than human force upon their assailants, they depended on strength more than art for success. Their clubs were invariably aimed at the head, and often, with the lozenge-shaped weapon, they would *tapai*, or cleave, the skulls of their opponents. Their spears they directed against the body, and the *maui* was often a deadly thrust, piercing through the heart.

When the first warrior fell on either side, a horrid shout of exultation and of triumph was raised by the victors, which echoed along the line, striking a panic through the ranks of their antagonists, it being considered an intimation of the favour of the gods towards the victorious parties. Around the body the struggle became dreadful; and if the victors bore him away, he was despoiled of his ornaments, and then seized by the priests, or left to be offered to the gods at the close of the battle.

The first man seized on before quite dead was offered in sacrifice, and called *te mataahaetumu Taaroa*—the first rending of the root. The victim was not taken to the temple, but the head was bound round with sacred cinet brought from the temple, and the body laid alive upon a number of spears, and thus borne on men's shoulders along the ranks, in the midst or rear of the army, the priest of Oro walking by the side, offering his prayer to the god, and watching the writhings and involuntary agitation of the dying man. If a tear fell from his eye, it was said to be weeping for his land. If he clenched the fist, it was an indication that his party would resist to the last, and conquest to the captors was uncertain, &c. If these auguries were deemed favourable, he pronounced victory as certain. Such indications were considered most encouraging, as earnests of the god's co-operation. Sometimes the first victim was called *Te ivi o te vai o Tu:* the head was completely covered as low as the neck with successive bandages of cinet, carried to the temple, and burned before Taaroa; and was generally regarded as an earnest of the defeat of his party, and the destruction of his family.

When a distinguished chief or warrior fell, the party, to which he belonged, retired a short distance, collected some of their bravest men, and then, in a body, with fury and revenge rushed upon their antagonists, to *vaere toto*, clear away the blood. The shock was terrific when they met the opposing ranks, and numbers frequently fell on both sides. Two brothers, or intimate friends, often manifested in battle an affecting strength of attachment and constancy; they fought side by side, especially in the Duumata, in which no retreat was allowed; and if one was killed, the survivor dipped his hand in the blood of his slain brother, and rubbed it on his own person, to manifest his affection, alleviate his grief, and stimulate to revenge.

During the engagement, the parties often retreated, so that there was a considerable space between the ranks, as when proceeding to the onset. The slingers were then employed; who often advanced in front of the ranks to which they belonged, and with boasting threats warned their enemies to fly or fall. The most dangerous missile was the *uriti* or stone, from the *ma* or sling. The latter was prepared with great care, and made with finely braided fibres of the cocoa-nut husk, or filaments of the native flax, having a loop to fasten it to the hand at one end, and a wide receptacle for the stone in the centre. The sling was held in the right hand, and, armed with the stone, was hung over the right shoulder, and caught by the left hand on the left side of the back. When thrown, the sling, after being stretched across the back, was whirled round over the head, and the stone discharged with great force.

The most expert slingers, as well as the most renowned among the warriors, were celebrated through the islands; and when one of these presented himself, a cry ran through the opposite ranks: Beware, or be vigilant, *e ofai mau omea*—an adhering stone is such a one; or *e ofai tano e ofai buai*—a sure or a powerful stone is such an one. The stones, which were usually about the size of a hen's egg, were either smooth, being polished by friction in the bed of a river, or sharp, angular, and rugged; these were called *ofai ara*—faced or edged stones. When thrown with any degree of elevation, they were seen and avoided, but they were generally thrown horizontally four or five feet from the ground, when they were with difficulty seen, and often did much execution. The slingers were powerful and expert marksmen.

The custom of the warriors sitting on the ground to wait for the combat, was not the only singular practice of the Tahitians in proceeding to battle. There was another, which they called *pito*. When two leading chiefs marched together to the onset, they not only walked side by side, but arm in arm. In this manner, Pomare-vahine, and Mahine, the chiefs of Huahine and Eimeo, marched to the battle of Narii. This was designed to shew their union, and that they would conquer or fall together. When a single chief led on his own men, he also walked in *pito* with his principal *aito* or warriors, two on each side, the nearest to him having hold of his arms. On approaching the enemy they separated, but fought near the person of their chieftain, whose life it was considered their special duty to defend, at the exposure of their own.

The battle sometimes terminated by both parties retreating, to recover, and prepare for a fresh campaign, but it was more frequently continued till the flight of one party left the other master of the field.

The carnage and destruction which followed the *fati* or breaking, and *hea* or flying, of one of the armies, was dreadful. It was called *tahaea*, and in it the gods were supposed to engage as well as the men. Those who were *vi*, or beaten, fled to their canoes, or to their *paris* or fastnesses in the mountains, while the victors, who were called *upoatia*, erect heads, pursued them with reckless slaughter. A prostrate warrior, as he lay at the feet of his antagonist, wounded or disarmed, would perhaps supplicate mercy, exclaiming *Tahitia iau ia ora wau*—Spare me, may I live. If the name of the king or chief, of the victor, was invoked, the request was often granted; but frequently a reproach or taunt, and a deadly blow or thrust, was the only reply.

The slaughter of the routed army was continued till the evening closed on the scene of murder and of blood, or until the fugitives had either reached their fortifications and strongholds in the mountains, or had eluded the pursuit of their enemies.— When the men went to battle, the women generally remained; but some of them fearlessly attended their husbands to the field, and either followed in the rear, or fought in the midst of the ranks. They carried the same kind of weapons as the men, but frequently used only their nails and their hands. Many were slain in the field, or during the retreat.

By whatever considerations civilized and enlightened nations may be influenced in the practice of war, and upon whatever principles they may desire to conduct it, war, barbarous, murderous, unrelenting war, is the delight of savages; and among no portion of the most cruel and warlike of the human race has it perhaps prevailed more extensively, or proved a greater scourge, than among the interesting inhabitants of the islands of the Pacific. With the Society and Sandwich Islanders, it has, since the introduction of Christianity, ceased. In the Friendly, Figi, and other groups, it still prevails: in the Marquesas, and New Zealand, it rages with unabated violence, and spreads devastation and wretchedness among the infatuated and hapless people.

Among the Society Islanders, in consequence of the influence of the climate, luxurious mode of living, and effeminacy of character induced thereby, the obstinacy and the continuance of actual combat were not equal to that which obtained in other tribes; yet we learn from the frequency of its occurrence, and the deadly hatred which was cherished, that the passion for war was not less powerful with them than with the New Zealander or the Marquesian; and its consequent cruelties and demoralization were perhaps unequalled in any other part of the world. Their wars were most merciless and destructive. Invention itself was tortured to find out new modes of inflicting suffering; and the total extermination of their enemies, with the desolation of a country, was often the avowed object of the war. This design, horrid as it is, has been literally accomplished: every inhabitant of an island, excepting the few that may have escaped by flight in their canoes, has been slaughtered; the bread-fruit trees have been cut down, and left to rot; the cocoa-nut trees have been killed by cutting off their tops or crown, and leaving the stems in desolate leafless ranks, as if they had been shivered by lightning.

Their wars were not only sanguinary, but frequent; yet from a variety of ceremonies, which preceded the expeditions, they were seldom prompt in commencing hostilities. What they were prior to the first visits of foreigners, we have not the means of correctly ascertaining, but since that time, the only period during which correct dates can be affixed to events in their history, the short and simple annals of Tahiti are principally filled with notices of destructive wars; and the effects of desolation still visible, prove that they have not been less frequent in the other islands.

The occasions of hostility were also at times remarkably trivial, though not so their consequences. The removal of a boundary mark; the pulling down of the king's flag; the refusing to acknowledge the king's son as their future sovereig; speaking disrespectfully of the gods, the king, or the chiefs; the slightest insult to the king, chiefs, or any in alliance or friendship with them; with a variety of more insignificant causes—were sufficient to justify an appeal to arms, or an invasion of the offender's territory with fire and spear. Although there were no standing armies or regular troops in the South Sea Islands, nor any class of men exclusively trained and kept for military purposes, war was followed as a profession as much as any other, and considered by many as one to which every other should be rendered subservient.

CHAP. XII.

Estimation in which fighting men were held—Weapons—Dress—Ornaments—Various kinds of helmet and armour—Ancient arms, &c. superseded by the introduction of fire-arms—Former ideas respecting the musket, &c.—Divination or augury—Savage and merciless conduct of the victors—Existence of wild men in the mountains Account of one at Bunaauïa who had fled from the field of battle—Treatment of the captives and the slain—Division of the spoil, and appropriation of the country—Maritime warfare—Encampments—Fortifications—Instance of patriotism—Methods of concluding peace—Religious ceremonies and festivities that followed—Present sentiments of the people in reference to war—Triumph of the principles of peace—Incident at Rurutu.

Provision for war was attended to when every other consideration was disregarded. In the perpetration of the unnatural crime of infanticide, boys were more frequently spared than female children, solely with a view to their becoming warriors. In all our schools, we were surprised at the disproportion between the boys and the girls that attended, and at the small number of women in the adult population; and on inquiring the cause, were invariably told that more girls than boys were destroyed, because they would, if spared, be comparatively useless in war. War therefore, being esteemed by the majority as the most important end of life, every kind of training for its successful pursuit was held in the highest repute.

In times of war, all capable of bearing arms were called upon to join the forces of the chieftain to whom they belonged, and the farmers, who held their land partly by feudal tenure, were obliged to render military service whenever their landlord required it. There were, besides these, a number of men celebrated for their valour, strength, or address in war, who were called *aito*, fighting-men or warriors. This title, the result of achievements in battle, was highly respected, and proportionably sought by the daring and ambitious. It was not, like the chieftainship and other prevailing distinctions, confined to any class, but open to all; and many from the lower ranks have risen, as warriors, to a high station in the community.

Originally their weapons were simple, and formed of wood; they consisted of the spear, which the natives called *patia* or *tao*, made with the wood of the cocoa-nut tree, or of the *aito*, iron-wood, or casuarina. It was twelve or eighteen feet long, and about an inch or an inch and a half in diameter at the middle or the lower end, but tapering off to a point at the other. The spears of the inhabitants of Rurutu, and other of the Austral Islands, are remarkable for their great length and elegant shape, as well as for the high polish with which they are finished.

The *omore*, or club, was another weapon used by them; it was always made of the *aito*, or iron-wood, and was principally of two kinds, either short and heavy like a bludgeon, for the purpose of close combat, or long, and furnished with a broad lozenge-shaped blade. The Tahitians did not often carve or ornament their weapons, but by the inhabitants of the southern islands they were frequently very neatly, though partially, carved. The inhabitants of the Marquesas carve their spears, and ornament them with human hair;* and the natives of the Hervey Islands, with the Friendly and Figian islanders, construct their weapons with taste, and carve them with remarkable ingenuity.

The *paeho* was a terrific sort of weapon, although it was principally used at the *heva*, or seasons of mourning. It resembled, in some degree, a club; but having the inner side armed with large sharks' teeth, it was not used for striking a blow, but for almost embowelling those assailed. Another weapon of the same kind resembled a short sword, but, instead of one blade it had three, four, or five. It was usually made of a forked *aito* branch; the central and exterior branches, after having been pointed and polished, were armed along the outside with a thick line of sharks' teeth, very firmly fixed in the wood. This was only used in close combat, and, when applied to the naked bodies of the combatants, must have been a terrific weapon. The bowels or lower parts of the body were attacked with it, not for the purpose of piercing, as a dagger is used, but drawn across like a saw.

They do not use the *patia*, or dagger, of the Sandwich Islands, but substitute an equally fatal weapon, the *aero fai*, a serrated back-bone of the sting-ray, and the *hoto*, a short dart-like weapon, barbed and pointed with this or other fish-

---

* This practice corresponds with that of the Malayans, among whom Dr. Buchanan saw a chief, the top of whose spear was ornamented with a tuft of hair, which he had taken from a vanquished foe, as he lay dying or dead at his feet.

bones, which being rugged on the edges, and barbed towards the point, is very destructive in a dexterous hand. Some of the natives of the Palliser Islands used the *ihi*, javelin or short spear, while fighting at a distance, and the South Sea Islanders use the *tiora*, a polished dart about three feet long, cast from the hand generally in their naval engagements, but occasionally on land. The *paro*, or large mother-of-pearl oyster shell, was also used in cutting the throats, or severing the head from the bodies, of those who were overcome.

The dress and ornaments of the warriors of Tahiti, and the adjacent islands, were singular, and unlike those of most savage nations, being often remarkably cumbersome. Their helmets, though less elegant and imposing than the fine Grecian-formed helmet of the Hawaiians, were adapted to produce considerable effect. Some of the Tahitians wore only a fillet or bandage round the temples, but many had a quantity of cloth bound round in the form of a high turban, which not only tended to increase their apparent stature, but broke the force of a blow from a club, or a thrust from a spear.

The most elegant head-dresses, however, were those worn by the inhabitants of the Austral Islands, Tubuai, Rurutu, &c. Their helmets were considerably diversified in form, some resembling a tight round cap, fitted closely to the head, with a light plume waving on the summit. Those used by the natives of Tubuai, and High Island, resembled an officer's cocked hat, worn with the ends projecting over each shoulder, the front beautifully ornamented with the green and red wing and tail feathers of a species of paroquet. The

Rurutuan helmet* is graceful in appearance, and useful in the protection it affords to the head of the wearer. It was a cap fitted to the head, and reaching to the ears, made with thick stiff native cloth, on a cane frame-work. The lower part of the front is ornamented with bunches of beautiful red and green feathers, tastefully arranged, and above these a line of the long slender tail-feathers of the tropic, or man-of-war bird, is fixed on a wicker-frame; the hinder part of the cap is covered with long flowing human hair, of a light brown or tawny colour, said to be human beard; this is fastened to a slight net-work attached to the crown of the helmet, and, being detached from any other part, often floats wildly in the wind, and increases the agitated appearance of the wearer.

On each side, immediately above the ears, numerous pieces of mother-of-pearl, and other shells, are fastened, not as plates or scales, but depending in a bunch, and attached to the helmet by a small strong cord, similar to those passing under the chin, by which the helmet is fastened to the head. These shells, when shaken by the movements of the wearer's head, produce a rattling noise, which heightens the din of savage warfare.

The Rurutuan helmet, though more complete and useful, was far less imposing than the *fau* worn by the Georgian and Society Islanders. This was also a cap fitted closely to the head, surrounded by a cylindrical structure of cane-work, ornamented with the dark glossy feathers of aquatic birds. The hollow crown frequently towered

* A Rurutuan helmet, a number of spears, a paeho, and many of the implements of war here described, have been deposited in the Missionary Museum, Austin Friars, London.

two or three feet above the head, and, being curved at the top, appeared to nod or bend with every movement of the wearer.

This was a head-dress in high esteem, and worn only by distinguished men, who were generally sought out by the warriors in the opposing army. To subdue or kill a man who wore a fau, was one of the greatest feats. I have been often told, by a gigantic man who resided some time in my house, and was one of the warriors of Eimeo, that when the army of the enemy has come in sight, they used to look out for the fau rising above the rest of the army, and when they have seen one, pointing to it, animate each other by the exclamation, "The man with the fau; ha! whosoever shall obtain him, it will be enough." But, however imposing in appearance these high helmets may have been, they afforded no defence; and, although formed only of cane-work and feathers, must have been inconvenient.

The slingers, and the most light and agile among the fighting men, wore, in battle, only a maro, a loose mantle, or ahubu.

Some of the fighting men wore a kind of armour of net-work, formed by small cords, wound round the body and limbs, so tight, as merely to allow of the unencumbered exercise of the legs and arms, and not to impede the circulation of the blood: or the Ruuruu, a kind of wooden armour for the breast, back, and sides, covered with successive folds of thick cloth, bound on with ropes. Over this a costly cloth was spread. The head was guarded with a corresponding quantity of cloth; and thus defended, the warrior, secure against either club or spear, was generally stationed with the main body of the army, though so encumbered as to render retreat impracticable, and, in the event of the defeat of his companions, was invariably captured or slain. In general, the dress of the Tahitian warriors must have been exceedingly troublesome. To make an imposing appearance, and defend their persons, seem to have been the only ends at which they aimed; differing greatly in this respect from the Hawaiians, who seldom thought of guarding themselves, but adopted a dress that would least impede their movements.

The Tahitians went to battle in their best clothes, sometimes perfumed with fragrant oil, and adorned with flowers; and whether they wore only the light *tiputa*, or the cumbrous *ruuruu*, which left only the arms at liberty, the whole was bound round the waist with a finely braided sash or girdle. On the breast they wore a handsome military gorget, ingeniously wrought with mother-of-pearl shells, white and coloured feathers, and dog's hair.

Their ancient dresses and weapons have, since their intercourse with Europeans, been superseded in a great degree by the introduction of fire-arms, the bayonet, and the sword. *Pupuhi* is the general name for gun. *Puhi* signifies to blow with the mouth, *pupuhi* to blow repeatedly, and this name has been given to a musket, from the circumstance of the foreigners, whom the natives first saw firing, bending down the head on one side to take aim, and bringing the mouth nearly in contact with the piece, into or through the barrel of which they supposed the person blew, and thus produced the explosion; hence it is called the blower.

They imagined that the first ships they saw were islands; their inhabitants supernatural, vindictive, and revengeful beings. The flag of one of the first vessels hanging from the ship into the water, a native approached, and took a piece of it away; this being perceived, he was fired at, and wounded, as they all supposed, by the thunder.

When we consider this, we shall not be surprised at their ideas of the source of motion in the ball. The opinion of its being blown from the mouth of the musketeer, has long been corrected; still the name is retained, and a cannon is called *pupuhi fenna*, to blow land, or country, from its contents spreading over a wide tract of country; the musket they call *pupuhi roa*, long gun; the blunderbuss *vaharahi*, wide or great mouth; the pistol *pupuhi teuumu*; a swivel, *pupuhi tioi*, turning gun; the bullets or balls they call *ofai*, or stones. Arms, ammunition, and ardent spirits, were formerly the principal articles in demand by all classes; and being the most valuable kinds of barter, they maintained a high price. Ten or twelve hogs, worth at least from one to two pounds a head, was, for a long time, the regular price of a musket; and one hundred pigs have been paid for a cannon. I have seen upwards of seventy tied up on the beach, at Fa-re, as the price of a single old cannon, which had been preserved from the wreck of an English vessel, at another island. These articles have, however, long ceased to be in demand among the Tahitians.

It does not appear that their wars were more sanguinary and cruel when they fought at a distance with muskets, than when they grappled hand to hand with club and spear. The numbers killed might be greater, but fewer were wounded. Although familiar with the musket during their last wars, they are by no means expert marksmen:

they understand little about taking aim, and often fire without placing the butt-end of the musket against the shoulder, or presenting their piece. They grasp it in the most awkward manner, holding it above the head, or by the side, and in this singular position fire it off. I was once with a party of natives, when one of them fired at a bullock but a few yards distant, and missed it.

War was seldom proclaimed or commenced with promptitude, being always considered as one of the most important matters in which the nation could engage. Hence the preparatory deliberations were frequent and protracted.

The greatest importance was always attached to the will of the gods: if they were favourable, conquest was regarded as sure; but if they were unfavourable, defeat, if not death, was as certain. Divination, or enchantment, was employed for the purpose of knowing their ultimate decision, and at these times they always pretended to follow implicitly supernatural intimation, though all this juggling and contrivance was designed only to deceive the people into a persuasion that the god sanctioned the views of the king and government. The divinations were connected with the offerings, and the success or failure of the expedition was often chiefly augured from the muscular action in the heart or liver of the animal offered, the involuntary acts and writhing contortions of the limbs of the human sacrifice in the agonies of death; or the appearance of the slaughtered victim, after it had been placed upon the altar.

When the murder and destruction of actual conflict terminated, and the vanquished sought security in flight, or in the natural strong-holds of the mountains, some of their conquerors pursued them to their hiding-places, while others repaired to the villages, and destroyed the wives, children, infirm and afflicted relatives, of those who had fled before them in the field. These defenceless wretches seldom made much resistance to the lawless and merciless barbarians, whose conduct betrayed a cowardly delight in torturing their helpless victims. Plunder and revenge were the principal objects in these expeditions. Every thing valuable they destroyed or bore away, while the miserable objects of their vengeance were deliberately murdered. No age or sex was spared. The infant that unconsciously smiled in its mother's arms, and the venerable gray-haired father or mother, experienced unbridled and horrid barbarity. The aged were at once despatched, though embowelling and every horrid torture was practised. The females experienced brutality and murder, and the tenderest infants were perhaps transfixed to the mother's heart by a ruthless weapon—caught up by ruffian hands, and dashed against the rocks or the trees—or wantonly thrown up in the air, and caught on the point of the warrior's spear, where it writhed in agony and died. A spear was sometimes thrust through the infant's head from ear to ear, a line passed through the aperture, and when the horrid carnage has been over, and the kindling brand has been applied to the dwellings, while the flames have crackled, the dense columns of smoke ascended, and the ashes mingled with the blood from the victims, the cruel warriors have retired with fiendish exultation, some bearing the spoils of plunder, some having two or three infants hanging on the spear they bore across their shoulders, and others dragging along the sand those that were strung together by a line through their heads, or a cord round their necks. This cruelty was not confined to the slain; the living captives, adults and children, were sometimes thus strung together by cords passed through the head from ear to ear, by holes made with the spears.

When those who had been vanquished in the field did not return to battle, but remained in their strong-holds, another religious ceremony was performed by the conquerors, called the Hora. A large quantity of property, the spoil of victory, was taken to the priests of Oro, partly as an acknowledgment for past success, but chiefly to encourage them to increased intercession that the destruction the god had commenced might not cease till their enemies were annihilated, for their wars were wars of extermination.

One singular result of their dreadful wars, and their horrid sacrifice of human beings is, the existence of a number of wild men inhabiting the fastnesses of the interior mountains of Tahiti. I have not heard of any having been seen in any other island, but they have been more than once met with in the neighbourhood of Atehuru. When I visited this station in 1821, I saw one of these men, who had been some time before taken in the mountains; he was comparatively tame, yet I shall not soon forget his appearance. He was above the middle size, large-boned, but not fleshy. His features and countenance were strongly marked; his complexion was not darker than those of many around, but his aspect was agitated and wild. His beard was unshaven, and his hair had remained uncut for many years. It appeared about a foot and a half in length, in some parts perhaps longer. He wore it parted in the middle of his forehead, but hanging uncombed an dishevelled on the other parts of his head. On the outside it was slightly curled, and hung in loose ringlets. The colour was singular; at the roots, or close to his head, it was dark brown or black, six inches from his head it was of a tawny brown, while the extremities exhibited a light and in some places bright yellow. Many attempts had been made to persuade him to have it cut, but to this he would never consent.

His only clothing was a *maro*, or girdle, with sometimes a light piece of cloth over his shoulder. His nails, for the sake of convenience, he had cut. He said but little, and though he came and looked at us once or twice, he seemed averse to observation, and retired when I attempted to converse with him. He had been driven to the mountains in a time of war, had remained in solitude for years, had been at length discovered by persons travelling in these regions, secured, and brought down, where with great difficulty he had been induced to remain. Mr. Darling said, he was very quiet, but appeared uninterested in most of what was passing around him.

Since Mr. Darling's residence at Bunaauïa, others have been seen in the mountains, and one was secured by the people of Burder's Point. They had gone to the mountains for the bark of the tiairi, which they use in dying native cloth; on their way they perceived a man lying on his side asleep, and exclaiming this is a *taehae*, a wild man, one of them went round among the bushes, in order to get on the opposite side, while the other was to advance slowly towards him: as they approached he awoke, and startled by their appearance, rose, flinging over his shoulders his hair, which the natives described as reaching to his waist, and darted into the woods; where he was stopped by one of the men who saw him, and finally secured. He was evidently enfeebled from recent illness, or, as the natives expressed themselves, they could neither have caught or retained him. Terror seemed to have absorbed every feeling. It was in vain they assured him that they meant him no injury, he appeared either not to understand, or not to regard any thing they said, but constantly exclaimed, "Ye are murderers, ye are murderers," occasionally supplicating them with, "Do not murder me, do not murder me." They conducted him to the settlement, gave him food and clothing, and, treating him with kindness, he appeared somewhat calmed, but still manifested a most restless apprehension, and for a long time the only sounds he uttered were, "Do not kill me." He was taken to the school and the chapel, but appeared distressed by the noise, yet pleased with letters, and ultimately even learned the elements of reading, but took the first opportunity of fleeing to the mountains. About a fortnight afterwards he was again secured, and brought to the settlement; but whether or not he has since returned to the woods, I have not the means of knowing. He is supposed to have originally fled for fear of being sacrificed to the gods, and, under the panic which seized those who were defeated in some of the battles that within the last fifty years have been fought in these portions of the island, to have retreated to the mountain fastnesses in its more central parts, where perhaps he had experienced a degree of mental aberration which had deprived him of memory, and induced him to wander like a demoniac among the lonely rocks and valleys.

On another occasion, some people from Bunaauia saw a large party, four or five, with two women and some children. These, the persons who saw them thought it most prudent to leave unmolested, and, though a large party have since sought them, I have not heard of their being met with. It is reported by the natives, that others have been seen, and that some of the inhabitants of the lowlands have been in danger of losing their lives from coming in contact with them. After the evidence of the facts above mentioned, we cannot doubt the existence of such unhappy victims; but at the same time, the circumstance of their being so seldom seen, warrants the hope that they are not numerous.

The captives taken in war, called *ivi* or *titi*, were murdered on the spot, or shortly afterwards, unless reserved for slaves to the victors. The bodies of the slain were treated in a most savage manner; they were pierced with their spears; and at times the conduct of the victors towards their lifeless remains was inconceivably barbarous. They were regarded as belonging to the king, and were disposed of according to his direction, and either left on the field, or taken to the places appropriated to the bodies of the slain.

On the day following the battle, the *bure taata* was performed. This consisted in collecting the bodies of the slain, and offering them to Oro, as trophies of his prowess, and in acknowledgment of their dependence upon his aid. Prayers were preferred, imploring a continuance of his assistance.

The bodies were usually left exposed to the elements, and to the hogs or wild dogs, and the crab that preyed upon them.—The victors took

CANNIBALISM.

away the lower jaw-bones of the most distinguished among the slain, as trophies, and often the bones of the arms or legs, forming with them tools for building canoes, or fish-hooks, while others converted the skulls of the slain into drinking vessels to be used at the feast of victory. Sometimes they piled the bodies in a heap, and built the skulls into a kind of wall around the temple, as at Opoa, but they were commonly laid in rows near the shore, or in front of the camp, their heads all in the same direction. Here the skulls were often so battered with the clubs, that no trace of the countenance or human head remained. The bodies of females slain in war were presented to two of the daughters of Taaroa, and were treated with equal barbarity, and a degree of brutality, as inconceivable as it was detestable.

In addition to the preceding indignities, their bodies were sometimes laid in rows along the beach, and used as rollers, over which they dragged their canoes, on landing, or launching them after a battle. We do not know that the Tahitians ever feasted on the bodies of the slain in a regular banquet, although this is practised by the Marquesians on the one side, and the New-Zealanders on the other—by the inhabitants of the Dangerous Archipelago in the immediate neighbourhood of the Georgian Islands in the east—and in several of the Hervey Islands in the west, especially Aitutake, where it continued till the abolition of idolatry in 1823.

Here the warriors were animated to the murderous combat by allusions to the inhuman feast it would furnish at the close. In New-Zealand, it is stated that a warrior has been known, when exulting over his fallen antagonist, to sever his head from his body, and, while the life-blood has flowed warm from the dying trunk, to scoop it up in his hands, and, turning to his enemies with fiend-like triumph, drink it before them. The Tahitians were not, however, altogether free from cannibalism; and, occasionally, a warrior, out of bravado or revenge, has been known to eat two or three mouthfuls of a vanquished foe, generally the fat from the inner side of the ribs.

Besides the *otore*, embowelling, which was frequently inflicted, they sometimes practised what they called *tiputa taata*. When a man had slain his enemy, in order fully to satiate his revenge, and intimidate his foes, he sometimes beat the body flat, and then cut a hole with a stone battle-axe through the back and stomach, and passed his own head through the aperture, as he would through the hole of his tiputa or poncho; hence the name of this practice. In this terrific manner, with the head and arms of the slain hanging down before, and the legs behind him, he marched to renew the conflict. A more horrific act and exhibition it is not easy to conceive of, yet I was well acquainted with a man in Fare, named Taiava, who, according to his own confession, and the declaration of his neighbours, was guilty of this deed during one of their recent wars. The bodies of celebrated warriors were often *pinihia* for the amusement of the spectators. The legs and arms were broken, round the feet and hands a kind of fringe of ti-leaves was tied, a rope was tied round the neck, by which the body was drawn up towards the branch of a tree, from which it remained suspended; a small cord, attached to one of the feet, was held in the hand of the exhibitor; by means of these cords the body was drawn up and down: other dead bodies were placed on the ground beneath, and beaten with the stalk of the cocoa-nut leaf, in the place of drums; to the horrid music, thus produced, the suspended body was made to move, for the mirth of the thousands who assembled to witness the sport; and such was the interest of these exhibitions, that the natives say they never thought of taking food at the time.

Other brutalities were practised towards the slain, which I never could have believed, had they not been told by the individuals who had been engaged in them, but which, though I do not doubt their authenticity, are improper to detail. I should not have dwelt so long on the distressing facts that have been given, but to exhibit in the true, though by no means strongest colours, the savage character and brutal conduct of those, who have been represented as enjoying, in their rude and simple state, a high degree of happiness, and cultivating all that is amiable and benevolent.

The bodies of the slain being now abandoned by the victors, they turned their attention to the division of the spoils, the appropriation of the country, &c. In connexion with this, the *rani arua* was performed, and was indeed considered as a part of the ceremony of devoting the slain to the gods. A human sacrifice was procured, and offered, principally to secure the return of the occupations and amusements of peace; feasting, dancing, &c. The burden of the prayer was—*Tutavae aua i te po, Roonui arena homai te ao*, &c. and which may be rendered, " Let the god of war return to the world of night : Let Roo the god of peace preside in the world, or place of light," &c.

The local situation of the people, and their

familiarity with the sea, led them to feel at home upon the water, and on this element many of their bloodiest battles were fought. A description of their *pahis*, or war canoes, has been already given. Their fleets were often large. The Huahinian expedition, according to the account of those still living who were in the battle of Hooroto, amounted to " ninety ships, each twenty fathoms long," on which it is probable a number of smaller canoes were in attendance. When the engagement took place within the reefs, the canoes were often lashed together in a line, the stem of one being fastened to the stern of the canoe before it. This they called *api*, and adopted it to prevent the breaking of their line, or retreat from the combat. The opposing fleet was, perhaps, lashed or fastened in the same way; and thus the two fleets, presenting one continued line of canoes, with the *revas* or streamers flying, were paddled out to sea, the warriors occupying the platform raised for their defence, and enabling them to command each part of the canoe.

At a distance, stones were slung; on a nearer approach, light spears or javelins were hurled, until they came close alongside of each other, when, under the excitement of rage, infatuation, ambition, or despair, they fought with the most obstinate fury.

It is not easy to imagine a conflict more sanguinary and horrid than theirs must have been. Although the victors, when *faatini'd* or supplicated, sometimes spared the fallen, it was rarely they gave any quarter. Retreat there was none—and, knowing that death or conquest must end the fray, they fought under the influence of desperation.

At times, both fleets retired, as at Hooroto; but when victory was evidently in favour of one, the warriors in that fleet sometimes swept through the other, slaughtering all who did not leap into the sea, and swim toward the canoe of some friend in the opposing fleet. I have been informed by some of the chiefs of Huahine, who have been in their battles, that they have seen a fleet towed to the shore by the victors, filled with the wounded and the dead—the few that survived being inadequate to its management.

When the canoes of a fleet were not fastened together, as soon as the combatants perceived that they were overpowered, they sought safety in flight, and, if pursued, abandoned their canoes on reaching the shore, and hastened to their fortress in the mountains.

They did not enclose their temporary encampments in the open field, but each party considered a fortification as a security against invasion, and a refuge after defeat in action.

Their places of defence were rocky fortresses improved by art—narrow defiles, or valleys sheltered by projecting eminences—passes among the mountains, difficult of access, yet allowing their inmates a secure and extensive range, and an unobstructed passage to some spring or stream. The celebrated Pare, in Atehuru, was of this kind; the mouth of the valley in which it was situated was built up with a stone wall, and those who fled thither for shelter, were generally able to repel their assailants.

Sometimes they cut down trees, and built a kind of stage or platform called *pafata*, projecting over an avenue leading to the *pare;* upon this they collected piles of stone and fragments of rock, which they hurled down on those by whom they were attacked. In some of the Hervey Islands they planted trees around their places of encampment, and thus rendered them secure against surprise.—These enclosures they called *pa*, the term which is used to designate a fort in the Sandwich Islands.

If those who had been routed on the field of battle were allowed by their pursuers time to wall up the entrances of their places of refuge, they were seldom exposed to assault, though they might be decoyed from them by stratagem, or induced to leave from hunger. The *pari* in Boraboro, and some places in Tahiti, are seldom excelled as natural fortresses. Several of these places were very extensive; that at Maeva, in Huahine, bordering on a lake of the same name, and near Mounatabu, is probably the best artificial fortification in the islands. Being a square of about half a mile on each side, it encloses many acres of ground well stocked with bread-fruit, containing several springs, and having within its precincts the principal temple of their tutelar deity. The walls are of solid stonework, in height twelve feet. They are even and regularly paved at the top. On the top of the walls, (which in some places were ten or twelve feet thick,) the warriors kept watch, and slept. Their houses were built within, and it was considered sufficiently large to contain the whole of the population. There were four principal openings in the wall, at regular distances from each other, that in the west being called the king's road. They were designed for ingress and egress, but during a siege were built up with loose stones, when it was considered a *pari haabuea*, an impregnable fortress, or, as the term indicates, place of refuge and life.

Such as fled to the rocks or mountains were called *meho*.

If those who had escaped were numerous, and the conquering army wished to subdue them, the war often assumed a protracted form. When the assailants had determined on reducing them, they endeavoured to decoy them out; if they failed, they seldom succeeded in scaling or forcing their ramparts. Famine often reduced the besieged to the greatest distress, so that they ate the *pohue*, or wild convolvolus stalks, and other rude kinds of food. They frequently made desperate sallies, but were often driven back with great slaughter.

In a sally made during one of the wars which occurred in the year 1802, called in the annals of Tahiti, " the war of Rua," this chief, and a number of his fighting-men, were taken, and killed on the spot by the king's order. The next day the king marched to the fortress, but found it well manned, and the greatest determination to resist manifested by the warriors.

An ambassadress, with a flag of truce, passed between the parties, but the besieged manifested an uncommon degree of dauntless obstinacy. When told of the numbers and the persons slain, they appeared as if but little affected by it, pretended not to know them, excepting the chief, who, they said, it was far more likely had been drowned in the river, than that he had fallen into their hands. This they evidently did, to shew that what they thought would induce them to make an unconditional surrender, had not so subdued them; and the survivor, Taatahee, directed the ambassadress to say to Pomare, " When I have experienced the same fate as Rua then, and not till then, he may expect peace."

When the reduction of a fortress was a matter of importance, the co-operation of the gods was again invoked, and the Hiamoea performed. This was a religious ceremony, in which the finest mats, cloth, and other valuable spoils, were taken by the victorious party, as near to the fortress as it was safe to approach. Here they took the different articles of property in their hands, and, holding them up, offered them to the gods, who, it was supposed, had hitherto favoured the besieged; the priests frequently exclaiming to the following effect— *Tane* in the interior or fortress, *Oro* in the interior or fortress, &c. come to the sea, here are your offerings, &c. The priests of the besieged, on the contrary, endeavoured to detain the gods, by exhibiting whatever property they possessed, if they considered the god likely to leave them. A warrior would sometimes offer himself, and say, *Eiaha e haere*, " Leave us not, here is your offering, O Oro! even I!" It is hardly possible to avoid admiring the patriotism evinced on such occasions. It was a devotion worthy of a better cause.

Although the besieged might offer their human sacrifices, they must perform what, under these circumstances, would be called *Taaraa-moua*, the fall from the mountain, and which they carried as near the temple of the tutelar deity as their enemies would allow them to approach, when, having deposited their offering, they fled to the fortress, determined to defend it; yet, if the property which the victors had there offered, and devoted as it were to the gods, was valuable and abundant, the besieged became dispirited, believing that the gods had left them, and gone to the party by whom these offerings had been made. They always imagined that the gods were influenced by motives similar to those which governed their own conduct; and when once the vanquished party imbibed the impression that the gods had forsaken them, their defence was comparatively feeble, and they consequently fell a prey to their enemies, who were often indebted more to the superstitious apprehensions of their foes, than to their own skill or power. It is amusing (were it not too serious a subject) to notice the absurdity, and childish conduct occasionally exhibited. When a party wished for peace, they sometimes offered the *taata o meia roa*, a young plantain tree, taken up by the roots, put in a basket, and carried to the temple, as they were accustomed to carry a human victim. The men who bore it, shouting to the god, exclaimed, "Here is the man, long plantain; give us peace in abundance. Compassionate your devotees—cause the war to cease. If you do not attend, we will not worship you again. Compassionate your pigs, feeders, pearl divers, scarlet feather seekers. If you do not deliver us, you are an evil working god."

If the conquered party surrendered at discretion, their land and property were divided by the conquerors, and the captives either murdered, reduced to slavery, or reserved for sacrifices when the gods might require human victims. The bodies of such as were killed in their forts, were treated with the same indignity as those slain in the field; parts of the bodies were *eaten* by the priests, the rest piled up in heaps on the sea-coast, where the effects of decomposition have been so offensive, that the people have forborne to fish in the adjacent parts of the sea. On the contrary, when neither party had been subdued, and, by intimation from the gods, or any other cause, one party desired peace, an ambassador was sent with a flag of truce which was usually of native cloth, a bunch of the sacred miro, or a bunch of feathers fixed to the end of a reed, and called the *manufaiti*, and proposals of peace. If the other party were favourable, an interview followed between the leaders, attended by the priests and national orators.

They usually sat in council on the ground, either under a shady grove, or on the sandy beach. The orators of those who had sent the proposals made the first harangue; this was followed by a reply from the orator of the other party, who was sitting on the ground opposite, and ten or twenty yards distant. Each held in his hand a bunch of the sacred miro. The king or chiefs sat beside them, while the people stood around, at some distance. When the terms were agreed upon, the wreath of peace was woven with two or three green boughs, furnished by each, as the bond of reconciliation and friendship. Two young dogs were then exchanged by the respective parties, and the *apa pia* brought; this was sometimes a long strip of *apa*, or cloth, white on one side, and red on the other; the cloth was joined together, by both parties, in token of their union, and imprecations were invoked on those who should *hae*, or rend, the *apaa pia*, or band of peace. The apaa pia and the green boughs were then offered to the gods, and they were called upon to avenge the treachery of those who should rend the band, or break the wreath. Divinations were also used, to know whether it would be of a long or short continuance. Sometimes a chief desirous of peace, sent a herald with the red and yellow feathers, and the apaa pia fastened at opposite ends of a cane, saying, " Fly to the dark water, (opposing army) with this manufaiti;" which was also called the restorer of peace, by which the dark sky became bright and cloudless.

Feasting followed the ceremony, together with the usual native games; besides which, religious rites were performed. The first was the *maioi*, when vast quantities of food were taken to the king, and large offerings to the gods, together with prayers for the establishment and prosperity of the reign. Another was called the *oburoa na te arii*, and consisted also in offerings to the gods, with prayers for their support, and a large present of food to the principal warrior chief, under the king, as an acknowledgment of his important service in the recent struggles, and his influence in establishing the king in his government.

But the most important ceremony, in connexion with the ratification of peace, was the *upoofaataa*, &c. It was commemorative of the establishment of the new government, and designed to secure its perpetuity, and the happiness of the community. A leading raatira was usually the chief proprietor of the entertainment, and master of the ceremonies. The festival was convivial and religious. Food and fruits, in the greatest profusion, were furnished for the altars of the gods, and the banquet of the king.

A *heiva*, or grand dance, formed a part of this ceremony. It was called the dance of peace, and was performed in the presence of the king, who, surrounded by a number of chiefs and warriors, sat at one end of the large house in which it took place. A number of men, and sometimes women, fantastically dressed, danced to the beating of the drum and the warbling of the *vivo*, or flute; and though the king was surrounded by a number of attendants as body-guards, towards the close of the exhibition the men sought to approach the king's person, and kiss his hand, or the females to salute his face; when one or the other succeeded in this, the heiva, or dance, was complete, and the performance discontinued.

This, however, was only part of the ceremony, for while they were thus employed, the priests were engaged in supplicating the gods that these amusements might be continued, and their enjoyments in feasting, dancing, and the pursuits connected with them, might not be again suspended or disturbed by war. Peace was now considered as established, the club and spear were cleaned, varnished, and hung up in their dwellings; and the festive entertainments, pagan rites, and ordinary avocations of life, resumed, till some fresh quarrel required an appeal to their weapons, and again led them to the field of plunder and of death.

I have dwelt longer on this subject than I intended, and perhaps than it required; but the former frequency of war, the motives influencing the parties engaging in the ceremonies connected with it, and the manner in which it was prosecuted, were all adapted to convey, next to their mythology, a correct idea of the national character of the people, who made war, paganism, and vicious amusements, the business of life. In all our converse with them relative to their former state, no subject was so frequently introduced. No event in history, no character in their biography, appeared unconnected with some warlike expedition, or feat of arms; and almost all the illustrations of the most powerful and striking expressions which we sought to investigate, were drawn from the wars.

CHAP. XIII.

General view of Polynesian mythology—Ideas relative to the origin of the world—Polytheism—Traditionary theogony—Taaroa supreme deity—Different orders of gods—Oro, Hiro, &c. gods of the wind—Power of spirits to raise tempests—Gods of the ocean, &c.—Supposed cause of an eclipse.—Gods of artificers and fishermen—Oramatuas, or demons—Emblems—Images—Uru, or feathers—Temples—Worship—Prayers—The awakening of the gods—Offerings—Sacrifices—Occasional and stated festivals and worship—Rau-mata-vehi-raa Maui-fata—Rites for recovery from sickness—Offering of first-fruits—The pae atua—The ripening of the year, a religious ceremony—Singular rites attending its close.

Whatever attention the Tahitians paid to their occupations or amusements, and whatever energies have been devoted to the prosecution of their barbarous wars, the claims of all were regarded as inferior to those of their religion. On this every other pursuit was dependent, while each was alike made subservient to its support. In an account of the former state of the people, their system of religion requires therefore particular notice.

Like that of all the ancient idolatrous nations, the mythology of the South Sea Islanders is but an assemblage of obscure fables brought by the first settlers, or originated in remarkable facts of their own history, and handed down by tradition through successive generations. If so much that is mysterious and fabulous has been mingled with the history of those nations among whom hieroglyphics or the use of letters has prevailed, it might be expected to exist in a greater degree, where oral communication, and that often under the fantastic garb of rude poetry, is the only mode of preserving the traditional knowledge of former times.

Distinguished, however, as the Polynesian mythology is by confusion and absurdity, it is not more so than the systems of some of the most enlightened and cultivated pagan nations, of the past or present time. It was not more characterized by mystery and fable, than by its abominations and its cruelty. Its objects of worship were sometimes monsters of iniquity. The islanders had "lords many and gods many," but seldom attributed to them any moral attributes. Among the multitude of their gods, there was no one whom they regarded as a supreme intelligence or presiding spiritual being, possessing any moral perfections, resembling those which are inseparable from every sentiment we entertain of the true God.

Like the most ancient nations, they ascribe the origin of all things to a state of chaos, or darkness, and even the first existence of their principal deities refer to this source. Taaroa, Oro, and Tane, with other deities of the highest order, are on this account said to be *fanau po*, born of Night. But the origin of the gods, and their priority of existence in comparison with the formation of the earth, being a matter of uncertainty even among the native priests, involves the whole in obscurity.

Taaroa, the Tanaroa of the Hawaiians, and the Tangaroa of the Western Isles, is generally spoken of by the Tahitians as the first and principal god, uncreated, and existing from the beginning, or from the time he emerged from the *po,* or world of darkness.

Several of their taata-paari, or wise men, pretend that, according to other traditions, Taaroa was only a man who was deified after death. By some he is spoken of as the progenitor of the other gods, the creator of the heavens, the earth, the sea, man, beasts, fowls, fishes, &c.; while by others it is stated, that the existence of the land, or the universe, was anterior to that of the gods.

There does not appear to be any thing in the Tahitian mythology corresponding with the doctrine of the Trinity, or the Hindoo tradition of Brahma, Vishnou, and Siva. Taaroa was the former and father of the gods; Oro was his first son: but there were three classes or orders between Taaroa and Oro. As in the theogony of the ancients, a bird was a frequent emblem of deity; and in the body of a bird they supposed the god often approached the marae, where it left the bird, and entered the *too,* or image, through which it was supposed to communicate with the priest.

The inferior gods and men, the animals, the air, earth, and sea, were by some supposed to originate in the procreative power of the supreme god. One of the legends of their origin and descent, furnished to some of the Missionaries, by whom it has been recorded, states, that Taaroa was born of Night, or proceeded from Chaos, and was not made by any other god. His consort, Ofeufeumaiterai, also uncreated, proceeded from the *po*, or night. Oro, the great national idol of Raiatea, Tahiti, Eimeo, and some of the other Islands, was the son of Taaroa and Ofeufeumaiterai. Oro took a goddess to wife, who became the mother of two sons. These four male and two female deities constituted the whole of their highest rank of divinities, according to the traditions of the priests of Tahiti—though the late king informed Mr. Nott that there was another god, superior to them all, whose name was Rumia; he did not, however, meet with any of their priests or bards who knew any thing about him. The tradition most generally received in the Windward Islands, ascribed the origin of the world, and all that adorn or inhabit it, to the procreative power of Taaroa, who is said to have embraced a rock, the imagined foundation of all things, which afterwards brought forth the earth and sea. It states, that soon after this, the heralds of day, the dark and the light blue sky, appeared before Taaroa, and solicited a soul for his offspring; the then inanimate universe. The foundation of all replied, It is done, and directed his son, the Sky-producer, to accomplish his will. In obedience to the mandate of Taaroa, his son looked up into the heavens, and the heavens received the power of bringing forth new skies, and clouds, sun, moon, and stars, thunder and lightning, rain and wind. He then looked downwards, and the unformed mass received the power to bring forth earth, mountains, rocks, trees, herbs and flowers, beasts, birds and insects, fountains, rivers, and fish. Raitubu, or Sky-producer, then looked to the abyss, and imparted to it power to bring forth the purple water, rocks and corals, and all the inhabitants of the ocean. Some of the gods are said to have been produced in the same way, namely, by the god Taaroa looking at the goddess his wife, who afterwards became the mother of his children.

Raa was also ranked among the principal deities; although inferior to Taaroa and Oro, and he was supposed to be an independent being; but nothing of consequence is ascribed to him in the native fables. His wife, Otupapa, who was also a divinity, bore him three sons and two daughters. Tane, the tutelar idol of Huahine, was also numbered among the uncreated gods, considered as having proceeded from the state of Night, or Chaos. His goddess was called Taufairei. They were the parents of eight sons, who were all classed with the most powerful gods, and received the highest honours. Among the sons of Tane was Temeharo, the tutelar deity of Pomare's family.

The most popular traditions in the Leeward Islands differed in several minor points from the above, which prevailed in the Windward group. According to one, for which I am indebted to my friend Mr. Barff, Taaroa, who was supreme here as well as in Tahiti, was said to be *Toivi*, or without parents, and to have existed from eternity. He was supposed to have a body, but it was invisible to mortals. After innumerable seasons had passed away, he cast his *paa*, shell or body, as birds do their feathers, or serpents their skins; and by this means, after intervals of innumerable seasons, his body was renewed. In the *reva*, or highest heavens, he dwelt alone. His first act was the creation of Hina, who is also called his daughter. Countless ages passed away, when Taaroa and his daughter made the heavens, the earth, and the sea. The foundation of the world was a solid rock; which, with every part of the creation, Taaroa was supposed to sustain by his invisible power.—It is stated, that the Friendly Islanders suppose that the earth is supported on the shoulders of one of their gods, and that when an earthquake takes place, he is transferring it from one shoulder to the other.

Having, with the assistance of Hina, made the heavens, earth, and sea, Taaroa *oriori*, or created, the gods. The first was Rootane, the god of peace. The second was Toahitu, in shape like a dog; he saved such as were in danger of falling from rocks and trees. *Te fatu* (the lord) was the third. *Te iria*, (the indignant,) a god of war, was the fourth. The fifth, who was said to have had a bald head, was called Ruanuu. The sixth was a god of war. The seventh, Tuaraatai, Mr. Barff thinks was the Polynesian Neptune. The eighth was Rimaroa, (long arms,) a god of war. The ninth in order were the gods of idiots, who were always considered as inspired. The tenth was *Tearii tabu tura*, another Mars. These were created by Taaroa, and constituted the first order of divinities.

A second class were also created, inferior to these, and employed as heralds between the gods and men. The third order seems to have been the descendants of Raa; these were numerous and varied in their character, some being gods of war, others among the Esculapiuses of the nation.

Oro was the first of the fourth class, and seems to have been the medium of connexion between celestial and terrestrial beings. Taaroa was his father. The shadow of a bread-fruit leaf, shaken by the power of the arm of Taaroa, passed over Hina, and she afterwards became the mother of Oro. Hina, it is said, abode in Opoa at the time of his birth; hence that was honoured as the place of his nativity, and became celebrated for his worship. Taaroa afterwards created the wife of Oro, and their children were also gods.

After the birth of Oro, Taaroa had other sons, who were called brothers of Oro, among whom were the gods of the Areois. These were the four orders of celestial beings worshipped in the Leeward Islands. The different classes only have been mentioned; an enumeration of the individual deities, and their offices or attributes, would be tedious and useless.

These objects of fear and worship were exceedingly numerous, and may be termed the chief deities of the Polynesians. There was an intermediate class between the principal divinities and the gods of particular localities or professions, but they are not supposed to have existed from the beginning, or to have been born of Night. Their origin is veiled in obscurity, but they are often described as having been renowned men, who after death were deified by their descendants. Roo, Tane, Teiri, probably Tairi, the principal idol of the Sandwich Islanders, Tefatu, Ruanuu, Moe, Teepa, Puaua, Tefatuture, Opaevai, Haana, and Taumure. These all received the homage of the people, and were on all public occasions acknowledged among Tahiti's gods.

Their gods of the ocean were not less numerous; this was to be expected amongst a people almost amphibious in their habits, dwelling in islands, and deriving a great part of their sustenance from the sea. The names of fourteen principal marine divinities were communicated by the first Missionaries; others have been subsequently added, but it is unnecessary to enumerate them here. They are not supposed by the people to be of equal antiquity with the *atua fauau po*, or night-born gods.

They were probably men who had excelled their contemporaries in nautical adventure or exploit, and were deified by their descendants. Hiro is conspicuous amongst them, although not exclusively a god of the sea. The most romantic accounts are given in their *aai*, or tales, of his adventures, his voyages, his combat with the gods of the tempests, his descent to the depth of the ocean, and residence at the bottom of the abyss, his intercourse with the monsters there, by whom he was lulled to sleep in a cavern of the ocean, while the god of the winds raised a violent storm, to destroy a ship in which his friends were voyaging. Destruction seemed to them inevitable—they invoked his aid—a friendly spirit entered the cavern in which he was reposing, roused him from his slumbers, and informed him of their danger. He rose to the surface of the waters, rebuked the spirit of the storm, and his followers reached their destined port in safety.

The period of his adventures is probably the most recent of any thus preserved, as there are more places connected with his name in the Leeward Islands than with any other. A pile of rocks in Tahaa is called the Dogs of Hiro; a mountain ridge has received the appellation of the Pahi, or Ship of Hiro; and a large basaltic rock near the summit of a mountain in Huahine, is called the Hoe or Paddle of Hiro.

Tuaraatai and Ruahatu, however, appear to have been the principal marine deities. Whether this distinction resulted from any superiority they were supposed to possess, or from the conspicuous

SHARKS CONSIDERED SACRED.

part the latter sustains in their tradition of the deluge, is not known; but their names are frequently mentioned. They were generally called *atua mao*, or shark gods; not that the shark was itself the god, but the natives supposed the marine gods employed the sharks as the agents of their vengeance.

The large blue shark was the only kind supposed to be engaged by the gods; and a variety of the most strange and fabulous accounts of the deeds they have performed are related by their priests. These voracious animals were said always to recognize a priest on board any canoe, to come at his call, retire at his bidding, and to spare him in the event of a wreck, though they might devour his companions, especially if they were not his maru, or worshippers. I have been repeatedly told by an intelligent man, formerly a priest of an atua mao, that the shark through which his god was manifested, swimming in the sea, carried either him or his father on its back from Raiatea to Huahine, a distance of twenty miles. The shark was not the only fish the Tahitians considered sacred. In addition to these, they had gods who were supposed to preside over the fisheries, and to direct to their coasts the various shoals by which they were periodically visited. Tahauru was the principal among these; but there were five or six others, whose aid the fishermen were accustomed to invoke, either before launching their canoes, or while engaged at sea. Matatini was the god of fishing-net makers.

Next in number and importance to the gods of the sea, were those of the aerial regions, sometimes worshipped under the figure of a bird. The chief of these were *Veromatautoru* and *Tairibu*, brother and sister to the children of Taaroa, their dwelling was near the great rock, which was the foundation of the world. Hurricanes, tempests, and all destructive winds, were supposed to be confined within them, and were employed by them to punish such as neglected the worship of the gods. In stormy weather their compassion was sought by the tempest-driven mariner at sea, or the friends of such on shore. Liberal presents, it was supposed, would at any time purchase a calm. If the first failed, subsequent ones were certain of success. The same means were resorted to for procuring a storm, but with less certainty. Whenever the inhabitants of one island heard of invasion from those of another, they immediately carried large offerings to these deities, and besought them to destroy by tempest the hostile fleet whenever it might put to sea. Some of the most intelligent people still think evil spirits had formerly great power over the winds, as they say there have been no such fearful storms since they abolished idolatry, as there were before. There were also gods of the *peho te moua te pari e te faa*, the valleys, the mountains, the precipices, and the dells or ravines. The names of twelve of the principal of these are preserved by the Missionaries; but as few of them are indicative of the character or attributes of these gods, their insertion is unnecessary.

I have often thought, when listening to their fabulous accounts of the adventures of their gods, which, when prosecuting our researches in their language, manners, customs, &c. we have sometimes with difficulty induced them to repeat, that, had they been acquainted with letters, these would have furnished ample materials for legends rivalling in splendour of machinery, and magnificence of achievement, the dazzling mythology of the eastern nations. Rude as their traditions were, in the gigantic exploits they detail, and the bold and varied imagery they employ, they are often invested with an air of romance, which shews that the people possessed no inferior powers of imagination.

By their rude mythology, each lovely island was made a sort of fairy-land, and the spells of enchantment were thrown over its varied scenes. The sentiment of the poet that—

"Millions of spiritual creatures walk the earth,
Unseen, both when we wake, and when we sleep,"

was one familiar to their minds; and it is impossible not to feel interested in a people who were accustomed to consider themselves surrounded by invisible intelligences, and who recognized in the rising sun—the mild and silver moon—the shooting star—the meteor's transient flame—the ocean's roar—the tempest's blast, or the evening breeze—the movements of mighty spirits. The mountain's summit, and the fleecy mists that hang upon its brows—the rocky defile—the foaming cataract—and the lonely dell—were all regarded as the abode or resort of these invisible beings.

An eclipse of the moon filled them with dismay; they supposed the planet was *natua*, or under the influence of the spell of some evil spirit that was destroying it. Hence they repaired to the temple, and offered prayers for the moon's release. Some imagined that on an eclipse, the sun and moon were swallowed by the god which they had by neglect offended. Liberal presents were offered, which were supposed to induce the god to abate his anger, and eject the luminaries of day and night from his stomach.

The shape and stability of their islands they regarded as depending on the influence of spirits. The high and rocky obelisks, and detached pieces of mountain, were viewed as monuments of their power. The large mountain on the left-hand side of the entrance to Opunohu, or Taloo harbour, which separates this bay from Cook's harbour, and is only united to the island by a narrow isthmus, was ascribed by tradition to the operations of those spirits, who, like the spirits in most other parts of the world, prefer the hours of darkness for their achievements. This mountain, it is stated, was formerly united with the mountains of the interior, and yielded in magnitude to none; but one night, the spirits of the place determined to remove it to the Leeward Islands, nearly one hundred miles distant, and accordingly began their operations, but had scarcely detached it from the main land, when the dawn of day discovered their proceedings, and obliged them to leave it where it now stands, forming the two bays already named. An aperture in the upper part of a mountain near Afareaitu, which appears from the lowland like a hole made by a cannon-ball, but which is eight or nine feet in diameter, is said to have been made by the passage of a spear, hurled by one of these supernatural beings.

Amusement was in part the business of a Tahitian's life; and with his games, as well as with every other institution, idolatry was connected. Five or six gods were imagined to preside over the upaupa, or games, of which Urataetae was one of the principal.

The most benevolent of their gods were Roo or Tane, Temaru, Feimata, and Teruharuhatai. These were invoked by the tahua faatere, or expelling priests; and were supposed to be able to restrain the effects of sorcery, or expel the evil spirits, which, from the incantations of the sorcerer, had entered the sufferer. They had also patron deities of the healing art. Tama and Tetuahuruhuru were the gods of surgery; and their assistance was implored in reducing dislocations, healing fractures, bruises, &c.; while Oititi, or Rearea, was their Esculapius, or god of physic.

In addition to these, there were gods who presided over the mechanic arts. The first was Oihanu, or Ofanu, the god of husbandry; the chief of the others was Taneetehia, the god of carpenters, builders, canoe-wrights, and all who wrought in wood. Nenia and Topea, the gods of those who thatched houses, and especially of those who finished the angles where the thatch on each side joined. With these, others of a more repulsive character might be associated, but I shall only mention Heva, the god of ghosts and apparitions, and Hiro the god of thieves. To the list, from which the greater part of the above are taken, including nearly one hundred of the objects formerly worshipped by the nation, a number of the principal family idols of the king and chiefs might be added, as every family of any antiquity or rank had its tutelar idol.

The general name by which their objects of worship were designated was *atua*, which is perhaps most appropriately translated god. This word is totally different in its meaning, as well as sound, from the word *varua*, spirit, although that is sometimes applied to the gods: when the people were accustomed to speak disrespectfully of them, they called them *varaua ino*, bad or evil spirits. It is also different in its signification from the word which is used to designate an image, and the spirits of departed children or relations, and frequently those evil genii to whom the sorcerers addressed their incantations.

Atua, or akua, is the name for god, without any exception, throughout the whole of the eastern part of Polynesia. The first *a* appears to be a component part of the word, though in many sentences it is omitted, in consequence of the preceding word terminating in a vowel. It is then pronounced tua; and though but little light is thus thrown on the origin of the people, it is interesting to trace the correspondence between the *taata* or *tangata*, first man, in Polynesia, and *tangatanga*, a principal deity among the South Americans; the *atua*, or *tua*, of the South Sea islanders, and the *tev*, which is said to be the word for god in the Aztec or Mexican language, the *deviyo* of the Singhalese, and the *deva* of the Sanscrit.

The objects of worship among the Tahitians, next to the *atua* or gods, were the *oramatuas tiis* or spirits. These were supposed to reside in the *po*, or world of night, and were never invoked but by wizards or sorcerers, who implored their aid for the destruction of an enemy, or the injury of some person whom they were hired to destroy. They were considered a different order of beings from the gods, a kind of intermediate class between them and the human race, though in their prayers all the attributes of the gods were ascribed to them. The *oramatuas* were the spirits of departed fathers, mothers, brothers, sisters, children, &c. The natives were greatly afraid of them, and presented offerings, to avoid being cursed or destroyed, when they were employed by the sorcerers.

They seem to have been regarded as a sort of demons. In the Leeward Islands, the chief oramatuas were spirits of departed warriors, who had distinguished themselves by ferocity and murder, attributes of character usually supposed to belong to these evil genii. Each celebrated tii was honoured with an image, through which it was supposed his influence was exerted. The spirits of the reigning chiefs were united to this class, and the skulls of deceased rulers, kept with the images, were honoured with the same worship. Some idea of what was regarded as their ruling passion, may be inferred from the fearful apprehensions constantly entertained by all classes. They were supposed to be exceedingly irritable and cruel, avenging with death the slightest insult or neglect, and were kept within the precincts of the temple. In the marae of *Tane* at Maeva, the ruins of their abode were still standing, when I last visited the place. It was a house built upon a number of large strong poles, which raised the floor ten or twelve feet from the ground. They were thus elevated, to keep them out of the way of men, as it was imagined they were constantly strangling, or otherwise destroying, the chiefs and people. To prevent this, they were also treated with great respect; men were appointed constantly to attend them, and to keep them wrapped in the choicest kinds of cloth, to take them out whenever there was a pae atua, or general exhibition of the gods; to anoint them frequently with fragrant oil; and to sleep in the house with them at night. All this was done, to keep them pacified. And though the office of calming the angry spirits was honourable, it was regarded as dangerous, for if, during the night or at any other time, these keepers were guilty of the least impropriety, it was supposed the spirits of the images, or the skulls, would hurl them headlong from their high abodes, and break their necks in the fall. The figures marked No. 5, in the engraving of the Idols, represent the images of two tiis or oramatuas; whose form and appearance convey no inappropriate exhibition of their imagined malignity of disposition.

Among the animate objects of their worship, they included a number of birds as well as fishes, especially a species of heron, a kingfisher, and one or two kinds of woodpecker, accustomed to frequent the sacred trees growing in the precincts of the temple. These birds were considered sacred, and usually fed upon the sacrifices. The natives imagined the god was imbodied in the bird, when it approached the temple to feast upon the offering; and hence they supposed their presents were grateful to their deities. The cries of those birds were also regarded as the responses of the gods to the prayers of the priests.

They supposed their gods were powerful spiritual beings, in some degree acquainted with the events of this world, and generally governing its affairs; never exercising any thing like benevolence towards even their most devoted followers, but requiring homage and obedience, with constant offerings; denouncing their anger, and dispensing destruction on all who either refused or hesitated to comply. But while the people supposed they were spiritual beings, they manufactured images either as representations of their form, and emblems of their character, or as the vehicle or instrument through which their communications might be made to the god, and his will revealed to them.

The idols were either rough unpolished logs of the aito, or casuarina tree, wrapped in numerous folds of sacred cloth; rudely carved wooden images; or shapeless pieces covered with curiously netted cinet, of finely braided cocoa-nut husk, and ornamented with red feathers. They varied in size, some being six or eight feet long, others not more than as many inches. These, representing the spirits they called *tii;* and those, representing the national or family gods, *toos.* Into these they supposed the god entered at certain seasons, or in answer to the prayers of the priests. During this indwelling of the gods, they imagined even the images were very powerful: but when the spirit had departed, though they were among the most sacred things, their extraordinary powers were gone.

I had repeated conversations with a *tahua-tarai-too*, a maker of gods, whom I met with on a visit to Raiatea. As he appeared a serious inquirer after truth, and I could place some confidence in what he related, I was anxious to know his own opinion as to the idols it had been his business to make,—whether he really believed they were the powerful beings which the natives supposed; and if so, what constituted their great power over the other parts of the tree from which they were hewn? He assured me, that although at times he thought it was all deception, and only practised his trade to obtain the payment he received for his work; yet at other times he really thought the gods he himself had made, were powerful beings. It was not, he said, from the alteration his tools had effected in the appearance of the wood, or the carving with which they were ornamented, but because they had been taken to the temple, and were filled with the atua, that they became so powerful. The images of aito-wood were only exceeded in durability by those of stone. Some of the latter were calcarious or silicious, but the greater part were rude, uncarved, angular columns of basalt, various in size, and destitute of carving or polish; they were clothed or ornamented with native cloth.

The sacred flag was also used in processions, and regarded as an emblem of their deities.

Throughout Polynesia, the ordinary medium of communicating or extending supernatural powers, was the red feather of a small bird found in many of the islands, and the beautiful long tail-feathers of the tropic, or man-of-war bird. For these feathers the gods were supposed to have a strong predilection; they were the most valuable offerings that could be presented; to them the power or influence of the god was imparted, and through them transferred to the objects to which they might be attached. Among the numerous ceremonies observed, the *paeatua* was conspicuous. On these occasions, the gods were all brought out of the temple, the sacred coverings removed, scented oils were applied to the images, and they were exposed to the sun. At these seasons, the parties who wished their emblems of deity to be impregnated with the essence of the gods, repaired to the ceremony with a number of red feathers, which they delivered to the officiating priest.

The wooden idols being generally hollow, the feathers were deposited in the inside of the image, which was filled with them. Many idols, however, were solid pieces of wood, bound or covered with finely-braided fibres of the cocoa-nut husk;

to these the feathers were attached on the outside by small fibrous bands. In return for the feathers thus united to the god, the parties received two or three of the same kind, which had been deposited on a former festival in the inside of the wooden or inner fold of the cinet idol. These feathers were thought to possess all the properties of the images to which they had been attached, and a supernatural influence was supposed to be infused into them. They were carefully wound round with very fine cord, the extremities alone remaining visible. When this was done, the new-made gods were placed before the larger images from which they had been taken; and, lest their detachment should induce the god to withhold his power, the priest addressed a prayer to the principal deities, requesting them to abide in the red feathers before them. At the close of his *ubu*, or invocation, he declared that they were dwelt in or inhabited, (by the gods,) and delivered them to the parties who had brought the red feathers. The feathers, taken home, were deposited in small bamboo-canes, excepting when addressed in prayer. If prosperity attended their owner, it was attributed to their influence, and they were usually honoured with a *too*, or image, into which they were inwrought; and subsequently, perhaps, an altar and a rude temple were erected for them. In the event, however, of their being attached to an image, this must be taken to the large temple, that the supreme idols might sanction the transfer of their influence.

Polynesian temples were either national, local, or domestic. The former were depositories of their principal idols, and the scenes of all great festivals; the second were those belonging to the several districts; and the third, such as were appropriated to the worship of family gods. *Marae* was the name for temple, in the South Sea Islands. All were uncovered, and resembled oratories rather than temples. The national places of worship were designated by distinct appellations. *Tabutabu-a-tea* was the name of several in the South Sea Islands, especially of those belonging to the king: the word may mean wide-spread sacredness. The national temples consisted of a number of distinct maraes, altars, and sacred dormitories, appropriated to the chief pagan divinities, and included in one large stone enclosure of considerable extent. Several of the distinct temples contained smaller inner-courts, within which the gods were kept. The form of the interior or area of their temples was frequently that of a square or a parallelogram, the sides of which extended forty or fifty feet. Two sides of this space were enclosed by a high stone wall; the front was protected by a low fence; and opposite, a solid pyramidal structure was raised, in front of which the images were kept, and the altars fixed. These piles were often immense. That which formed one side of the square of the large temple in Atehuru, according to Mr. Wilson, by whom it was visited when in a state of preservation, was two hundred and seventy feet long, ninety-four wide at the base, and fifty feet high, being at the summit one hundred and eighty feet long, and six wide. A flight of steps led to its summit; the bottom step was six feet high. The outer stones of the pyramid, composed of coral and basalt, were laid with great care, and hewn or squared with immense labour, especially the *tiavá*, or corner stones.

Within the enclosure, the houses of the priests, and keepers of the idols, were erected. Ruins of temples are found in every situation: on the summit of a hill, as at Maeva, where Tane's temple, nearly one hundred and twenty feet square, enclosed with high walls, is still standing, almost entire; on the extremity of a point of land projecting into the sea; or in the recesses of an extensive and overshadowing grove. The trees growing

within the walls, and around the temple, were sacred; these were the tall cypress-like casuarina, the *tamanu*, or callophyllum, *miro*, or thespesia, and the *tou*, or cordia. These were, excepting the casuarina-trees, of large foliage and exuberant growth, their interwoven and dark umbrageous branches frequently excluded the rays of the sun; and the contrast between the bright glare of a tropical day, and the sombre gloom in the depths of these groves, was peculiarly striking. The fantastic contortions in the trunks and tortuous branches of the aged trees, the plaintive and moaning sound of the wind passing through the leaves of the casuarina, often resembling the wild notes of the Eolian harp—and the dark walls of the temple, with the grotesque and horrific appearance of the idols—combined to inspire extraordinary emotions of superstitious terror, and to nurture that deep feeling of dread which characterized the worshippers of Tahiti's sanguinary deities.

The priests of the national temples were a distinct class; the office of the priesthood was hereditary in all its departments. In the family, according to the patriarchal usage, the father was the priest; in the village or district, the family of the priest was sacred, and his office was held by one who was also a chief. The king was sometimes the priest of the nation, and the highest sacerdotal dignity was often possessed by some member of the reigning family. The intimate connexion between their false religion and political despotism, is, however, most distinctly shown in the fact of the king's personifying the god, and receiving the offerings brought to the temple, and the prayers of the supplicants, which have been frequently presented to Tamatoa, the present king of Raiatea. The only motives by which they were influenced in their religious homage, or service, were, with very few exceptions, superstitious fear, revenge towards their enemies, a desire to avert the dreadful consequences of the anger of the gods, and to secure their sanction and aid in the commission of the grossest crimes.

Their worship consisted in preferring prayers, presenting offerings, and sacrificing victims. Their *ubus*, or prayers, though occasionally brief, were often exceedingly protracted, containing many repetitions, and appearing as if the suppliants thought they should be heard for their much speaking. The petitioner did not address the god standing or prostrate, but knelt on one knee, sa cross-legged, or in a crouching position, on a broad flat stone, leaning his back against an upright basaltic column, at the extremity of a smooth pavement, usually six or ten yards from the front of the idol. He threw down a branch of sacred miro on the pavement before the image or altar, and began his *tarotaro*, or invocation, preparatory to the offering of his prayer. *Pure* is the designation of prayer, and *haamore* that of praise, or worship.

Small pieces of *niau*, or cocoa-nut leaf, were suspended in different parts of the temple, to remind the priest of the order to be observed. They usually addressed the god in a shrill, unpleasant, or chanting tone of voice, though at times the worship was extremely boisterous. That which I have often heard in the northern islands was peculiarly so; and on these occasions, when we have induced the priest to repeat any of the prayers, they have always recited them in these tones.

I have several of their prayers, but they are vain and unmeaning recitations, or abound so much in expressions and images of licentiousness and crime, as to be unfit for translation. The following is an outline of one of the least exceptionable. It was the morning prayer, and is called the awaking, or awakening, of the gods.

"Awake Roo—awake Tane—awake unnumbered progeny of Tane—awake Tuu—awake Tuaratai." Thus the gods, to the number of twenty, are called upon by name, and are directed to the birds and to Roo, the god of morning, and the parent of clouds — to the formation and increase of clouds — to the blue cloud, the red cloud, and the low hungry cloud, and the horned or pointed cloud. They are then directed to mark the progress of Roo, the property or offerings of Roo, the platted cocoa-nut leaf of Roo, the medium through which his influence or power was conveyed to his image, or through which he received the spirit of the offerings. All the gods are then invoked to enter their tapau or cocoa-nut leaves, and to open wide their mouths. Each one is addressed by name, and it is declared, " Here is the food and offering, in or from the land or the sea." The gods are then invoked to take off the sacredness or restriction, and to hold it fast, probably that men may securely attend to their avocations. The gods are then supposed to be awakened, and the priest retires.

Their offerings included every kind of valuable property: — the fowls of the air, the fishes of the sea, the beasts of the field, and the fruits of the earth, together with their choicest manufactures, were presented. The sacrifice was frequently called *Taraehara*, a compound term, signifying disentangling from guilt; from *tara*, to untie or loosen, and *hara*, guilt. The animals were taken either in part or entire. The fruits and other eatables were generally, but not always, dressed. Portions of the fowls, pigs, or fish, considered sacred, dressed with sacred fire within the temple, were offered; the remainder furnished a banquet for the priests and other sacred persons, who were privileged to eat of the sacrifices. Those portions appropriated to the gods were deposited on the *fata* or altar, which was of wood. Domestic altars, or those erected near the corpse of a departed friend, were small square wicker structures; those in the public temple were large, and usually eight or ten feet high. The surface of the altar was supported by a number of wooden posts or pillars, often curiously carved, and polished. The altars were covered with sacred boughs, and ornamented with a border or fringe of rich yellow plantain leaves. Besides these, there were smaller altars connected with the temples; some resembling a small round table, supported by a single post fixed in the ground. Occasionally, the carcase of the hog presented in sacrifice, was placed on the large altar, while the heart and some other internal parts were laid on this smaller altar, which was called a *fata aiai*. The pigs, &c. when presented alive, received the sacred mark, and ranged the district at liberty; when slain, they were exceedingly anxious to avoid breaking a bone, or disfiguring the animal. One method of killing them was by holding the pig upright on its legs, placing a strong stick horizontally under its throat, and another across upon its neck, and then pressing them together until the animal was strangled. Another plan was, by bleeding the pig to death, washing the carcase with the blood, and then placing it in a crouching position on the altar. Offerings and sacrifices of every kind, whether dressed or not, were placed upon the altar, and remained there, until decomposed. The heat of the climate, and frequent rain, accelerated this process, yet the atmosphere in the vicinity of the maraes was frequently most offensive.

Animals, fruits, &c. were not the only articles presented to their idols; the most affecting part of their sacrificing was the frequent immolation of human victims. These, in the technical language of the priests, were called *fish*. They were offered in seasons of war, at great national festivals, during the illness of their rulers, and on the erection of their temples. I have been informed by several of the inhabitants of Maeva, that the foundation of some of the buildings, for the abode of their gods, was actually laid in human sacrifices; that at least the central pillar, supporting the roof of one of the sacred houses at Maeva, was planted upon the body of a man, who had

Altar, and Offerings.

been offered as a victim to the sanguinary deity afterwards to be deposited there. The unhappy wretches selected were either captives taken in war, or individuals who had rendered themselves obnoxious to the chiefs or the priests. When they were wanted, a stone was, at the request of the priest, sent by the king to the chief of the district from which the victims were required. If the stone was received, it was an indication of an intention to comply with the requisition. It is a singular fact, that the cruelty of the practice extended not only to individuals, but to families and districts. When an individual had been taken as a sacrifice, the family to which he belonged was regarded as *tabu* or devoted; and when another was required, it was more frequently taken from that family than any other: and a district from which sacrifices had been taken, was, in the same way, considered as devoted; and hence, when it was known that any ceremonies were near, on which human sacrifices were usually offered, the members of tabu families, or others who had reason to fear they were selected, fled to the mountains, and hid themselves in the caverns till the ceremony was over. At a public meeting in Raiatea, Paumoana, a native chieftain, alluded to this practice in terms resembling these: —How great our dread of our former gods! Are there not some here who have fled from their houses, to avoid being taken for sacrifices? Yes! I know the cave in which they were concealed.

In general, the victim was unconscious of his doom, until suddenly stunned by a blow from a club or a stone, sometimes from the hand of the very chief on whom he was depending as a guest for the rights of hospitality. He was usually murdered on the spot—his body placed in a long basket of cocoa-nut leaves, and carried to the temple. Here it was offered, not by consuming it with fire, but by placing it before the idol. The priest, in dedicating it, took out one of the eyes, placed it on a plantain leaf, and handed it to the king, who raised it to his mouth as if desirous to eat it, but passed it to one of the priests or attendants, stationed near him for the purpose of receiving it. At intervals during the prayers some of the hair was plucked off, and placed before the god; and when the ceremony was over, the body was wrapped in the basket of cocoa-nut leaves, and frequently deposited on the branches of an adjacent tree. After remaining a considerable time, it was taken down, and the bones were buried beneath the rude pavement of the marae. These horrid rites were not unfrequent, and the number offered at their great festivals was truly appalling.

The seasons of worship were both stated and occasional. The latter were those in which the gods were sought under national calamities, as the desolation of war, or the alarming illness of the king or chiefs. In addition to the rites connected with actual war, there were two that followed its termination. The principal of these, *Rau mata vehi raa*, was designed to purify the land from the defilement occasioned by the incursions or devastations of an enemy, who had perhaps ravaged the country, demolished the temples, destroyed or mutilated the idols, broken down the altars, and used as fuel the *unus*, or curiously carved pieces of wood marking the sacred places of interment, and emblematical of tiis or spirits. Preparatory to this ceremony, the temples were rebuilt, new altars reared, new images, inspired or inhabited by the gods, placed in the maraes, and fresh unus erected.

At the close of the rites in the new temples, the parties repaired to the sea-beach, where the chief priest offered a short prayer, and the people dragged a small net of cocoa-nut leaves through a shallow part of the sea, and usually detached small fragments of coral from the bottom, which were brought to the shore. These were denominated fish, and were delivered to the priest, who conveyed them to the temple, and deposited them on the altar, offering at the same time an *ubu* or prayer, to induce the gods to cleanse the land from pollution, that it might be pure as the coral fresh from the sea. It was now supposed safe to abide on the soil, and appropriate its produce to the purposes of support; but had not this ceremony been performed, death would have been anticipated.

The *maui fata*, altar-raising, was connected with the preceding rites. No human victim was slain, but numbers of pigs, with abundance of plantains, &c. were placed upon the altars, which were newly ornamented with branches of the sacred miro, and yellow leaves of the cocoa-nut tree. These rites extended to every marae in the island, and were designed to secure rain and fertility for the country gained by conquest, or recovered from invasion.

Besides these, the chief occasional services were those connected with the illness of their rulers, which was supposed to be inflicted by the gods for some offence of the chiefs or people. Long and frequent prayers were offered, to avert their anger, and prevent death. But, supposing the gods were always influenced by the same motives as themselves, they imagined that the efficacy of their prayers would be in exact proportion to the value of the offerings with which they were accompanied. Hence, when the symptoms of disease were violent and alarming, if the sufferer was a chief of rank, the fruits of whole fields of plantains, and a hundred or more pigs, have been taken to the marae, and frequently, besides these, a number of men, *with ropes round their necks*, have been also led to the temple, and presented before the idol. The prayers of the priests have often been interrupted by the ejaculatory addresses of the men, calling on the god by name, and exclaiming, " Be not angry, but let thy wrath be appeased; here we are: look on us, and be satisfied," &c. It does not appear that these men were actually sacrificed, but probably they appeared in this humiliating manner with ropes about their necks, to propitiate the deity, and to shew their readiness to die, if it should be required.

While these ceremonies were observed, the progress of the disease was marked, by the friends of the afflicted, with intense anxiety. If recovery followed, it was attributed to the pacification of the deities; but if the disease increased, or terminated fatally, the god was regarded as inexorable, and was usually banished from the temple, and his image destroyed.

Religious rites were connected with almost every act of their lives. An *ubu* or prayer was offered before they ate their food, when they tilled their ground, planted their gardens, built their houses, launched their canoes, cast their nets, and commenced or concluded a journey. The first fish taken periodically on their shores, together with a number of kinds regarded as sacred, were conveyed to the altar. The first-fruits of their orchards and gardens were also *taumaha*, or offered, with a portion of their live-stock, which consisted of pigs, dogs, and fowls, as it was supposed death would be inflicted on the owner or the occupant of the land, from which the god should not receive such acknowledgment.

The *bure arii*, a ceremony in which the king acknowledged the supremacy of the gods, was attended with considerable pomp; but one of the principal stated festivals was the *pae atua,* which was held every three moons. On these occasions all the idols were brought from their sacred depository, and *meheu*, or exposed to the sun; the cloth in which they had been kept was removed, and the feathers in the inside of the hollow idols were taken out. The images were then anointed with fragrant oil; new feathers, brought by their worshippers, were deposited in the inside of the hollow idols, and folded in new

sacred cloth; after a number of ceremonies, they were carried back to their dormitories in the temple. Large quantities of food were provided for the entertainment, which followed the religious rites of the pae atua.

The most singular of their stated ceremonies was the *muoa raa matahiti*, ripening or completing of the year. This festival was regularly observed in Huahine: although I do not know that it was universal, vast multitudes assembled. In general, the men only engaged in pagan festivals; but men, women, and children, attended at this: the females, however, were not allowed to enter the sacred enclosure. A sumptuous banquet was held annually at the time of its observance, which was regulated by the blossoming of reeds.

Their rites and worship were in many respects singular, but in none more so than in the ripening of the year, which was regarded as a kind of annual acknowledgment to the gods. When the prayers were finished at the marae, and the banquet ended, a usage prevailed much resembling the popish custom of mass for souls in purgatory. Each individual returned to his home, or to his family marae, there to offer special prayers for the spirits of departed relatives, that they might be liberated from the *po*, or state of night, and ascend to *rohutunoanoa*, the mount Miru of Polynesia, or return to this world, by entering into the body of one of its inhabitants.

They did not suppose, according to the generally received doctrine of transmigration, that the spirits who entered the body of some dweller upon earth, would permanently remain there, but only come and inspire the person to declare future events, or execute any other commission from the supernatural beings on whom they imagined they were constantly dependent.

CHAP. XIV.

Description of Polynesian idols—Human sacrifices—Anthropophagism—Islands in which it prevails—Motives and circumstances under which it is practised—Tradition of its existence in Sir Charles Sanders' Island—Extensive prevalence of Sorcery and Divination—Views of the natives on the subject of satanic influence—Demons—Imprecations—Modes of incantation—Horrid and fatal effects supposed to result from sorcery—Impotency of enchantment on Europeans—Native remedies for sorcery—Native oracles—Buaatapena—Means of inspiration—Effects on the priest inspired—Manner of delivering the responses—Circumstances at Rurutu and Huahine—Intercourse between the priest and the god—Augury by the death of victims—Augury by the stars and clouds—Divination for the detection of theft.

The system of idolatry, which prevailed among a people separated from the majority of their species by trackless oceans, and possessing the means, not only of subsistence but of comfort, in an unusual degree, presents a most affecting exhibition of imbecility, absurdity, and degradation. Whether we consider its influence over the individual, the family, or the nation, through the whole period of life—its oppressive exactions, its frequent and foolish rites, its murderous sacrifices, the engines of its power, and the objects of its homage and its dread—it is impossible to contemplate it without augmented thankfulness for the blessings of revelation, and increased compassion for those inhabiting "the dark places of the earth."

The idols of the heathen are in general appropriate emblems of the beings they worship and fear; and if we contemplate those of the South Sea Islanders, they present to our notice all that is adapted to awaken our pity. The idols of Tahiti were generally shapeless pieces of wood, from one to four feet long, covered with cinet of cocoa-nut fibres, ornamented with yellow and scarlet feathers. Oro was a straight log of hard casuarina wood, six feet in length, uncarved, but decorated with feathers. The gods of some of the adjacent islands exhibit a greater variety of form and structure. The accompanying wood-cut contains several of these.

The figure in the centre, No. 1. exhibits a correct front view of Taaroa, the supreme deity of Polynesia; who is generally regarded as the creator of the world, and the parent of gods and men. The image from which this was taken, is nearly four feet high, and twelve or fifteen inches broad, carved out of a solid piece of close, white, durable wood. In addition to the number of images or demigods forming the features of his face, and studding the outside of his body, and which were designed to shew the multitudes of gods that had proceeded from him; his body is hollow, and when taken from the temple at Rurutu, in which for many generations he had been worshipped, a number of small idols were found in the cavity. They had perhaps been deposited there, to imbibe his supernatural powers, prior to their being removed to a distance, to receive, as his epresentatives, divine honours. The opening to the cavity was at the back; the whole of which,

might be removed. No. 2. is Terongo, one of the principal gods, and his three sons. No. 3. is an image of Tebuakina, three sons of Rongo, a principal deity in the Hervey Islands. The name is probably analogous to Orono in Hawaii, though distinct from Oro in Tahiti. No. 4. exhibits a sacred ornament of a canoe from the island of Huahine. The two figures at the top, are images worshipped by fishermen, or those frequenting the sea. The two small idols at the lower corners of the plate, No. 5. are images of oramatuas, or demons. The gods of Rarotogna were some of them much larger; Mr. Bourne, in 1825, saw fourteen about twenty feet long, and six feet wide.

Such were the objects the inhabitants of these islands were accustomed to supplicate; and to appease or avert the anger of which, they devoted not only every valuable article they possessed, but murdered their fellow-creatures, and offered their blood. Human victims were sacrificed to Taaroa, Oro, and several others. The eye was presented to the king. The natives state, that they regarded the eye as the organ or emblem of power. It has been supposed, that the circumstance of the priests' offering the eye, the most precious part of the victim, to the king, who appeared to eat it, indicated their having formerly devoured the men they had sacrificed. I do not regard this fact as affording any very strong evidence, although I have not the least doubt that the inhabitants of several of the South Sea Islands have eaten human flesh.

From the many favourable traits in their character, we have been unwilling to believe they had ever been cannibals; the conviction of our mistake has, however, been impressed by evidence so various and multiplied, as to preclude uncertainty. Their mythology led them to suppose, that the spirits of the dead are eaten by the gods or demons; and that the spiritual part of their sacrifices is eaten by the spirit of the idol before whom it is presented. Birds resorting to the temple, were said to feed upon the bodies of the human sacrifices, and it was imagined the god approached the temple in the bird, and thus devoured the victims placed upon the altar. In some of the islands, "man-eater" was an epithet of the principal deities; and it was probably in connexion with this, that the king, who often personated the god, appeared to eat the human eye. Part of some human victims were eaten by the priests.

The Marquesians are known to be cannibals; the inhabitants of the Palliser or Pearl Islands, in the immediate neighbourhood of Tahiti, to the eastward, are the same. A most affecting instance of their anthropophagism is related by recent visitors; who state that a captive female child, pining with hunger, on begging a morsel of food from the cruel and conquering invaders of her native island, received a piece of her own father's flesh!

The bodies of prisoners in war, or enemies slain in battle, appear to have been eaten by most of the Hervey Islanders, who reside a short distance to the west of the Society group. There were several inducements to this horrid practice. The New Zealanders ate the bodies of their enemies, that they might imbibe their courage, &c. Hence, they exulted in their banquet on a celebrated warrior; supposing that, when they had devoured his flesh, they should be imbued with his valiant and daring spirit. I am not certain that this was the motive by which the eastern Polynesians were influenced, but one principal design of their wars was to obtain men to eat. Hence, when dwelling in their encampment, and clearing the brushwood, &c. from the place in which they expected to engage the enemy, they animated each other to the work in the following terms, "Clear away well, that we may kill and eat, and have a good feast to-day." To "kill and eat," was the haughty warrior's threat; and to be "killed and eaten," the dread of the vanquished and the exile. In the island of Rarotogna, they cut off the heads of the slain, piled them in heaps within the temple, and furnished the banquet of victory with their bodies.

The desire of revenge, or the satisfaction resulting from actually devouring an enemy, was not their only motive. The craving of nature, and the pangs of famine, often led to this unnatural crime. It was the frequent inducement in the Marquesas, and also in the Hervey Islands. In Maute, Metiaro, and Atiu, seasons of scarcity are severely felt; and, to satisfy their hunger, a number of persons, at the hour of midnight, have stolen a man from a neighbouring residence, killed, and eaten him at once. Mr. Bourne, who visited the islands in 1825, states, that members of the same family are not safe; and so awful is their wretchedness, that this horrid cruelty is practised towards those who, in civilized communities, are the objects of most endearing attachment: the husband has preyed upon the body of his wife, and the parent upon his child, in a most revolting manner, without subjecting it to any previous preparation. These facts are too painful and barbarous to admit detail. Another, and perhaps more criminal motive than either revenge or want, led some to the perpetration of these appalling deeds: this was, the indulgence of their depraved and vitiated appetite.

In the little island of Tapuaemanu, between Eimeo and Huahine, tradition states that there were formerly cannibals. In the reign of Tamatafetu, an ancestor of the present ruler, it is related, that when a man of stout or corpulent habit went to the island, or lowland on the reef, he was seldom heard of afterwards. The people of the island imagined those thus missing were destroyed by the sharks: but for many years, the servants of the king followed them to the island on the reef, and having murdered, baked them there. When the bodies were baked, they wrapped them in leaves of the hibiscus and plantain, as they were accustomed to wrap their eels, or other fish, taken and cooked on the island; they then carried them to the interior, where the king and his servants feasted on them. Their deeds were at length discovered by Feito, the wife of the king. She was in the house on one occasion, and, as they supposed, asleep, when she overheard the king and his servants planning the death of Tebuoroo, her brother. Anxious to save her brother's life, she revealed to him the purpose of the chief. He communicated it to the raatiras, or farmers, who immediately repaired to the marae of Taaroa, to inquire what they should do; and left with a unanimous determination to destroy their chief. Two men, Mehoura and Raiteanui, were appointed to hide themselves near his place of bathing; and when the chief came to bathe, they killed him with stones. A native of this island related the above statement within the last two years, at a public meeting held near the place where it is reported to have occurred, and afterwards in private stated that it was according to their traditions. Mr. Barff, to whom I am indebted for the tradition, adds, "The people affirmed it to be true." This unnatural crime does not appear to have been general; and the above is the only direct account that we have of its existence in what are properly the Society Islands. It is not probable that it will ever be revived, and, at a recent public meeting, in alluding to it, as illustrative of the former, and contrasting it with the present state of the people, the native speaker concluded by saying, "Behold, under the gospel of Jesus Christ, this land, where man-eaters have dwelt, has become a land of neighbours and of brethren."

No people in the world, in ancient or modern times, appear to have been more superstitious than the South Sea Islanders, or to have been more entirely under the influence of dread from imaginary demons, or supernatural beings. They had not only their major but their minor demons, or spirits, and all the minute ramifications of idolatry. Sorcery and witchcraft were extensively practised. By this art, the sorcerers pretended to be able to inflict the most painful maladies, and to deprive of life the victims of their mysterious rites.

It is unnecessary now to inquire whether satanic agency affects the bodies of men. We know this was the fact at the time our Saviour appeared on earth. Many of the natives of these islands are firmly persuaded, that while they were idolaters, their bodies were subject to most excruciating sufferings, from the direct operation of satanic power. In this opinion they might be mistaken, and that which they regarded as the effect of super-human agency, might be only the influence of imagination, or the result of poison. But considering the undisputed exercise of such an influence, recognized in the declarations and miracles of our Lord and of his apostles, existing not only in heathen, but Jewish society, and considering, in connexion with this, the undisputed dominion, moral and intellectual, which the powers of darkness held over those who were entirely devoted to the god of this world, it does not appear impossible, or inconsistent with the supreme government of God, that these subordinate powers should be permitted to exert an influence over their persons, and that communities, so wholly given to idolatry of the most murderous and diabolical kinds, should be considered corporeally, as well as spiritually, to be lying " in the wicked one." In addition to the firm belief which many who were sorcerers, or agents of the infernal powers, and others who were the victims of incantation, still maintain, some of the early Missionaries are disposed to think this was the fact. Since the natives have embraced Christianity, they believe they are now exempt from an influence, to which they were subject during the reign of the evil spirit.

Individuals, among the most intelligent of the people, sometimes express their deliberate conviction, that it is because they live under the dispensation or government of Jesus Christ, that they are now exempt from those bodily sufferings to which they were exposed while they were willing and zealous devotees of idols. It is, I believe, also an indisputable fact, that those kinds of violent, terrific, and fatal corporeal agony, which they attributed to this agency, have - altogether ceased, since the subversion of that system, of which it was so dreadful a part. I am not prepared to pronounce the opinions many of the natives still hold, as altogether imaginative: at the same time, the facts that have come to my knowledge, during my residence among them, have led me to desire the most satisfactory evidence for rejecting them.

Witchcraft and sorcery they considered the peculiar province of an inferior order of supernatural beings. The names of the principal oramatuas were, Mau-ri, Bua-rai, and Tea-fao. They were considered the most malignant of beings, exceedingly irritable and implacable; they were not confined to the skulls of departed warriors, or the images made for them, but were occasionally supposed to resort to the shells from the sea-shore, especially a beautiful kind of murex, the *murex ramoces*. These shells were kept by the sorcerers, and the peculiar singing noise perceived on applying the valve to the ear, was imagined to proceed from the demon it contained.

These were the kinds of beings invoked by the wizards or sorcerers. Different names were applied to their arts, according to the rites employed, or the effects produced. Tahu, or tahutahu, natinatiaha, or pifao, were the general terms employed, both for sorcery and the performance of it. *Tahu*, in general, signifies to kindle, and is much the same in import as *ahikuni*, the word for sorcery in the Sandwich Islands. The application of fire was common to both. *Natinati* signifies involved, entangled, and knotted: *aha*, is cinet; and the persons afflicted with this, were supposed to be possessed by a demon, who was twisting and knotting their inside, and thus occasioning most excruciating pain and death. *Pifao* signifies a hook or barb; and is also indicative of the condition of those, under the visitation of evil spirits, who were ling them in agony, as severe as if transfixed a barbed spear or hook.

ncantations sometimes commenced with an imprecation or curse, either by the priest or the offended party, and it was usually denounced in the name of the gods of the party, or of the king, or some oramatua. The poor people entertained the greatest horror of this mode of vengeance, as it was generally considered fatal, unless, by engaging a more powerful demon, its effects could be counteracted.

This dreadful system of iniquity, and demon tyranny, was complex and intricate. The party using sorcery against another, whose destruction they designed, employed a tahutahu, or a taata-obu-tara, whose influence with the demons procured their co-operation, and was supposed to induce the *tii*, or spirit, to enter into the victim of their malice.

Prayers, offerings, and the accustomed mysteries, however numerous, were not sufficient for this purpose. It was necessary to secure something connected with the body of the object of vengeance. The parings of the nails, a lock of the hair, the saliva from the mouth, or other secretions from the body, or else a portion of the food which the person was to eat. This was considered as the vehicle by which the demon entered the person, who afterwards became possessed. It was called the *tubu*, growing, or causing to grow. When procured, the *tara* was performed; the sorcerer took the hair, saliva, or other substance that had belonged to his victim, to his house or marae, performed his incantations over it, and offered his prayers; the demon was then supposed to enter the tubu, and through it the individual, who suffered from the enchantment. If it was a portion of food, similar ceremonies were observed, and the piece of bread-fruit, fish, &c., supposed by this process to be impregnated by the demon, was placed in the basket of the person for whom it was designed; and, if eaten, inevitable destruction was expected to follow.

The use of the portable spittoon by the Sandwich Island chiefs, in which the saliva was carefully deposited, carried by a confidential servant, and buried every morning, and the custom of the Tahitians in scrupulously burning or burying the hair when cut off, and also furnishing to each individual his distinct basket for food, originated in their dread of sorcery by any of these means. When the tara had been performed, and the tubu secured, the effects were violent, and death speedy. The most acute agonies and terrific distortions of the body were often experienced; the wretched sufferer appeared in a state of frantic madness, or, as they expressed it, torn by the evil spirit, while he foamed and writhed under his dreadful power.

On one occasion, Mr. Nott sent two native boys, who were his servants, from Eimeo to Tahiti, for *taro,* or arum-roots. The man, under whose care it was growing, was a sorcerer: he was from home, I believe—but the boys, according to the directions they had received, went to the field, and procured the roots for which they had been sent. Before they had departed, the person who had charge of the field returned, and was so enraged, that he pronounced the most dreadful imprecations upon one, if not both of them, threatening them with the *pifao.* The boys returned to Eimeo, but apparently took no notice of the threatening. One of them was shortly afterwards taken ill; and the imprecation of the sorcerer being made known to his friends, it was immediately concluded that he was possessed by the evil spirit. Alarming symptoms rapidly increased, and some of the Missionaries went to see him in this state. On entering the place where he lay, a most appalling spectacle was presented. The youth was lying on the ground, writhing in anguish, foaming at the mouth, his eyes apparently ready to start from his head, his countenance exhibiting every form of terrific distortion and pain, his limbs agitated with violent and involuntary convulsions. The friends of the boy were standing round, filled with horror at what they considered the effects of the malignant demon; and the sufferer shortly afterwards expired in dreadful agonies. In general, the effects of incantations were more gradual in their progress, and less sudden, though equally fatal in their termination.

The belief of the people in the power of the sorcerers remained unshaken, until the renunciation of idolatry, and the whole population were consequently kept in most humiliating and slavish fear of the demons. No rank or class was supposed to be exempt from their fatal influence. The young prince of Taiarabu, Te-arii-na-vahoroa, brother of the late king, was by many of the people considered as destroyed, by Metia, a prophet of Oro, and a celebrated sorcerer, who had sometimes been known to threaten even the king himself with the effects of his indignation. "Give up, give up," was the language he on one occasion employed, when addressing the king, "lest I bend my strong bow;" in allusion it is supposed, to his pretended influence with the demon. Whole families were sometimes destroyed. In Huahine, out of eight, one individual alone survives; seven, it is imagined, having been cut off by one sorcerer.

The imprecation was seldom openly denounced, unless the agent of the powers of darkness imagined his victim had little prospect of escape, and that his family were not likely to avenge his death. In general, these mysteries were conducted with that secrecy, which best comported with such works of darkness. Occasionally the tahutahu employed his influence with the evil spirit, to revenge some insult or injury he or his relatives had received; but more frequently he exercised it for hire. From his employers he received his fee and his directions, and having procured the tubu, or instrument of acting on his victim, repaired to his own rude marae, performed his diabolical rites, delivered over the individual to the demon he invoked, imploring the spirit to enter into the wretch, and inflict the most dreadful bodily sufferings, terminate at length the mortal existence, and then hurry the spirit to the *po*, or state of night, and there pursue the dreadful work of torture. These were the infernal labours of the tahutahu or the pifao, the wizard or the sorcerer; and these, according to the superstitions of the people, their terrific results.

It is possible that in some instances these sufferings may have been the effects of imagination, and a deep impression on the mind of the afflicted individual, that he was selected as the victim of some insatiable demon's rage. Imagining he was already delivered to his power, hope was abandoned, death deemed inevitable, and the infatuated sufferer became the victim of despair. It is also possible that poison, of which the natives had several kinds, vegetable and animal, (some few of which they have stated as capable of destroying human life,) might have produced the violent convulsions that sometimes preceded dissolution. It is probable that into the piece of food—over which the sorcerer performed his enchantments—he introduced a portion of poison, which would prove fatal to the individual by whom it should be eaten. Indeed, some of the sorcerers, since their conversion to Christianity, and one of them on his deathbed, confessed that this had been practised, and that they supposed the poison had occasioned the death which had been attributed to their incantations. Others, however, still express their belief, that they were so completely under the dominion of the evil spirit, that his power extended to the body as well as to the mind. I offer no opinion on this matter, but confine myself to stating the sentiments of the people, and some of the facts connected with the same. It has been a subject of frequent conversation with several of the most reflecting among the natives, who, since they have become Christians, have expressed their deliberate belief that their bodies were subject to satanic agency.

It is a singular fact, that while the practice continued, with all its supernatural influence, among the natives, the sorcerers invariably confessed that incantations were harmless when employed upon Europeans: several have more than once been threatened with sorcery, and there is reason to believe it has been put to the test upon them. The sorcerers have always declared, that they could not prevail with the white men, because such were under the keeping of a more powerful Being than the spirits *they* could engage against them, and therefore were secure. The native Missionaries, in different islands, have also been threatened with sorcery from the idolaters among whom they have endeavoured to introduce Christianity. They have always defied the sorcerers and their demons, telling them that Jehovah would protect them from their machinations; and though frequently exposed to incantations, have never sustained the slightest injury.

The sentiments entertained by the natives relative to the character of these supernatural beings, led them to imagine them to be such as they were themselves, only endowed with greater powers. They supposed that in all their actions they were influenced by motives exactly corresponding with those that operated upon their own minds; hence they believed, that even spirits could be diverted from their purposes by the offer of a larger bribe than they had received to carry it into effect, or that the efforts of one tii could be neutralized or counteracted by those of another more powerful.

Under the influence of these opinions, when any one was suffering from incantations, if he or his friends possessed property, they immediately employed another sorcerer. This person was frequently called a *faatere*, causing to move or slide, who, on receiving his fee, was generally desired, first to discover who had practised the incantations which it was supposed had induced the sufferings: as soon as he had accomplished this, he was employed, with more costly presents, to engage the aid of his demons, that the agony and death they had endeavoured to inflict upon the subject of their malignant efforts, might revert to themselves

—and if the demon employed by the second party was equally powerful with that employed by the first, and their presents more valuable, it was generally supposed that they were successful.

How affecting is the view these usages afford, of the mythology of these rude untutored children of nature! How debasing their ideas of those beings on whom they considered themselves dependent, and whose service they regarded as the principal business of their lives!—how degrading and brutalizing such sentiments, and how powerful their effect must have been, in cherishing that deadly hatred which often found but too congenial a home in their bosoms! They were led to imagine that these super-human beings were engaged in perpetual conflict with each other, employing their dreadful powers, at the instigation of their priests, in afflicting with deepest misery, and ultimately destroying, the devotees of some rival demon.

A mythology so complicated, and a system of idolatry so extensive and powerful, as that which prevailed in the South Sea Islands, led the people not only to consider themselves as attended and governed by the gods, but also induced to seek their direction, and submit to their decision, in every event of interest or importance. Every island had its oracle; and divination, in various forms, was almost universally practised by the priests.

In many respects, the oracles of the Polynesians resembled those of the ancients; in some they differed. Oro, the great national idol, was generally supposed to give the responses to the priests, who sought to know the will of the gods, or the issue of events; and at Opoa, this being considered as the birth-place of the god, was the most celebrated oracle of the people. It does not appear that there were any persons specially appointed to consult the gods. The priest, who officiated in other services, presented the offerings, and proposed the inquiries of those who thus sought supernatural direction.

No event of importance was determined, nor any enterprise of hazard or consequence undertaken, without, in the first instance, inquiring of the gods its result. The priest was directed, as they expressed it, to spread the matter before the idol, and to wait the intimation of his will, or the prediction of its consequences. The priest, who was called *taura*, or *tairoiro*, repaired to the temple, presented the offerings, and proposed the inquiry, while the parties by whom he was employed anxiously waited his report.

In all matters of great and national importance, however, the gods were generally consulted by the *buaa tapena*, or dedicated hog. The animal was strangled, the hair singed or burnt off by the application of torches of reeds, and the hog was conveyed to the sacred pavement, in front of the depository of the idol. It was there embowelled, and if the movements of the entrails, after being taken out, were quick or continued, it was regarded as an omen of success. This mode of consulting the god was generally resorted to, prior to engaging in war, or during the existence of hostilities. The hog was now bathed with its own blood, and the priest offered his prayers over it, and then laid the sacred cocoa-nut leaf round it, as the tapâu, or means by which the god might enter, and through the sacrifice manifest his will. The heart and its appurtenances were placed on the small altar, while the carcase was placed with great care in an upright position on the large altar. The priest then preferred the claims of the people, and the several orders of diviners took their station near the victim, to watch the indications of the god's designs, while the men, women, and children of the island waited without, to know the result. The following were the principal omens. If the hog continued for a given period without exhibiting any change, it was an indication of continued conquest and spoil to the party offering it. If the hinder parts of the pig sunk, while the fore-part remained stationary, it was regarded as an indication that the enemy was restrained by the gods, and that peace might be concluded; and such intimation was invariably attended to. If the middle of the back sunk while the fore and hindparts remained stationary, it was an indication that neither army should be overcome, but that both, after sustaining some loss, should claim the victory. If some parts of the surface of the animal which had been covered with blood, changed colour, while other parts continued red, it signified that both armies should alternately experience victory and defeat. If the back was bent to one side, it indicated that the front rank of both armies should be destroyed, but the rear escape. If one eye closed, it shewed that the opposing chiefs should be conquered, or one of them taken. If the hinder parts of the sacrifice became enlarged, it indicated that the party offering it would be overcome, and consequently predisposed them to retreat, or sue for peace.

In the Sandwich Islands, the king, personating the god, uttered the responses of the oracle, from his concealment in a frame of wicker-work. In the southern islands, the priest usually addressed the image, into which it was imagined the god entered when any one came to inquire his will. Sometimes the priest slept all night near the idol, expecting his communication in a dream; at other times it was given in the cry of a bird, whose resort was in the precincts of his temple; in the sighing of the breeze among the entwining branches of the tall and slender trees around the temple; or in the shrill, squeaking articulations of some of the priests. When the priest returned to those by whom he had been employed, if an unfavourable answer had been given, the project was at once abandoned, however favourable other circumstances might appear. If the answer was propitious, arrangements were forthwith made for its prosecution; but if no answer had been given, no further steps were then taken, it was considered to be restrained by the idol, and was left in abeyance with him.

Appearing to the priest in a dream of the night, though a frequent, was neither the only nor the principal mode by which the god intimated his will. He frequently entered the priest, who, inflated as it were with the divinity, ceased to act or speak as a voluntary agent, but moved and spoke as entirely under supernatural influence. In this respect there was a striking resemblance between the rude oracles of the Polynesians, and those of the celebrated nations of ancient Greece.

As soon as the god was supposed to have entered the priest, the latter became violently agitated, and worked himself up to the highest pitch of apparent frenzy, the muscles of the limbs seemed convulsed, the body swelled, the countenance became terrific, the features distorted, and the eyes wild and strained. In this state he often rolled on the earth, foaming at the mouth, as if labouring under the influence of the divinity by whom he was possessed, and, in shrill cries, and violent and often indistinct sounds, revealed the will of the god. The priests, who were attending, and versed in the mysteries, received, and reported to the people, the declarations which had been thus received.

When the priest had uttered the response of the oracle, the violent paroxysm gradually subsided, and comparative composure ensued. The god did not, however, always leave him as soon as the communication had been made. Sometimes the same *taura*, or priest, continued for two or three days possessed by the spirit or deity; a piece of native cloth, of a peculiar kind, worn round one arm, was an indication of inspiration, or of the indwelling of the god with the individual who wore it. The acts of the man during this period were considered as those of the god, and hence the greatest attention was paid to his expressions, and the whole of his deportment.

In the year 1808, during the civil war between the king and rebel chiefs, of whom Taute was the leader, the priest of Oro, who was known to be not only attached to the king's interests, but a personal friend of Pomare, left the royal camp, and went over to that of the enemy. Many of Pomare's friends endeavoured to persuade him to remain with them, but no one dared to use force, as it was supposed that he acted under the inspiration of his god. This circumstance greatly discouraged the king and his friends, and probably prepared the way for their discomfiture and flight, as they supposed the god had forsaken them, and fought with their enemies.

On an occasion, of more recent date, the god and the prophet were not treated with quite so much respect, but were rather rudely handled. The natives of Rurutu having determined to renounce idolatry, it was proposed by the native teachers that the people should meet together at the sacred enclosure, near the idol temple, where both sexes would unitedly partake of those kinds of food which had heretofore been regarded as sacred, and the eating of which by any female, especially in such a place, the gods would have punished with death.

At a previous meeting, Auura, one of the chiefs, had told a priest, who pretended to be inspired, that he was the very foundation of the deceit, and that he should never deceive them again. The priests, however, appeared at the appointed meeting; and one of them, pretending to be inspired, began denouncing, in the name of his god, the most awful punishment upon those that had violated the sacred place. One or two of the natives of Raiatea went up to him, and told him to desist, and not attempt to deceive them any longer, that the people would not tolerate their imposition. The priest answered, that it was the god that was within him, and that he was the god. When *uruhia*, (under the inspiration of the spirit,) the priest was always considered as sacred as the god, and was called, during this period, *atua*, god, though at other times only denominated *taura*, or priest. Finding him determined to persist in his imprecations, one of the christian boatmen from Raiatea said, " If the god is in, we will try and pinch, or twist, him out." Immediately seizing the priest, who already began to shew symptoms of violent convulsive muscular action, they prevented his throwing himself on the ground. For a long time, the priest and one of the Raiateans struggled together; when the god, insulted at the rude liberty taken with his servant, left him, and the priest silently retired from the assembly.

When one of the priests was exhibiting all the violent gestures of inspiration in Huahine, a by-stander observed, that it was all deceit, and that if they were to open the body of the priest, they should not find any god within. The multitude, however, appeared struck with horror at the startling proposal, and seemed to think the individual who had dared to utter it would not escape the signal vengeance of the powerful spirit.

Although so much ceremony, and such extraordinary effects, attended the public or formal intercourse between the god and the people, through the medium of the priest, the communications between the priest and the god were sometimes of an opposite character, and ludicrously colloquial. Mr. Davies, when itinerating round the island of Eimeo, in the early part of his missionary labour in that island, arrived at a village near Tiatae-pua, where he endeavoured to purchase provisions from the inhabitants. Vegetables were procured with facility, but the only animals were a number of fowls, and these belonged to the priest of the adjacent temple. Application was made to this individual, who looked at the articles (scissors, looking-glasses, &c.) offered in exchange, and seemed desirous to barter his fowls for them, but he said they belonged to the god, having been presented as offerings, and that without his leave he durst not part with any.

Again he examined the articles, and then said he would go and ask if the god was willing to part with any of the fowls. He proceeded to the temple, whither he was followed by Mr. Davies, who heard his address to the object of hope and fear, in words to the following effect: "O my atua, (or god,) here is some good property, knives, scissors, looking-glasses, &c. *e hoo paha vau, na moa na taua;* perhaps I may sell some of the fowls belonging to us two, for it. It will be good property for you and me." After waiting a few moments, he pretended to receive an answer in the affirmative, and returned, stating that the god had consented to the appropriation. The sacred fowls were accordingly hunted by a number of boys and dogs, and several secured, and sold for the above-mentioned articles.

It has already been stated, that the oracle was not the only method by which the people were accustomed to consult the gods; nor was the inspiration of the priests the exclusive manner by which supernatural direction was revealed to the people. Divination, or augury, was practised in a variety of modes, and by these means it was thought that future events were made known, and information was communicated. Much of their augury was connected with the sacrifices they offered. They had also a singular method of cutting a cocoa-nut, and, by minutely examining its parts, of ascertaining their portentous indications. These ceremonies were generally practised in the temple.

There were others, however, performed elsewhere, as the *patu*, which consisted in dividing a ripe cocoa-nut into two equal parts, taking the half opposite to that to which the stalk was attached, and proceeding with it in a canoe to some distance from the shore; here the priest offered his prayers;

and then placing the cocoa-nut in the sea, continuing his prayers, and narrowly watching its descent, he thereby pretended to ascertain the result of any measures in which those by whom he was employed were interested. The patu was frequently resorted to while negociations for peace were carried on between parties who had been engaged in war. The situation of the stars was also regarded as foreshewing future events. When Venus and any other conspicuous planet appeared above the horizon at sunset, for several successive nights, it was viewed as an indication that two chiefs were planning each others downfall. When the horns of the new moon were in an upright direction, it was supposed to indicate the secret formation of two hostile parties. Such an aspect was called an angry or savage moon. If three or more spiral clouds were seen in the west about the setting of the sun, it indicated division of councils, and conflicts. If one conspicuous cloud appeared, it foretold the death of some powerful chief. When the sky was red over Borabora at sunset, the inhabitants of Huahine imagined it proceeded from preparations for invasion by the Boraborans, and they prepared accordingly. Divination was employed to discover the cause or author of sickness, or to ascertain the fate of a fleet or a canoe that might have commenced a distant or hazardous voyage. This latter was often used in the islands to the westward of the Society group.

The natives had also recourse to several kinds of divination, for discovering the perpetrators of acts of injury, especially theft. Among these was a kind of water ordeal. It resembled in a great degree the *wai haruru* of the Hawaiians. When the parties who had been robbed wished to use this method of discovering the thief, they sent for a priest, who, on being informed of the circumstances connected with the theft, offered prayers to his demon. He now directed a hole to be dug in the floor of the house, and filled with water; then, taking a young plantain in his hand, he stood over the hole, and offered his prayers to the god, whom he invoked, and who, if propitious, was supposed to conduct the spirit of the thief to the house, and place it over the water. The image of the spirit, which they imagined resembled the person of the man, was, according to their account, reflected in the water, and being perceived by the priest, he named the individual, or the parties, who had committed the theft, stating that the god had shewn him the image in the water. The priests were rather careful how they fixed on an individual, as the accused had but slight prospect of escaping, if unable to falsify the charge; but when he could do this, the credit of the god, and the influence of the priest, were materially diminished.

Sometimes the priest, after the first attempt, declared that no answer had been returned, and deferred till the following day the repetition of his enchantments. The report, however, that this measure had been resorted to, generally spread among the people, and the thief, alarmed at the consequences of having the gods engaged against him, usually returned the stolen property under cover of the night, and by this superseded the necessity for further inquiries. — Like the oracles among the nations of antiquity, which gradually declined after the propagation of Christianity, the divinations and spells of the South Sea Islanders have been laid aside since their reception of the gospel. The only oracle they now result is the Sacred Volume; and multitudes, here is reason to believe, give to its divine communications unreserved credence, and yield to its requirements the most cheerful and conscientious obedience.

The religion, of which some account has been given, although established among a people scarcely above the rudest barbarism—destitute of letters, hieroglyphics, and symbols, and by their isolated situation deprived of all intercourse with the rest of the world—is, as a system, singularly complete.

The invention displayed in the fabrication and adjustment of its several parts, the varied and imposing imagery under which it was exhibited, and the mysterious and complicated machinery which sustained its operations, were remarkable and, in the standard of virtue which it fixed, in the future destinies it unfolded, and in its adaptation to the untutored but ardent mind, the Polynesian mythology will not suffer by comparison with any systems which have prevailed among the most polished and celebrated nations of ancient or modern times.

In some respects, the mythology of Tahiti presents features peculiarly its own: in others we trace a striking analogy to that of the nations of antiquity. In each, the light of truth occasionally gleams through a mass of darkness and error. The conviction that man is the subject of supernatural dominion, is recognized in all, and the multiplied objects of divine homage, which distinguished the polytheism of the ancients, marked also that of the rude islanders. Nor was the fabulous religion of the latter deficient in the mummeries of sorcery and witchcraft, the delusion of oracles, and the influence of other varieties of juggling, and oppressive spiritual domination.

We are not surprised, that, to the enlightened, benevolent, but transient visitor, the South Sea Islanders appeared under circumstances peculiarly favourable to happiness, but their idolatry exhibits them as removed to the farthest extreme from such a state. The baneful effects of their delusion was increased by the vast preponderance of malignant deities, frequently the personifications of cruelty and vice. They had changed the glory of God into the image of corruptible things, and instead of exercising those affections of gratitude, complacency, and love, towards the objects of their worship, which the living God supremely requires, they regarded their deities with horrific dread, and worshipped only with enslaving fear.

While this system shews the distance to which those under its influence departed from the knowledge and service of the true God; it also furnishes additional confirmation of the fact, that polytheism, whether exhibited in the fascinating numbers of classic poetry, the splendid imagery of eastern fable, or the rude traditions of unlettered barbarians, is equally opposed to all just views of the being and perfections of the only proper object of religious homage and obedience; and that, whether invested with the gorgeous trappings of a cumbrous and imposing superstition, or appearing in the naked and repulsive deformity of rude idolatry, it is alike unfriendly to intellectual improvement, moral purity, individual happiness, social order, and national prosperity.

CHAP. XV.

Tahitian prophets—Ancient predictions relative to the arrival of ships—Traditions of the Deluge corresponding with the accounts in sacred and profane writings—General ideas of the people relative to death and a future state—Death the consequence of Divine displeasure — State of spirits—Miru, or heaven—Religious ceremonies for ascertaining the causes of death—Embalming—The burying of the sins of the departed—Singular religious ceremony—Offerings to the dead—Occupation of the spirits of the deceased—Superstitions of the people—Otohaa, or lamentation—Wailing—Outrages committed under the paroxysms of grief—Use of sharks' teeth—Elegies—The heva—Absurdity and barbarism of the practice.

BESIDES the priests who made known the will of the gods, and pretended to foretell the issue of those enterprises in which the people might be engaged, or were about to commence, there have been at different periods individuals who have foretold events that were to take place in periods yet more remote, but which at the time appeared incomprehensible. There are some which regarded the destiny of the people, but the most remarkable (because, according to the interpretation of the natives themselves, they have received a partial fulfilment) were those referring to the strange ships that should arrive. Among the native prophets of former times, there appear to have been several of the name of *Maui*. One of the most celebrated of this name resided at Raiatea, and on one occasion, when supposed to be under the inspiration of the god, he predicted that in future ages a *vaa ama ore*, literally an "outriggerless canoe," would arrive at the islands from some foreign land. Accustomed to attach that appendage to their single canoes, whatever might be their size or quality, they considered an outrigger essential to their remaining upright on the water, and consequently could not believe that a canoe without one would live at sea. The absence of this has ever appeared to the South Sea Islanders as one of the greatest wonders connected with the visits of the first European vessels. At one of the Hervey Islands, where they had never seen a vessel until recently visited by a Missionary, when the boat was lowered down to the water, and pushed off by the rowers from the ship's side, the natives simultaneously and involuntarily exclaimed—"It will overturn and sink, it has no outrigger."

The chiefs and others, to whom Maui delivered his prophecy, were also convinced in their own minds, that a canoe would not swim without this necessary balance, and charged him with foretelling an impossibility. He persisted in his predictions, and, in order to remove their scepticism as to its practicability, launched his umete, or oval wooden dish, upon the surface of a pool of water near which he was sitting, and declared that in the same manner would the vessel swim that should arrive.

We have not been able to ascertain the period when this prediction was delivered. It was preserved among the people by oral tradition, until the arrival of Captain Wallis's and

Cook's vessels. When the natives first saw these, they were astonished at their gigantic size, imposing aspect, and the tremendous engines on board. These appearances induced them first to suppose the ships were islands inhabited by a supernatural order of beings, at whose direction lightnings flashed, thunders roared, and the destroying demon slew, with instantaneous but invisible strokes, the most daring and valiant of their warriors. But when they afterwards went alongside, or ventured on board, and saw that they were floating fabrics of timber, borne on the surface of the waters, and propelled by the winds of heaven, they unanimously declared that the prediction of Maui was accomplished, and the canoes without outriggers had arrived. They were confirmed in this interpretation, when they saw the small boats belonging to the ships employed in passing to and fro between the vessel and the shore. These being simple in their structure, and approaching their own canoes in size, yet conveying in perfect safety those by whom they were manned, excited their astonishment, and confirmed their convictions that Maui was a prophet.

When a boat or a vessel has been sailing in or out of the harbour, I have often heard the natives, while gazing at the stately motion, exclaim, *Te vaa a Maui e! Ta vaa ama ore.* "Oh the canoe of Maui! the outriggerless canoe!" They have frequently asked us how he could have known such a vessel would arrive, since it was at that time considered by all besides as an impossibility. We have told them it was probable he had observed the steadiness with which his umete, or other hollow wooden vessel, floated on the water, and had thence inferred that at some future period they might behold larger vessels equally destitute of any exterior balancing power. They in general consider the use of boats and shipping among them as an accomplishment of his prediction.

The islanders also state, that there is another prediction, still to be fulfilled; and although it appears to them as great an improbability as the former, yet the actual appearance of one, leads many to think that possibly they may witness the other. This remaining prediction also has reference to a ship, and declares that after the arrival of a canoe without an outrigger, *e vaa taura ore*, a boat, or vessel, without ropes or cordage, shall come among them. What idea Maui designed to convey by this declaration, it is perhaps not easy to ascertain; but the people say it is next to impossible that the masts should be sustained, the sails attached, or the vessel worked, without ropes or cordage. They say, however, that one prediction respecting the vessels has been accomplished, but that the other remains to be realized. I have often thought, when contemplating the little use of rigging on board our steam-vessels, that should a specimen of this modern invention ever reach the South Sea Islands, although the natives would not, perhaps, like the inhabitants of the banks of the Ganges, be ready to fall down and worship this wonderful exhibition of mechanical skill, they would be equally astonished at that power within itself by which it would be propelled, and would at once declare that the second prediction of Maui was accomplished, and the vessel without rigging or cordage had arrived.

They have other predictions, but less circumstantial or probable, yet I could not learn that they have ever been led, from the declarations of their wise men, to anticipate the arrival of any distinguished personage in their country. The expectation of some wise and great prince or ruler rising up among them, or coming from some distant region, which has prevailed among many nations, and is generally supposed to refer to the appearance of the Saviour, does not seem to have existed among them; unless we suppose the anticipated return of Rono to the Sandwich Islands, an *Avatar* of whom, the inhabitants supposed Captain Cook to be, refers to this event.

Traditions of the deluge, the most important event in reference to the external structure and appearance of our globe that has occurred since its creation, have been found to exist among the natives of the South Sea Islands, from the earliest periods of their history. Accounts, more or less according with the scripture narrative of this awful visitation of Divine justice upon the antediluvian world, have been discovered among most of the nations of the earth; and the striking analogy between those religiously preserved by the inhabitants of the islands of the Pacific, and the Mosaic account, would seem to indicate a degree of high antiquity belonging to this isolated people.

The principal facts are the same in the traditions prevailing among the inhabitants of the different groups, although they differ in several minor particulars. In one group the accounts state, that in ancient times Taaroa, the principal god, (according to their mythology, the creator of the world,) being angry with men on account of their disobedience to his will, overturned the world into the sea, when the earth sunk in the waters, excepting a few *aurus*, or projecting points, which remaining above its surface, constituted the present cluster of islands. The memorial preserved by the inhabitants of Eimeo, states, that after the inundation of the land, when the water subsided, a man landed from a canoe near Tiataepua, in their island, and erected an altar, or marae, in honour of his god.

The most circumstantial tradition preserved among the Windward Islands, of this remarkable event, is one, for the original of which I am indebted to Mr. Orsmond: the following is a literal translation:—

"Destroyed was Tahiti by the sea; no man, nor hog, nor fowl, nor dog, remained. The groves of trees, and the stones, were carried away by the wind. They were destroyed, and the deep was over the land. But these two persons, the husband and the wife, (when it came in,) the wife took up her young chicken; the husband took up his young pig; the wife took up her young dog and the kitten; the husband took up that. [These were all the animals formerly known to the people, and the term *fanaua*, young, is both singular and plural, so that it may apply to one, or to more than one chicken, &c.] They were going forth, and looking at Orofena:* the husband said, 'Up, both of us, to yonder mountain high.' The wife replied, 'No, let us not go thither.' The husband said, 'It is a high or long rock, and will not be reached by the sea:' but the wife replied, 'Reached will be it by the sea yonder, we two on the mountain round as a breast, O Pitohito; it will not be reached by the sea.' They two arrived there. Orofena was overwhelmed by

* The high mountain in Tahiti.

the sea; that mountain, Pito-hiti, (alone) remained, that was their abode.

"There they watched nights ten,[*] the sea ebbed, and they two saw the little heads of the mountains in their elevation. When the sea dried or retired, the land remained without produce, without man, and the fish were putrid in the caves and holes of the rocks. They said, 'Dig a hole for the fish in the sea.' The wind also was becoming feeble, and when it was dead or calm, the stones and the trees began to fall from the heavens: thither they had been carried by the wind. All trees of the land had been torn up, and carried high by the wind. They two looked about, and the woman said, 'Safe are we two from the sea, but death, or hurt, comes now in these stones that are falling. Where shall we abide?' Torn by the roots up had been all the trees, and carried above the pathway of the rain in the heavens.

"'Dig a hole for us two, a dwelling-place.' The hole was dug, covered with grass the bottom of the hole or cave; stones were spread on the top of the hole, and these covered over with earth. While these two were sitting within, they heard with terror the loud voice of the falling stones. Now they fell more thinly, then one little stone at a time fell, and afterwards ceased entirely.

"The woman said, 'Arise you, and advance without, and see if the stones fall.' The man replied, 'I go not out, I shall die.' He waited till night and till day, and then said, 'The wind is truly dead, and the stones and the trunks of trees cease to fall, neither is there the sound of the stones.' They went out, and like a small

[*] The native mode of reckoning time is by nights, instead of days.

mountain was the heap or collection of the stones and the wood. The earth and the rocks remained of the land; the shrubs were destroyed by the sea. They descended, and gazed with astonishment: There were no houses, nor cocoa-nuts, nor palm-trees, nor bread-fruit, nor hibiscus, nor grass; all was destroyed by the sea. They two dwelt together. The woman brought forth two children; one was a son, the other a daughter. They grieved that there was no food for their children. Again the mother brought forth, but still there was no food. The children grew up without food; then the bread-fruit bore fruit, and the cocoa-nut, and every other kind of food. In three days encircled or covered was the land with food. The land became covered with men. From two persons, the father and the mother, filled was the land."

The principal facts of this singular and curious account, though blended together by the natives in the order in which they are here given, probably refer to two distinct events. The total inundation of the land is perhaps a relic of the account of the deluge, and the tearing up and falling of the trees and stones, to some violent hurricane or volcanic eruption.

The tradition, which prevails in the Leeward Islands, is intimately connected with the island of Raiatea. According to this, shortly after the first peopling of the world by the descendants of Taata, *Ruahatu*, the Neptune of the South Sea Islanders, was reposing among the coralline groves in the depths of the ocean, on a spot that, as his resort, was sacred. A fisherman, either through forgetfulness or disregard of the tabu, and sacredness of the place, paddled his canoe upon the forbidden waters, and lowered his hooks among the branching corals at the bottom. The hooks became entangled in the hair of the sleeping god. After remaining some time, the fisherman endeavoured to pull up his hooks, but was for a long period unable to move them. At length they were suddenly disentangled, and he began to draw them towards the surface. In an instant, however, the god, whom he had aroused from his slumbers, appeared at the surface of the water, and, after upbraiding him for his impiety, declared, that the land was criminal, or convicted of guilt, and should be destroyed.

The affrighted fisherman prostrated himself before the god of the sea, confessed his sorrow for what he had done, and implored his forgiveness, beseeching him that the judgment denounced might be averted, or that he might escape. Ruahatu, moved by his penitence and importunity, directed him to return home for his wife and child, and then proceed to a small island called Toamarama, which is situated within the reefs on the eastern side of Raiatea. Here he was promised security, amid the destruction of the surrounding islands. The man hastened to his residence, and proceeded with his wife and child to the place appointed. Some say he took with him a friend who was residing under his roof, with a dog, a pig, and a pair of fowls, so that the party consisted of four individuals, besides the only domesticated animals known in the islands.

They reached the refuge appointed, before the close of the day; and as the sun approached the horizon, the waters of the ocean began to rise, the inhabitants of the adjacent shore left their dwellings on the beach, and fled to the mountains. The waters continued to rise during the night, and the next morning the tops of the mountains only appeared, above the wide-spread sea. These were afterwards covered, and all the inhabitants of the land perished. The waters subsequently retired, the fisherman and his companions left their retreat, took up their abode on the main land, and became the progenitors of the present inhabitants.

Toamarama, the ark in which those individuals are stated to have been preserved, is a small and low coralline island, of exceedingly circumscribed extent, while its highest parts are not more than two feet above the level of the sea. Whether, on the occasion above referred to, it was raised by Ruahatu to a greater elevation than the summits of the lofty mountains on the adjacent shore, or whether the waters, when, according to their representations, they rose several thousand feet above their present level, formed a kind of cylindrical wall around Toamarama, the natives do not pretend to know, and usually decline discussing this circumstance. Their belief in the event was, however, unshaken; and whenever we have conversed with them on the subject, they have alluded to the *farero*, coral, shells, and other marine substances, occasionally found near the surface of the ground, on the tops of their highest mountains. These, they say, would never have been carried there by the people, and could not have originally existed in the situations in which they are now found, but must have been deposited there by the waters of the ocean, when the islands were inundated.—We do not consider these marine substances as evidences that the islands were overflowed at the deluge, but have generally been accustomed to attribute to the whole a formation, if not posterior, yet not of more than equal antiquity with that event. We have usually viewed the coral, shells,

&c. which do not appear to be fossils, as indications of the submarine origin of the mountains, and have supposed they were deposited on the rocks, near the surface of which they are now found, when those rocks formed the bed of the ocean, and prior to those violent explosive convulsions by which they were raised to their present elevation, and formed the groups of islands now under consideration.

These are but mere speculative opinions, and however strong the indications of such an origin might appear to our own minds, we could not demonstrate that the different islands now existing had not formerly belonged to one large island. Neither could we shew that they were not the remains of a continent, originally stretching across the Pacific, and uniting Asia and America, which, having been overflowed by the waters of the deluge, might have disappeared after those disruptions had taken place, by which the fountains of the great deep were broken up. Such speculations would have been useless, and we should only have perplexed the minds of the people with our own opinions. In general, we endeavoured to direct them to the records of that great event preserved in the Scriptures; in the traditionary accounts of which, perpetuated, as they were likely to be, by the descendants of the family of Noah for many generations, their own traditions, with those of the Sandwich Islanders, and other neighbouring tribes, had probably originated. I have frequently conversed with the people on the subject, both in the northern and southern groups, but could never learn that they had any accounts of the windows of heaven having been opened, or the rain having descended. In the legend of Ruahatu, the Toamarama of Tahiti, and the Kai of Kahinarii in Hawaii, the inundation is ascribed to the rising of the waters of the sea. In each account, the anger of the god is considered as the cause of the inundation of the world, and the destruction of its inhabitants. The element employed in effecting it is the same as that mentioned in the Bible; and in the Tahitian tradition, the boat or canoe being used, as the means of safety to the favoured family, and the preservation of the only domestic animals found on the islands, appear corrupted fragments of the memorial of Noah, the ark, and its inmates. These, with other minor points of coincidence between the native traditions and the Mosaic account of the deluge, are striking, and warrant the inference, that although the former are deficient in many particulars, and have much that is fabulous in their composition, they yet refer to the same event.

The memorial of an universal deluge, found among all nations existing in those communities, by which civilization, literature, science, and the arts, have been carried to the highest perfection, as well as among the most untutored and barbarous, preserved through all the migrations and vicissitudes of the human family, from the remote antiquity of its occurrence to the present time, is a most decisive evidence of the authenticity of revelation. The brief yet satisfactory testimony to this event, preserved in the oral traditions of a people secluded for ages from intercourse with other parts of the world, furnishes strong additional evidence that the scripture record is irrefragable. In several respects, the Polynesian account resembles not only the Mosaic, but those preserved by the earliest families of the postdiluvian world, and supports the presumption that their religious system has descended from the Arkite idolatry, the basis of the mythology of the gentile nations. The mundane egg is conspicuous in the cosmogony of some of the most ancient nations. One of the traditions of the Hawaiians states, that a bird deposited an egg (containing the world in embryo) upon the surface of the primeval waters. If the symbol of the egg be supposed to refer to the creation, and the bird be considered a corrupted memorial of the event recorded in the sacred writings, in which it is said, "The Spirit of God moved upon the face of the waters," the coincidence is striking. It is no less so, if it be referred to the ark, floating on the waters of the deluge. The sleep of Ruahatu accords with the slumber of Bramah, which was the occasion of the crime that brought on the Hindoo deluge. The warning to flee, and the means of safety, resemble a tradition recorded by Kœmpfer, as existing among the Chinese. The canoe of the Polynesian Noah has its counterpart in the traditions of their antipodes, the Druids, whose memorial states the bursting of the waters of the lake Lleon, and the overwhelming of the face of all lands, and drowning all mankind excepting two individuals, who escaped in a naked vessel, (a vessel without sails,) by whom the island of Britain was re-peopled. The safety which the progenitors of the Peruvian race are said to have found in caves, or the summits of the mountains, when the waters overflowed the land, bears a resemblance to the Hawaiian; and that of the Mexican, in which Coxcox, or Tezpi, and his wife, were preserved in a bark, corresponds with the Tahitian tradition. Other points of resemblance between the Polynesian account, and the memorial of the deluge, preserved among the ancient nations, might be cited; but these are sufficient to shew the agreement in the testimony to the same event, preserved by the most distant tribes of the human family.

Before closing the account of the ancient state of the people, their views in relation to the origin of those maladies with which they were afflicted, the cause of death, and their ideas of a future state, require to be noticed. Some of their usages and opinions on these subjects were remarkably curious. Every disease was supposed to be the effect of direct supernatural agency, and to be inflicted by the gods for some crime against the tabu, of which the sufferers had been guilty, or in consequence of some offering made by an enemy to procure their destruction. Hence, it is probable, in a great measure, resulted their neglect and cruel treatment of their sick. The same ideas prevailed with regard to death, every instance of which they imagined was caused by the direct influence of the gods.

The natives acknowledged that they possessed articles of poison, which, when taken in the food, would produce convulsions and death, but those effects they considered more the result of the god's displeasure, operating by means of these substances, than the effects of the poisons themselves. Those who died of eating fish, of which several kinds found on their coasts are at certain seasons unsuitable for food, were supposed to die by the influence of the gods; who, they imagined, had entered the fish, or rendered it poisonous. Several Europeans have been affected by these fish, though only slightly, usually causing swelling of the body, a red colour diffused on the skin, and a distressing head-ache. Those who were killed in battle were also supposed to die from the influence of the gods, who, they fancied, had actually entered the weapons of their murderers. Hence, those who died suddenly were said to be seized by the god.

Their ideas of a future state were vague and indefinite. They generally spoke of the place to which departed spirits repaired on leaving the body, as the *po*, state of night. This also was the abode or resort of the gods, and those deified spirits that had not been destroyed. What their precise ideas of a spirit were, it is not easy to ascertain. They appear, however, to have imagined the shape or form resembled that of the human body, in which they sometimes appeared in dreams to the survivors.

When the spirit left the body, which they called *unuhi te varua e te atua*, the spirit drawn out by the god, (the same term, *unuhi*, is applied by them to the drawing a sword out of its scabbard,) it was supposed to be fetched, or sent for, by the god. They imagined that *oramatuas*, or demons, were often waiting near the body, to seize the human spirit as it should be drawn out (they supposed) from the head; and, under the influence of strong impressions from such superstitions, or the effects of a disordered imagination, when dying, the poor creatures have sometimes pointed to the foot of the mat or the couch on which they were lying, and have exclaimed, "There the *varua*, spirits, are waiting for my spirit; guard its escape, preserve it from them," &c.

On leaving the body, they imagined it was seized by other spirits, conducted to the *po*, or state of night, where it was eaten by the gods; not at once, but by degrees. They imagined, that different parts of the human spirit were scraped with a kind of serrated shell, at different times; that the ancestors or relatives of the deceased performed this operation; that the spirit thus passed through the god, and if it underwent this process of being eaten, &c. three different times, it became a deified or imperishable spirit, might visit the world, and inspire others.

They had a kind of heaven, which they called *Miru*. The heaven most familiar, especially in the Leeward Islands, is *Rohutu noanoa*, sweet-scented Rohutu. This was situated near *Tamahani unauna*, glorious Tamahani, the resort of departed spirits, a celebrated mountain on the north-west side of Raiatea. The perfumed Rohutu, though invisible but to spirits, was somewhere between the former settlement and the district of Tipaehapa on the north side of Raiatea. It was described as a beautiful place, quite an Elysium, where the air was remarkably salubrious, plants and shrubs abundant, highly odoriferous, and in perpetual bloom. Here the Areois, and others raised to this state, followed all the amusements and pursuits to which they had been accustomed in the world, without intermission or end. Here was food in abundance, and every indulgence. It is worthy of remark, that the misery of the one, and enjoyments of the other, debasing as they were, were the destiny of individuals, altogether irrespective of their moral character and virtuous conduct. The only crimes that were visited by the displeasure of their deities were the neglect of some rite or ceremony, or the failing to furnish required offerings. I have often, in conversations with the people, and sometimes with the priests, endeavoured to ascertain whether they had any idea of a person's condition in a future state being connected with his disposition and general conduct in this; but I never could learn that they expected, in the world of spirits, any difference in the treatment of a kind, generous, peaceful man, and that of a cruel, parsimonious, quarrelsome one. I am, however, inclined to think, from the great anxiety about a future state, which some have evinced when near death, that natural conscience, which I believe pronounced a verdict on the moral character of every action throughout their lives, is not always inactive in the solemn hour of dissolution, although its salutary effects were neutralized by the strength of superstition.

As soon as an individual was dead, the tahua tutera was employed, for the purpose of discovering the cause of the deceased person's death. In order to effect this, the priest took his canoe, and paddled slowly along on the sea, near the house in which the body was lying, to watch the passage of the spirit; which they supposed would fly upon him, with the emblem of the cause through which the person died. If he had been cursed by the gods, the spirit would appear with a flame, fire being the agent employed in the incantation of the sorcerers; if *pifaod*, or killed, by the bribe of some enemy, given to the gods, the spirit would appear with a red feather, the emblem or sign of evil spirits having entered his food. After a short time, the tahua, or priest, returned to the house of the deceased, and told the survivors the cause of his death, and received his fee, the amount of which was regulated by the circumstances of the parties.

The taata faatere, or faatubua, was then employed, to avert the destruction of the surviving members of the family. A number of ceremonies were performed and prayers offered, according to the cause of the death that had taken place; and when these were concluded, the priest, informing the family that he had been successful, and that the remaining members were now safe, received another fee, and departed.

The disposal of the corpse was the next concern. The bodies of the chiefs, and persons of rank and affluence, and those of the middle class, were preserved; the bodies of the lower orders unceremoniously buried, which was called the burial of a dog: when interred, the body was not laid out straight or horizontal, but placed in a sitting posture, with the knees elevated, the face pressed down between the knees, the hands fastened under the legs, and the whole body tied with cord or cinet wound repeatedly round. It was then covered over, and deposited not very deep'y in the earth.

However great the attachment between the deceased and the survivors might have been, and however they might desire to prolong the melancholy satisfaction resulting from the presence of the lifeless body, on which they still felt it some alleviation to gaze, the heat of the climate was such, as to require that it should be speedily removed, unless methods were employed for its preservation, and these were generally too expensive for the poor and middle ranks. They were therefore usually obliged to inter the corpse sometimes on the first, and seldom later than the second day after death. During the short period that they could indulge the painful sympathies connected with the retention of the body, it was placed on a sort of bier covered with the best white native cloth they possessed, and decorated with wreaths and garlands of the most odoriferous flowers. The body was also placed on a kind of bed of green fragrant leaves, which were also strewed over the floor of the dwelling. During the period which elapsed between the death and interment of the body, the relatives and surviving friends sat round the corpse, indulging in melancholy sadness, giving vent to their grief in loud and continued lamentations, often accompanied with the use of the shark's tooth; which they employed in cutting their temples, faces, and breasts, till they were covered with blood from their self-inflicted wounds. The bodies were frequently committed to the grave in deep silence, unbroken excepting by occasional lamentations of those who attended. But on some occasions, the father delivered an affecting and pathetic oration at the funeral of his son.

The bodies of the dead, among the chiefs, were, however, in general preserved above ground: a temporary house or shed was erected for them, and they were placed on a kind of bier. The practice of embalming appears to have been long familiar to them; and the length of time which the body was thus preserved, depended altogether upon the costliness and care with which the process was performed. The methods employed were at all times remarkably simple: sometimes the moisture of the body was removed by pressing the different parts, drying it in the sun, and anointing it with fragrant oils. At other times, the intestines, brain, &c. were removed; all moisture was extracted from the body, which was fixed in a sitting position during the day, and exposed to the sun, and, when placed horizontally, at night was frequently turned over, that it might not remain long on the same side. The inside was then filled with cloth saturated with perfumed oils, which were also injected into other parts of the body, and carefully rubbed over the outside every day. This, together with the heat of the sun, and the dryness of the atmosphere, favoured the preservation of the body.

Under the influence of these causes, in the course of a few weeks the muscles dried up, and the whole body appeared as if covered with a kind of parchment. It was then clothed, and fixed in a sitting posture; a small altar was erected before it, and offerings of fruit, food, and flowers, were daily presented by the relatives, or the priest appointed to attend the body. In this state it was preserved many months, and when it decayed, the skull was carefully kept by the family, while the other bones, &c. were buried within the precincts of the family temple.

It is singular that the practice of preserving the bodies of their dead by the process of embalming, which has been thought to indicate a high degree of civilization, and which was carried to such perfection by one of the most celebrated nations of antiquity, some thousand years ago, should be found to prevail among this people. It is also practised by other distant nations of the Pacific, and on some of the coasts washed by its waters.

In commencing the process of embalming, and placing the body on the bier, another priest was employed, who was called the *tahua bure tiapapau*, literally "corpse-praying priest." His office was singular: when the house for the dead had been erected, and the corpse placed upon the platform or bier, the priest ordered a hole to be dug in the earth or floor, near the foot of the platform.

Over this he prayed to the god, by whom it was supposed the spirit of the deceased had been required. The purport of his prayer was, that all the dead man's sins, and especially that for which his soul had been called to the *po*, might be deposited there, that they might not attach in any degree to the survivors, and that the anger of the god might be appeased.

The priest next addressed the corpse, usually saying, *Ei ia oe na te hara e vai ai*, "With you let the guilt now remain." The pillar or post of the corpse, as it was called, was then planted in the hole, perhaps designed as a personification of the deceased, to exist after his body should have decayed—the earth was thrown over, as they supposed, the guilt of the departed—and the hole filled up.

At the conclusion of this part of the curious rite, the priest proceeded to the side of the corpse, and, taking a number of small slips of the *fa maia*, plantain leaf-stalk, fixed two or three pieces under each arm, placed a few on the breast, and then, addressing the dead body, said, There are your family, there is your child, there is your wife, there is your father, and there is your mother, Be satisfied yonder, (that is, in the world of spirits.) Look not towards those who are left in this world.— The concluding parts of the ceremony were designed to impart contentment to the departed, and to prevent the spirit from repairing to the places of his former resort, and so distressing the survivors.

This was considered a most important ceremony, being a kind of mass for the dead, and necessary for the peace of the living, as well as the quiet of the deceased. It was seldom omitted by any who could procure the accustomed fees for the priest, which for this service were generally furnished in pigs and cloth, in proportion to the rank or possessions of the family.

All who were employed in embalming, which they called *miri*, were, during the process, carefully avoided by every person, as the guilt of the crime for which the deceased had died, was supposed in some degree to attach to such as touched the body. They did not feed themselves, lest the food defiled by the touch of their polluted hands, should cause their own death,—but were fed by others.

As soon as the ceremony of depositing the sins in the hole was over, all who had touched the body or the garments of the deceased, which were buried or destroyed, fled precipitately into the sea, to cleanse themselves from the pollution, called *mahuruhuru*, which they had contracted by touching the corpse; casting also into the sea, the clothes they had worn while employed in the work. Having finished their ablutions, they gathered a few pieces of coral from the bottom of the sea, and, returning with them to the house, addressed the dead body by saying, "With you may the *mahuruhuru*, or pollution, be," and threw down the pieces of coral on the top of the hole that had been dug for the purpose of receiving every thing contaminating, connected with the deceased.

The ceremonies in general were now finished, but if the property of the family was abundant, their attachment to the deceased great, and they wished his spirit to be conveyed to *Rohutu noanoa*, the Tahitian paradise, a fifth priest was employed. Costly offerings were presented, and valuable articles given to the priest of Romatane, the keeper of this happy place; Urutaetae was the guide of such as went thither, and the duty of the priest now employed was to engage him to conduct the spirit of the departed to this fancied region of enjoyment.

The Tahitians divide their history into two eras, the first they call the *hau hupehupe*, the rude or unpolished age: during this period the bodies of the dead were allowed to remain in the house in which they had lived, and which was still occupied by the survivors. A kind of stage or altar was erected in the house, on which the body was laid. But when the people became wiser, and society improved, the *hau una*, neat or polished age, commenced, which continued till the arrival of foreigners. It was in the commencement of this age, that separate houses were built for the dead.

The houses erected as depositories for the dead, were small and temporary buildings, though often remarkably neat. The pillars supporting the roof were planted in the ground, and were seldom more than six feet high. The bier or platform on which the body was laid, was about three feet from the ground, and was moveable, for the purpose of being drawn out, and of exposing the body to the rays of the sun. The corpse was usually clothed, except when visited by the relatives or friends of the deceased. It was, however, for a long time carefully rubbed with aromatic oils once a day.

A light kind of altar was erected near it, on which articles of food, fruits, and garlands of flowers were daily deposited; and if the deceased were a chief of rank or fame, a priest or other person was appointed to attend the corpse, and present food to its mouth at different periods during the day. When asked their reason for this practice, they have said they supposed there was a spiritual as well as a material part of food, a part which they could smell; and that if the spirit of the deceased returned, the spirit or scent of the offering would be grateful, or they were influenced by a wish to appease any desire the departed might have to return and partake of the enjoyments of life. Connected with the depositories of the dead, there was what they called the *aumiha*, a kind of contagious influence, of which they appeared to be afraid; and hence, at night especially, they avoided the place of sepulture. The family, district, or royal maraes were the general depositories of the bones of the departed, whose bodies had been embalmed, and whose skulls were sometimes preserved in the dwelling of the survivors. The marae or temple being sacred, and the bodies being under the guardianship of the gods, were in general considered secure when deposited there. This was not, however, always the case; and in times of war, the victors sometimes, not only despoiled the temples of the vanquished, and bore away their idol, but robbed the sacred enclosure of the bones of celebrated individuals. These spoils were appropriated to what the nation considered the lowest degradation, by being converted into chisels or borers, for the builders of canoes and houses, or transformed into fishing-hooks. In order to avoid this, they carried the bones of their chiefs, and even the recently deceased corpse, and deposited them in the caverns of some of the most inaccessible rocks in the lofty and fearful precipices of the mountain denles.

Notwithstanding the labour and care bestowed on the bodies of the dead, they did not last very long; probably the most carefully preserved could not be kept more than twelve months. When they began to decay, the bones, &c. were buried, but the skull was preserved in the family sometimes for several generations, wrapt carefully in native cloth, and often suspended from some part of the roof of their habitations. In some of the islands they dried the bodies, and, wrapping them in numerous folds of cloth, suspended them also from the roofs of their dwelling-houses.

The tribes inhabiting the islands of the Pacific were remarkably superstitious, and among them none more so than the inhabitants of the Georgian and Society Islands. They imagined they lived in a world of spirits, which surrounded them night and day, watching every action of their lives, and ready to avenge the slightest neglect, or the least disobedience to their injunctions, as proclaimed by their priests.

These dreaded beings were seldom thought to resort to the habitations of men on errands of benevolence. They were supposed to haunt the places of their former abode, to arouse the survivors from their slumbers by making a squeaking noise, to which, when the natives heard, they would sometimes reply, asking what they were, what they wanted, &c. Sometimes the spirits upbraided the living with former wickedness, or the neglect of some ceremonious enactment, for which they were unhappy.

When a person was seized with convulsions or hysterics, it was said to be from seizure by the spirits, who sometimes scratched their faces, tore their hair, or otherwise maltreated them. For some time after the death of Taaroarii we could seldom induce any of our servants to go out of the house after it was dark, under an apprehension that they should see, or be seized by, his spirit. They were, however, very ignorant young persons. The natives in general laugh at their former credulity. The whole system of their superstition seems to have been, in every respect, wonderfully adapted to debase the mind, and keep the people in the most abject subjection to the priests, who, in order to maintain their influence, had recourse to this extensive and imposing machinery of supernatural agency; and it must be confessed that, considering their isolated situation, their entire ignorance of science, of natural and experimental philosophy, their ardent temperament, the romantic nature of the country, and the adventurous character of many of their achievements, there was something remarkably imposing to an uncultivated mind in the system here inculcated.

Almost every native custom connected with the death of relations or friends, was singular, and none perhaps more so than the *otohaa*, which, though not confined to instances of death, was then most violent. It consisted in the most frantic expressions of grief, under which individuals acted as if bereft of reason. It commenced when the sick person appeared to be dying; the wailing then was often most distressing, but as soon as the spirit had departed, the individuals became quite ungovernable.

They not only wailed in the loudest and most affecting tone, but tore their hair, rent their garments, and cut themselves with shark's teeth or knives in a shocking manner. The instrument usually employed was a small cane, about four inches long, with five or six shark's teeth fixed in, on opposite sides. With one of these instruments every female provided herself after marriage, and on occasions of death it was unsparingly used.

With some this was not sufficient; they prepared a short instrument, something like a plumber's mallet, about five or six inches long, rounded at one end for a handle, and armed with two or three rows of shark's teeth fixed in the wood, at the other. With this, on the death of a relative or a friend, they cut themselves unmercifully, striking the head, temples, cheek, and breast, till the blood flowed profusely from the wounds. At the same time they uttered the most deafening and agonizing cries; and the distortion of their countenances, their torn and dishevelled hair, the mingled tears and blood that covered their bodies, their wild gestures and unruly conduct, often gave them a frightful and almost inhuman appearance. This cruelty was principally performed by the females, but not by them only; the men committed on these occasions the same enormities, and not only cut themselves, but came armed with clubs and other deadly weapons.

The otohaa commenced with the nearest relations of the deceased, but it was not confined to them; so soon as the tidings spread, and the sound of the lamentations was heard through the neighbourhood, the friends and relatives repaired to the spot, and joined in the tragic performance.

I am not prepared to say that the same enormities were practised here as in the Sandwich Islands at these times, but on the death of a king or principal chief the scenes exhibited in and around the house were in appearance demoniacal. The relatives and members of the household began; the other chiefs of the island and their relatives came to sympathize with the survivors, and, on reaching the place, joined in the infuriated conduct of the bereaved; the tenantry of the chiefs also came, and, giving themselves up to all the savage infatuation which the conduct of their associates or the influence of their superstitions inspired, they not only tore their hair, and lacerated their bodies till they were covered with blood, but often fought with clubs and stones till murder followed.

Auna has now some dreadful indentations on his skull from blows he received by stones on one of these occasions at Huahine; and in almost one of the last *otohaa* observed in the same island, a man was killed by the contents of the musket of another. Since the introduction of fire-arms, they have been used in these seasons; and the smoke and report of the guns must have added to the din and terrible confusion of the scene. I cannot conceive of a spectacle more appalling, than that which the infuriated rabble, smeared with their own blood, presenting every frightful distortion in feature, and frantic madness in action, must often have exhibited. This scene was sometimes continued for two or three successive days, or longer, on the death of a person of distinction.

I have often conversed with the people on their reasons for this strange procedure, and have asked them if it was not exceedingly painful to them to cut themselves as they were accustomed to do. They have always answered that it was very painful in some parts of the face—that the upper lip, or the space between the upper lip and the nostril, was the most tender, and a stroke there was always attended with the greatest pain—that it was their custom, and therefore considered indispensable, as it was designed to express the depth of their sorrow— that any one who should not do so, would be considered deficient in respect for the deceased, and also as insulting to his family. The acts of violence committed, they added, were the effects of the paroxysms of their sorrow, which made them *neneva*, or insensible. They continued till their grief was *ua maha*, or satisfied, which often was not the case till they had received several severe blows upon the tender part above mentioned.

The females on these occasions sometimes put on a kind of short apron of a particular sort of cloth, which they held up with one hand, while they cut themselves with the other. In this apron they caught the blood that flowed from the grief-inflicted wounds, until it was almost saturated. It was then dried in the sun, and given to the nearest surviving relations as a proof of the affection of the donor, and was preserved by the bereaved family as a token of the estimation in which the departed had been held.

Had the otohaa been confined to instances of death, or seasons of great calamity, it would not have appeared so strange, as it does in connexion with the fact, that it was practised on other occasions, when feelings the most opposite to those of calamity were induced. In its milder form, it was an expression of joy, as well as of grief; and when a husband or a son returned to his family, after a season of absence, or exposure to danger, his arrival was greeted, not only with the cordial welcome, and the warm embrace, but loud wailing was uttered, and the instrument armed with shark's teeth applied, in proportion to the joy experienced.

The early visitors, and the first Missionaries, were much surprised at this strange and contradictory usage; and, in answer to their inquiries, were informed, that it was the custom of Tahiti.

The wailing was not so excessive, or the duration so long, nor were the enormities committed so great, as in the event of a death. The otohaa appears to have been adopted by the people to express the violence or excess of their passion, whether joy or grief.

There was another custom associated with their bereavements by death, of an opposite character, and more agreeable to contemplate. This was their elegiac ballads, prepared by the bards, and recited for the consolation of the family. They generally followed the otohaa, and were often treasured up in the memory of the survivors, and eventually became a part of the ballads of the nation. Though highly figurative and beautiful in sentiment, breathing a pathetic spirit of sympathy and consolation, they were often historical, or rather biographical, recounting, under all the imagery of song, the leading events in the life of the individuals, and were remarkably interesting, when that life had been one of enterprise, adventure, or incident.

Scarcely had Taaroarii, the young chieftain of Huahine, been consigned to the tomb, when a ballad was prepared, after the ancient usage of his country. I heard it once or twice, and intended to have committed it to paper, but my voyage to the Sandwich Islands, shortly afterwards, prevented. It commenced in a truly pathetic manner; the first lines were—

> *Ua moe te teoto o Atiapii i roto te ana*
> *Ua rava e adu tona uuauna.*

"The pride of Atiapii* sleeps in the cavern;
Departed has its glory, or its brightness," &c.

---

* One of the names of the island of Huahine.

It was, throughout, adapted to awaken tenderness, and regret at the event, and sympathy with the survivors.

Soon after the decease of a chief or person of distinction, another singular ceremony, called a *heva*, was performed by the relatives or dependants. The principal actor in this procession was a priest, or relative, who wore a curious dress, the most imposing part of which was the head-ornament, or parae. A cap of thick native cloth was fitted close to the head; in front were two large broad mother-of-pearl shells, covering the face like a mask, with one small aperture through which the wearer could look. Above the mask a number of beautiful, long, white, red-tipped, tail feathers of the tropic bird, were fixed, diverging like rays; beneath the mask was a curved piece of thin yet strong board, six or nine inches wide in the centre, but narrow at the ends, which, turned upwards, gave it the appearance of a crescent.

Attached to this was a beautiful kind of network of small pieces of brilliant mother-of-pearl shell called the *ahu aua*, each piece being about an inch or an inch and a half long, and less than a quarter of an inch wide. Every piece was finely polished, and reduced to the thinness of a card; a small perforation was made at each corner, and the pieces fastened together by threads passed through these perforations. They were fixed perpendicularly to the board, and extended nearly from one end to the other. The depth varied according to the taste or means of the family, but it was generally nine inches or a foot.

The labour in making this part of the parae must have been excessive. The many hundred pieces of mother-of-pearl shell, that must have been cut, ground down to the required thickness, polished, and perforated, without iron tools, before a single line could be fixed upon the head-dress, required a degree of patience that is surprising. The manufacture was regarded as a sacred work; emblems of intercourse with the gods were required to be placed in front of the parae when it was made.

This part covered the breast of the wearer; a succession of pieces of black and yellow cloth fastened to the pearl-shell nctting, surrounded the body, and reached sometimes to the loins, to the knees, or even to the ankles. The beautiful mother-of-pearl shell net-work was fringed with feathers; a large bunch of man-of-war-bird's plumage was fixed at each end of the board, and two elegantly shaped oro-oro feather tassels, hanging from each end, were attached to the light board by cords, also covered with feathers.

In one hand the heva carried a paeho, a terrific weapon, about five feet long, one end rounded for a handle, the other broad and flat, and in shape not unlike a short scythe. The point was ornamented with a tuft of feathers, and the inner or concave side armed with a line of large, strong, sharks' teeth, fixed in the wood by the fibres of the tough *ieie*. In the other hand he held a *tete* or kind of clapper, formed with a large and a smaller pearl-oyster shell, beautifully polished.

The man thus arrayed led the procession, which came from the valley, whither, as if under the paroxysm of grief, the party had retired at the death of the person for whom this was used, and continued, as he walked along, to strike or jingle the shells against each other, to give notice of his approach. He was attended by a number of men and boys, painted with charcoal and red and white clay, as if they had endeavoured to render themselves as hideous as possible. They wore only a maro or girdle, and were covered with these coloured earths. Sometimes the body was painted red, with black and white stripes; at other times the face painted red or black, and the rest of the body red and white. The pigment was mixed with the gum of the bread-fruit tree, that it might adhere to the skin. They were armed with a club or cudgel, and proceeded through the district, seizing and beating every person they met with, who did not shew them the greatest respect; any one who should ridicule them would be unmercifully cut with the paeho. The only remedy was to fly to the king's temple, which was on this, as well as some other occasions, a kind of sanctuary, or place of refuge. In general, all who saw their approach instantly fled, or hid themselves.

They did not enter any of the dwellings, but often struck them as they passed by, to the great terror of those within. They appeared and acted as if they were deranged, and were supposed to be inspired by the spirit of the deceased, to revenge any injury he might have received, or to punish those who had not shewn due respect to his remains. It was often the means of commencing a war, which frequently proved fatal to multitudes before it terminated. Tuiheva was the god of this singular ceremony.

Date Due